CHURCH UNION AT MIDPOINT

Church Union at Midpoint

EDITED BY

PAUL A. CROW, Jr.

AND

WILLIAM JERRY BONEY

Association Press · *NEW YORK*

International Standard Book Number: 0-8096-1848-6
Library of Congress Catalog Card Number: 72-4341

Library of Congress Cataloging in Publication Data

Crow, Paul A
    Church union at midpoint.

    Bibliography: p.
    1. Consultation on Church Union—Addresses, essays, lectures. 2. Christian union—United States—Addresses, essays, lectures. I. Boney, William Jerry, joint author. II. Title.
BR516.5.C76   262′.001   72-4341
ISBN 0-8096-1848-6

PRINTED IN THE UNITED STATES OF AMERICA

To
Carol, Stephen, Susan,
and
Beth, Tommy, Paul,
and
Children like them
everywhere who deserve
unity for the healing
of their world

Contents

Preface

The purpose of *Church Union at Midpoint* is to help advance the discussion of those issues confronted in *A Plan of Union for the Church of Christ Uniting*, and to assist engagement in that process toward a new community among Christians which is the Consultation on Church Union. Behind these pages is the conviction that the questions posed to the churches by the Consultation on Church Union are not isolated to this ecumenical venture. They are questions put to every existing church body. Even more crucial, the questions are not only put to the churches by their fellow Christians in other COCU churches, but come with all power and directness from the biblical message and from the world.

As it exists at large, the discussion is many-sided and multifaceted, with striking elements of consensus, and with many shadings of agreement and disagreement among the participants. *Church Union at Midpoint* reflects this variety, as well as the high level at which the debate is proceeding in response to the issues. For this and much else, thanks go to the distinguished scholars and churchmen who have joined us in this venture.

The divisions of the book are, we hope, clear: past, present, and future —long-range and immediate—of the Consultation on Church Union, and so of ecumenism in the U.S.A. Such an agenda has obvious implications beyond the union of nine churches. It necessarily touches upon the unity of all Christians, and with deep intensity upon the unity and healing of mankind.

It is hoped this book will find many kinds of readers and uses. Certainly it will help to inform the general reader who wants to understand the milieu and major issues of COCU. It *is* a part of the discussion on COCU at its midpoint.

We trust that these contributions will engender a yet larger and fuller discussion of the issues of reconciliation, renewal, and reunion as the revision process continues, and as congregations in the COCU communions ask the pivotal question posed at the Denver plenary session, "What Does God Require of Us Now?" Perhaps this volume will find good use among study groups (ecumenically composed, we trust), especially those which have previously been through the first draft of A *Plan of Union.*

The present volume is an invitation to engage in COCU, to be stimulated by its challenge, and to help shape the future of the church. Those who will step in the stream of this process toward reconciliation, and encourage their fellow Christians to become participants, will find the church has a future of greater proportions than they or their churches have yet imagined.

Many people have been helpful to the editors in the early and/or preparatory stages of this book. We wish to thank: Joseph W. Sandifer, Jr., Lewis L. Wilkins, Carl L. Howard, Harold R. Johnson, Charles K. Johnson, John C. Cosby, Robert R. Wright, and especially Valerie Polhammer, Jocelyn Armstrong, and Doris Pettebone, three resident angels at the COCU offices in Princeton.

PAUL A. CROW, JR.
WILLIAM JERRY BONEY

I

A DECADE IN PERSPECTIVE

1

A Personal View of the
Consultation on Church Union

GEORGE G. BEAZLEY, JR.

The Consultation on Church Union is a gift of God's grace in a shattering era of church history. Of this, I am convinced. Some other church leaders might question this statement, but I am very sure about it and, as of now, I know COCU as well as any other living person.

I first heard of the Consultation on Church Union aboard a 707 jet flying over the Rocky Mountains to San Francisco. The date was December 2, 1960, and the Consultation was still in the womb of time, to be cast screaming into life two days later. My wife and I were flying to attend the triennial assembly of the National Council of Churches of Christ in the United States of America. Seated next to me was a Presbyterian minister who told me of the proposal which Eugene Carson Blake was planning to make in a sermon at Grace Cathedral (Episcopal) that coming Sunday. It never occurred to me that this sermon would reshape my life and become as important a factor in the ecumenical movement as the National Council, which I had long admired and in which I was about to be intimately involved.

I had just become the chief executive of the Council on Christian Unity for the Christian Church (Disciples of Christ), having assumed my office the previous day. This meant I would be that church's "ecumenical officer" (though the term had not come into common usage yet), relating its congregations to the conciliar manifestation of the ecumenical movement and working with them in all church union efforts in which they were involved. I was a new breed of ecumenical cat, for up to that time no American church had a full-time ecumenical officer. Within a few years almost every major church was to have one.

My seat companion, intrigued by my new job and realizing, better

than I did then, the significance of the Blake sermon, not only shared
this information, he also loaned me his copy of the *New York Times*
which contained an interview with Dr. Blake. This had taken place at
the airport in New York as he was leaving for the National Council of
Churches meeting and to preach this sermon in the cathedral where the
flamboyant James A. Pike then had his bishop's chair. By the time we
were lining up in our robes and hoods for the procession into the opening
session of the triennial assembly, everyone was discussing that sermon.
The next morning front-page stories were giving its content to the public. Within several days this proposal placed Eugene Carson Blake's
picture on the cover of *Time* magazine.

In the years that have followed, I have reread that sermon several
times. I am increasingly impressed with its insight. At the time it was
preached, its boldness was its most easily recognized characteristic. However, eleven years later, when, as chairman of the Consultation, I read it,
it is the author's insight which becomes most obvious.

Gene Blake has made two essential contributions to the world church,
in addition to many other merely important ones. One of these was providing a leadership for the World Council of Churches at a time when
it was in a state of shock from a tragic miscarriage in the process of
selecting a general secretary to succeed the irreplaceable W. A. Visser't
Hooft. Probably no one but Eugene Carson Blake could have taken the
council through that troubled period, for he was the one person on whom
all the factions were agreed. The second essential contribution was his
sermon in Grace Cathedral, popularly called the "Blake proposal." It
was given at the height of his powers as an American church leader, and
he seems to have intuitively sensed the coming tensions of the sizzling
sixties, when the church would be caught in the maelstrom of so many
conflicting forces. He seems to have known that the church would need
the Consultation for such hours.

The proposal itself was not as remarkable as some, unacquainted with
the details of the ecumenical movement, thought. Blake seems to have
selected for his target practically the same churches which fourteen years
before had created the Church of South India. One of the books which
was quite influential in the early days of COCU and on the suggested
reading list for the delegates at the second plenary at Oberlin, March 19–
21, 1963, was Lesslie Newbigin's *The Reunion of the Church*. The three
points from the catholic tradition and the four points from the reformed
tradition which Blake set forth in the body of the sermon as essentials
for any union arose from careful thinking by one immersed in the Faith
and Order discussions going on in the World Council of Churches. Those
issues set the agenda for the first four years of the Consultation on
Church Union, which culminated in *Principles of Church Union*, ap-

proved at the Dallas plenary, May 2–5, 1966, for transmission to the constituencies of the participating churches for study and comment. Gene Blake worked with some of the rest of us in the committee which formulated those principles, and then left shortly thereafter to begin his work as the General Secretary of the World Council of Churches. Into this consensus went the work of many people, especially Albert C. Outler, the late Elmer Arndt, Paul S. Minear, Stephen F. Bayne, Jr., Gerald Ensley, Paul Washburn, George L. Hunt, Paul A. Crow, Jr., and myself.

It was in the midst of this work that the first predominantly black church, the African Methodist Episcopal Church, sent the Rev. Richard Hildebrand to work on that committee. It was in the summer following the approval of the *Principles of Church Union* (1966) that the Conference on Church and Society, called by the World Council of Churches, met in Geneva and became a catalyst for all the elements that were combining into the new life-style that was to dominate the churches for the next five years.

Eugene Carson Blake did not rationally comprehend those forces and consider them in his sermon. Indeed, at that time no one could. However, like a good bird dog, he caught their scent and pointed toward them, though they were still hidden in the tall grasses of the future. This came out in a passage which was neglected by the clergy, but fastened on by the secular reporters, though they misunderstood its meaning. The passage reads:

> Another clear reason for moving toward the union of American Churches at this time came home to me with compelling force during the presidential campaign this fall. The religious issue was, you will remember, quite generally discussed even though all the high-level politicians attempted to avoid it as much as possible. Now that the election has been decided and nobody really knows how much the religious question figured in the result, I recall the issue to remind you that one result is clear. Every Christian Church, Protestant, Orthodox, Anglican, and Roman Catholic, has been weakened by it. Never before have so many Americans agreed that the Christian Churches, divided as they are, cannot be trusted to bring to the American people an objective and authentic word of God on a political issue. Americans more than ever see the Churches of Jesus Christ as competing social groups pulling and hauling, propagandizing and pressuring for their own organizational advantages.[1]

Some secular reporters thought Dr. Blake was indicating that the election of President John F. Kennedy had strengthened the position of the Roman Catholic Church in American life, and that Dr. Blake's proposal was designed to counterbalance that additional power. We must remember that the Second Vatican Council was only a proposal at this time.

Of course, Blake was not being narrowly Protestant. Most people had caught the sound of the distant thunder. Gene Blake sensed the coming storm and guessed the fury of it. He saw in the fact that the people of America did not consider religious affiliation a cogent factor in the presidential campaign a sign that many citizens of the United States were more secular than they had yet appeared and were about to write off the institutional church as a major factor in the real issues of life.

It was that reaction to the church and the polarization of the society around the issues of race, the various liberation movements, the Vietnam war, and the counterculture which were to set the context in which the Consultation was to operate for its next period. The Blake proposal had by April, 1962, become the Consultation on Church Union, created by the plenary bodies of the four churches he had suggested. By 1966, when it had adopted *Principles of Church Union,* it was a widespread movement in which eight churches were participants, while about twenty additional churches, as widely diverse as the Society of Friends and the Roman Catholic Church, were rather actively commenting observers. By 1967 it had its present participating members, though they were in ten bodies, not nine, as the union of the Methodist Church and the Evangelical United Brethren into the United Methodist Church made them. Through an additional four years they wrestled with the new shape of church union brought by this new context and formulated their conclusions in 1970 in that remarkable document, *A Plan of Union for the Church of Christ Uniting.* Then at the Denver plenary of 1971 this vital and creative movement, at the very moment when the fearful and the ghoulish were proclaiming it "dead," created a plenary discussion which could well be the most significant ecumenical meeting since the Church and Society Conference of 1966. That plenary suggested the contemporary church was about to transcend its "action kick" and lead its people into a new appreciation of the Gospel which would tell the old, old story with such freshness that its implications for both social justice and the tragic human condition would be seen by those who had thought they had discarded their Christian heritage and were living as "men come of age."

Surely, an ecumenical movement that did not grow weary, that did not marry the Gospel either to middle-class American culture or any of the subcultures which were in revolt against it, and that had a keen sense of identity and purpose in the chaos of our confused age is God's gift to his people for such a time as this.

The Consultation on Church Union is something far more than an attempt to unite nine church bodies, though it never has lost and, presumably, never will lose, sight of a goal for union as inclusive as possible. It is wrestling with the proper shape of the church in our age to enable the Gospel to have the maximum power to change human lives and societies. It is the quest for an expression of faith that is so comprehensive as to enable the church to transcend the definitions of that faith which have been institutionalized in the divided churches so that in a divided church the total Tradition is unavailable to anyone. The Consultation has produced *A Plan of Union,* which is now the catalyst of more interchurch study than the American scene has ever seen before. Out of these hours together has come for the participants a vision of their given unity in Christ, which is replacing the tolerance of theological indifference with the new wine of an excitement about the basic faith which they already hold in common. And, most surprising, out of the Consultation's willingness to hold itself open to the promptings of the Holy Spirit has come the suggestion of a new movement in theology which may bring a period of revitalization similar to the one Neo-Orthodoxy brought to the church in the period when our present ecumenical structures were coming into being.

The tragic shadow across this bright picture is that just at the moment when the Consultation on Church Union is being surprised by joy with all which God seems to be doing through it, many people in the church are so walled in by their preconceptions of the future and their rigid caricature of the nature of the union process that they are pronouncing as "dead" an ecumenical movement which might shatter our rigidities in rebellion and give opportunity for a genuine revolution in the life of the church, which would change not only outward institutions but also the heart of man.

"Born Free" is a favorite song in our age—not just the notes of that popular ballad, but the theme of all the liberation movements, which multiply like rabbits in a counterculture disillusioned with the patterns of our society. But, as Tony Tanner points out in his astute analysis of the American fiction of the fifties and the sixties, the form of rebellion is itself a pattern and can imprison just as surely as those established forms which it seeks to replace.[2] One evidence of the truth of this statement is the way in which many potentially creative elements in our society insist that the Consultation on Church Union is just another effort at ecclesiastical carpentry. To me, this means that either they are so imprisoned in their pattern of rebellion that they are unable to recognize new forms of freedom when they arise, or that they have merely scanned the material produced by COCU and quickly classified it as a repetition of union schemes out of the past, without looking at the process which produced this material, or at the process it is designed to produce in the local, regional, and national situations. It also means that some have become so fascinated in listening to the secular that they have turned contemporary theology into a new puritanism of the social scene, so that the transcendent element in the Gospel and its concern for man, caught in the twin toils of mortality and sin, is being jettisoned in favor of a utopia which will remain "nowhere."

The Consultation on Church Union is not so viewed in international circles. In its conversations with ecumenical leaders in the Roman Catholic Church and in its dialogue with other church union efforts in the world—e.g., in the conferences on church union set up by the Faith and Order Department of the World Council of Churches—COCU has been seen as a truly new venture in this endeavor. It is a hopeful breakthrough in the wall that is so easily erected between those concerns that are frequently labeled "Faith and Order" and those concerns that are tagged "Life and Work."

Perhaps the most exciting thing about COCU is that when many coalitions between white, black, and other minorities are breaking up, the Consultation has been able thus far to weather all the tensions created by these polarizations; that, when renewalists and traditionalists have been parting with flung anathemas in so many circles, in the Consultation they have been seeking some total in which both could find new meanings; and that, when so-called participatory democracy has been divorcing so many ecumenical efforts from the real sources of power in the denominations, where the conscious identity of so many Christians still lies, the Consultation has thus far found a way between by which all groups can have a voice, and yet by which the power structures of the participating churches can give a realism to the hopes created in decision.

Of course, the Consultation on Church Union remains a very fragile achievement. Indeed, our recent trips into space have reminded us that life itself is a very fragile achievement, possible only within a quite limited spectrum. The atrocities of our age with both systemic violence and anarchistic violence remind us that civilization and world culture are a very fragile achievement which could be easily lost. The teetering balance of terror which is characteristic of our world divided into competing blocks of countries, each group holding the ultimate weapons of destruction, reminds us of the possibility that, in the words of Shakespeare's Prospero:

> the great globe itself,
> Yea, all which it inherit, shall dissolve
> And, like this insubstantial pageant faded,
> Leave not a rack behind.

In such a world, it should surprise no one that an effort for church union which seeks at the same time relevance and renewal is in constant danger of death. Security is not for people who follow the Lord, nor for movements which seek to manifest that reconciliation which he has given the church as its stewardship. The nine years which I have spent with the Consultation on Church Union since the Christian Church (Disciples of Christ) became a participant and I first walked into its executive committee in December of 1962 have known few moments in which this fragile bark has not been threatened with swamping by the waves of rigid traditions and the tides of instant ecumenism, but it still sails bravely on. To those of us who have experienced its darkest hours and found them to be only the heralds of a new dawn, the sense of God's leading and of his saving power are very strong. We do not believe he will abandon our storm-tossed bark now, and we remember that it is our Savior Jesus Christ who says in all storms, "Be not afraid."

NOTES

1. Blake, Eugene Carson, "A Proposal Toward the Reunion of Christ's Church" (Philadelphia: General Assembly Office of the United Presbyterian Church in the U.S.A., 1961).
2. Tanner, Tony, *City of Words: American Fiction, 1950–1970* (New York: Harper and Row, 1971).

2

The Church—A New Beginning

PAUL A. CROW, JR.

I

In his *Areopagitica* John Milton confidently declared of his day, "God is decreeing to begin some new and great period in his church." Christian history is the story of new beginnings for the people of God. The creation-rebirth motif constantly recurs in the Bible. Christmas, Easter, Pentecost are its message, all new beginnings. God acts in specific events, persons, movements to give new life to the church and the human community. Down through the centuries the church has expressed itself in a series of new beginnings, some silent and unannounced, some dramatic and pronounced. Its life has been a sequence of birth, growth, maturity, decline, death, resurrection. Among all the things which can be said about the church, it is especially a community that knows through its history and experience that "though our outer nature is wasting away, our inner nature is being renewed every day" (II Corinthians 4:16).

This does not mean that the church is renewed automatically, or that every novel movement or plan is an instrument of rebirth. New beginnings sometimes get waylaid; they become victims of pious hesitations as well as realistic obstacles. The church union movement in America and other parts of the world has been vulnerable at this point. After more than half a century of ecumenical dialogue and cooperation, with some victories, the actual accomplishments toward church union on any large-scale basis remain few and far between. The most creative achievements are reserved for Christians in the so-called "younger churches" of South India, North India, Pakistan, and Zaire (formerly the Congo). The only actual reunions in the U.S.A. have occurred among those of the same confessional families. Baptists have united with Baptists, Presbyterians with Presbyterians, Lutherans and Methodists with the separated confreres in their family. The United Church of Christ, while bringing together churches with different polities and ethnic roots, is composed of those who share a reformed theology and doctrine of the church.

Prior to the Consultation on Church Union several heroic but unsuccessful attempts were made in this century to unite those of diverse traditions. The first attempt at a multilateral union in the United States was the Conference on Organic Union. In 1918, a time when the Western world was entrapped in the throes of the First World War, representatives from nineteen communions met at Philadelphia and authorized the preparation of the Philadelphia Plan of Union. The Philadelphia Plan intended to bring "evangelical" churches into a federation, called The United Churches of Christ in America, which would be the first stage toward full corporate union. This goal went unfilled when in 1920 the Presbyterian Church in the U.S.A., which initiated the movement, rejected the plan.

Another plan was set forth by Methodist evangelist E. Stanley Jones. Conceived in the mid-1930s while he was in India, Dr. Jones' plan for "union with a federal structure" was unveiled to his American audience in 1942. Modeled after the American federal system, this plan would eventuate in "The United Church of America," in which the various denominations would maintain their identity as branches. For nearly a decade this Plan of Federal Union benefited from the charismatic leadership and wide travels of Dr. Jones, but never claimed a place on the official agenda of the churches.

A third attempt at comprehensive church union arose in 1946 when the Congregational Christian Church called upon the Federal Council of Churches to convene a plenary to explore the possibility of union among those churches which "already accord one another mutual recognition of ministries and of sacraments." The intent was to limit the number of theological problems to be faced in these conversations. The Conference on Church Union, with nine participating churches, convened at Greenwich, Connecticut, in 1949, and created high hopes and enthusiasm at first. In 1951 *A Plan for a United Church in the United States,* popularly called the Greenwich Plan, was released for study. The basic author of the document was Charles Clayton Morrison, Disciples theologian and editor of *The Christian Century.* When the Presbyterian Church in the U.S.A. withdrew in 1953 and two other participating churches—the Congregational Christian and Evangelical and Reformed churches—united in 1957 to form the United Church of Christ, the loss of momentum was sufficient to result in the termination of the Conference on Church Union in 1958.

None of these three multilateral conversations brought forth a united church. Indeed, none even reached the stage of official voting, though each was not without its company of enthusiasts and its contributions to the ecumenical future. This nonproductive track record gives credence to an observation once made by Dietrich Bonhoeffer. After his brief visit to America in 1939, Bonhoeffer wrote an evaluative article entitled "Protestantism Without Reformation" which made this penetrating critique: "It has been granted to the Americans less than any other nation of the earth to realize on earth the visible unity of the church of God." [1] However, this same cautious history of past union initiatives makes COCU loom as "an audacious ecumenical venture without precedent." [2]

Any attempt at church union is influenced by the complexity of the church situation in its times. Upon examining the full spectrum of problems confronting the church today, many people are tempted to pronounce disparaging epithets, ranging from frustration, rejection, to pessimism about the church. Ecumenism—conciliar, bilateral conversations, secular, or church union—is not immune from this pessimism and its full partner, apathy. Advocates and doomsayers alike have offered a diagnosis stating that a particular model of ecumenism, or indeed the whole ecumenical movement, is stalled, in a slump, in the doldrums, in limbo, has developed a malaise, become non-essential, or is dead! Such sentiments are common to the Consultation, which at its inception and at nearly every plenary has been proclaimed on the verge of shipwreck. These pronouncements are not unimportant, especially if they represent a majority of Christians in America. Such diagnoses, however, tell us as much about the crises of faith, identity, and mission within the church today as they do about the health or stability of any ecumenical model. They could also be the defensive barrages of those who would want to forestall change in the church.

From the outset we should acknowledge that the *kairos* for church union is not the same as popular support for a united church. *Kairos* is a matter of God's time, openness to his purpose. The consideration of church union, therefore, is tested not only by the uninformed opinions of church constituencies, but by our faithfulness and obedience to God's reconciling act in Jesus Christ. COCU began with the conviction that God wills the visible reconciliation and unity of his people. If the prospects of genuine openness to study and a future decision are preconditioned merely by unresponsiveness and apathy, we can expect nothing other than divine judgment upon the churches.

COCU portends a new beginning for the church. Despite the assessments of skeptics—those radical traditionists opposed to change, those tired and disenchanted visionaries of previous decades, or the devotees of instant ecumenism—this decade of conversations has produced monumental achievements and gains which cannot be erased. These hard-won achievements need to be understood by those who may not have been aware of this venture, and replayed for those who have been deeply involved. In a real sense the Consultation's first decade reveals a potential for destiny, if church union is understood as a process of churches in search of faithfulness and obedience. A consideration of this first decade will give us the range of COCU's vision and intention.

II

The Consultation on Church Union's meteoric appearance is well known. The initial proposal was made in a sermon by Eugene Carson Blake on December 4, 1960, at Grace Cathedral (Episcopal), San Francisco. Entitled "A Proposal Toward the Reunion of Christ's Church," it proved to be an epochal event which captured the imagination of the American churches and communication media. Two ironies are related to that event. First, the proposal for COCU was made by the same man, then stated clerk of the United Presbyterian Church in the U.S.A., who had officially ended the Greenwich Plan by causing his church to withdraw. Second, while Dr. Blake's sermon was preached on the eve of the fifth triennial assembly of the National Council of the Churches of Christ in the U.S.A. and dominated the informal agenda of that meeting, the relations between COCU and the NCC have been marked at best by tangential relations and at worst by veiled suspicion and an oft-assumed incompatibility between church union and the conciliar principle.

The Blake sermon came after John XXIII's call of the Second Vatican Council (1959) but before the actual opening of the Council in 1962. It was, therefore, a signal part of the ecumenical milieu of the early 1960s, and shared in the generation of ecumenical optimism at the turn of the decade. While the content of the San Francisco sermon gave an able basis for what was to follow, it was the prophetic dimension of this proposal, unseen by most people until later, which was its deepest merit and which gave cruciality to the later COCU. In Blake's judgment, the time was right for the churches to transcend their historical disunities and to find a common life in a church "truly catholic, truly evangelical, and truly reformed."[3] A united church was essential for the immediate future. The present divided Christian churches would be rendered ineffective in mission and witness by the rising secularization and materialism of American life. As he noted nearly a year later:

> At present there is not a sufficient community of Christians either at the local or at the national level to make effective application of the Gospel of Jesus Christ to the crucial decisions being made in the social, economic, and political spheres of American life. American churches are generally (and are generally correctly judged by the world to be) competing pressure groups rather than channels to the mission of the grace of God.[4]

Similarly, the dual rationale of faithfulness and mission was articulated by the delegates after the first plenary in Washington:

> We came away convinced, all of us, that the same conditions that in the 16th century led the churches apart—that is, the concern for the church's renewal and for her purity, and the effectiveness of her witness—are now driving the churches together today, as we seek our unity visibly in Jesus Christ.[5]

The original perception by Dr. Blake and other early leaders of the Consultation proved to be painfully accurate, as in the next decade the ship was rocked by storms, assaulted by outsiders, imperiled by mutiny from within. This perception gave COCU a realism and clarity about the journey it was to begin in a revolutionary sea.

Consensus and Conflict: Exploring the Issues

The four churches originally proposed—United Presbyterian, Episcopal, Methodist, United Church of Christ—committed themselves to official consultation, and sent representatives to the first, exploratory plenary at Washington, D.C., in April, 1962. Forty-two representatives constituted themselves the "Consultation on Church Union," and then sought to isolate the theological and nontheological issues which needed study and clarification. If church union was to have theological integrity, these issues and the conflicts they have produced among the churches must be identified, faced, and resolved. Background papers were presented and committees dealt with the areas of faith, order, liturgy, education and public relations, social and cultural problems, and polity, organization and power structure. In addition, decisions were made about personnel and procedures which gave tangibility and set patterns for the future Consultation on Church Union. George L. Hunt served as part-time executive secretary (1962–1968). James I. McCord, President of Princeton Theological Seminary, was elected to serve a two-year term (1962–1964) as the first chairman. Those who followed in this capacity were Robert F. Gibson, Jr. (1964–1966), Bishop of the Episcopal Diocese of Virginia; David G. Colwell (1966–1968), the minister of the First Congregational Church, Washington, D.C.; James K. Mathews (1968–1970), Bishop of the Boston area of the United Methodist Church; George G. Beazley, Jr. (1970–1973), Ecumenical Officer of the Christian Church (Disciples of Christ).

Two sets of invitations were sent. The first was to the Christian Church (Disciples of Christ), the Evangelical United Brethren, and the Polish National Catholic Church to become full participants. The Disciples and the Evangelical United Brethren were already in official union conversations with the United Church of Christ and the Methodist Church, respectively; the Polish National Catholic Church is in full communion with the Episcopal Church. The Disciples and the Evangelical United Brethren accepted the invitation in 1962, but the Polish National Catholic Church declined.

A second invitation urged other churches in North America to become observer-consultants at the plenary meetings. Across the decade of conversations nearly twenty churches (virtually every major church family in America), councils, and church union conversations in other countries (Canada, Germany, South India, Jamaica, New Zealand, et al.) have shared this status; some have served as intimate counselors to the COCU deliberations.

The second official meeting of the Consultation was held at Oberlin, Ohio, in March, 1963. The presence of the Disciples and the Evangelical United Brethren as full participants broadened the spectrum of COCU and, as would be the case with the entry of all future participating churches, enlarged the possibilities of catholicity in any eventual united church. At Oberlin important explorations were made on worship and the sociological factors at work in the participating churches. Nevertheless, an unexpected consensus was reached on the crucial question of authority in the church, namely Scripture and Tradition. This theological breakthrough had far-reaching implications for consensus on other critical issues and for the possibilities of union. In previous centuries and situations, Scripture and Tradition had been regarded as contradictory authorities and thereby in opposition to each other. Now both could be affirmed in a relationship of interdependence within the church.

Oberlin's consenus gave new ecclesiological prospects. The Scriptures of Old and New Testaments have "a unique authority" because they witness to God's revelation. The center of the Holy Scriptures is Jesus Christ, "crucified and risen, the living Lord and Head of the church." In like manner "a historic Christian Tradition" was recognized as authoritative for the church. Tradition ("T") in this sense means "the whole life of the Church, ever guided and nourished by the Holy Spirit, and expressed in its worship, witness, way of life, and its order." [6]

At its third meeting at Princeton, New Jersey, in 1964, the Consultation received a prod and a jolt. On the one hand, it achieved significant consensus on the sacraments, but on the other hand was shaken by the denominational defensiveness revealed in two of the participating churches.

The theological discussion at the third plenary focused on the ministry, baptism, and the Lord's Supper—three major theological issues which previously constituted barriers to the formation of a united church. Because of its commitment to catholicity as well as the participation of the

Disciples, the Consultation faced the meaning of baptism and the historical existence of different modes. As the act of Christ in his church, baptism was acknowledged as the visible basis of Christian unity. The primary significance of baptism, said Princeton, "lies not in what we do but
in what God has already done for us in Jesus Christ, to which faith is
our response." [7] On this basis it was agreed that both infant and be-
liever's baptism could be accepted as alternate forms in the united church,
but neither could be required against the sincere conscience of a member
or a minister. Baptism is to be administered only once "since it is an act
of God in Christ and the sign of our entrance into the whole Church."
The fact of this mutual recognition of each other's membership was not
totally surprising, since the Faith and Order movement had helped the
churches move toward this consensus. Even Roman Catholic theologians
at this time were speaking of baptism as a symbol of the common unity
which all Christians share. What was surprising was the ease with which
consensus on a very sticky problem was reached in union conversations.

The Lord's Supper, also called the Eucharist, Holy Communion, is affirmed as central to the church's worship. It is an effective means whereby
God in Christ acts and is present with his people. There were obviously
different emphases about the meaning of the Supper. Although aware
of these divergencies, the Princeton statement on the Eucharist found a
central core of common belief:

> We in the united church must say what we can about the Eucharist, as
> Christians in every age have struggled to do. Yet we must recognize that
> human words can never fully express but only point toward redemptive
> mystery. The Church's action of sharing together in that mystery, in re-
> sponse to the Lord's invitation and command, is altogether more decisive
> than any effort on our part to think alike about it.[8]

Within the context of a total range of views about the Lord's Supper,
the Princeton meeting enumerated certain basic affirmations which represented a growing consensus among the churches. These affirmations of
Princeton were later made fundamental to the *Principles of Church
Union* and *A Plan of Union*. First, the Eucharist is recognized as an effective sign—i.e., the means whereby God in Christ acts and is present with
his people; second, the awareness of Christ's action, "accomplished in
his incarnation, atoning death, resurrection, and exultation" in this event
is affirmed; third, there is conviction about the presence of Christ in the
Eucharist. He is not only remembered by the church but also is, by God's
action, present among his people. "The Holy Communion is the presence
of Christ who has come, who comes to his people, and who will come
in glory." [9]

The Princeton meeting unexpectedly dealt with motivation and nature of commitment to the process as they related to certain of the participating churches. The Episcopal delegation restated the Anglican mandate under which their participation was limited—namely, the Chicago-Lambeth Quadrilateral—emphasizing particularly the historic episcopate as a necessary condition for the reconciliation of divided ministries. A more controversial crisis centered around the attitude of the Methodist delegation. The report of their Commission on Church Union, prepared for the forthcoming General Conference of the Methodist Church at Pittsburgh, was inadvertently unveiled (unearthed by the press!) at Princeton. The report carried two disconcerting implications. First, it revealed there was no intention to do as the previous plenary at Oberlin had requested of all participating churches—namely, to request the General Conference for authorization to engage in writing a plan of union. Second, the report isolated five major concerns about the other churches which led them to question the possibilities of Methodists uniting with these particular communions. The concerns laid out were the difference between Methodist and Episcopal concepts of the episcopate, the lack of appreciation of the connectional system, baptism by immersion, the value of world Methodist ties, and the use of alcoholic beverages by members of other churches. While this report did not reach the floor of the plenary, its handling by the public press did bring a candor to the discussions and surfaced a need for deeper commitment to the COCU process. This kind of report did not drastically influence the agenda of the Princeton meeting, but it did influence the revision of the Methodist delegation and resulted in a stronger involvement in the future.

Amid this unrest and disappointment—not uncommon emotions in a church union process—the closing statement at Princeton spoke of undaunted intentions:

> That difficulties, setbacks, and disappointments will come in the future, as they have already, we realize full well. Yet in obedience to Jesus Christ, and claiming his promise of the presence of the Holy Spirit, we pledge ourselves to press on for a union to the glory of God the Father.[10]

To some degree such sentiments can be judged as ecumenical euphoria. At the fullest, however, they convey a tenacity not to run when crises arise. The churches in the Consultation have made a covenant based on their given unity in Christ. All crises are faced within the covenant.

If the Princeton meeting in 1964 adjourned amid a pale uncertainty and anxiety, the fourth plenary at Lexington, Kentucky, in 1965 discovered renewed confidence. Responsible for this boldness were the strides made in a mutual understanding of ministry. Ministry is the rock upon which earlier church union efforts had been shipwrecked. At Lexington it was given full and open consideration; as a result, substantive agreement was reached. Consensus was reached on the meaning of ordination, the functions and the offices of the ordained ministers (presbyters, bishops, deacons), and a service of reconciling the divided ministries and memberships without questioning the reality of any previous ordinations. If the breakthrough at Oberlin on Christian authority gave the Consultation sure life in its infancy, the ability to come to agreement on ordained ministry at Lexington gave it a more secure adolescence.

Lexington transposed the normal formula for the unification of ministries. In the past, divided churches have considered the reconciling of the ordained ministries of the various communions as a prerequisite to and guarantor of a united church. Yet this approach had very dangerous implications about the church receiving its validity from the clergy; inherent also is an impoverished view of the role of ministry of lay people. At Lexington COCU recast the discussion, which was later embodied in *Principles of Church Union* and the service of reconciliation in *A Plan of Union*. Proposed as the first act is the reconciliation of the churches and their memberships (based on the mutual recognition of baptism), after which would follow—within the context of the united church—the authorization of a common ministry. Hence, the Consultation's participating churches insisted that ministry be understood and exercised in the context of the church.

The Lexington report accepted the three historic ministries of bishops, presbyters, and deacons. However, no single doctrine or theory of any office would be required. In each instance the idea is not merely to perpetuate existing forms, but to recover the full ministry which these offices have known in Christian history and could manifest within a fuller Christian community. More specific work on the nature and function of these offices had to await the preparation of *A Plan of Union* five years later.

Lexington articulated certain guidelines for a ministry truly catholic, truly evanegical, and truly reformed. A "catholic" ministry implies continuity which provides the contemporary ministry with a vital connection with the ministry of Jesus Christ, the apostolic community, and the church throughout its history. This continuity is made real and conserved by the faithful testimony of the whole Christian community. An "evangelical" ministry is grounded in God's saving act in Jesus Christ, commends personal obedience to the Lordship of Christ, and is concerned for Christian witness and mission in and for the world. A "reformed" ministry constantly stands under the judgment of the Holy Spirit as he works and witnesses through the Scriptures and in history, and gives priority to the inclusiveness of the Christian community. In other words, it is a ministry

committed to the varieties of Christian truth, but lives in the openness
of the Spirit.

The confidence revealed at the Lexington plenary led the delegates to authorize a Special Committee to prepare *Principles of Church Union,* which
would bring all the earlier agreements into a workable whole and would
serve as a basis for a future plan of union. Immediately a blue-ribbon
committee, chaired by Eugene Carson Blake, was appointed and brought
its fruits to the next plenary. In the work of this *Principles* committee
the first black church, the African Methodist Episcopal, began to function
in the activities of the Consultation.

Convergence and the Shape of the Church:
Testing the Consensus

The drama of the Dallas, Texas, plenary in 1966 was heightened by the
consideration and approval of *Principles of Church Union* and the increase of the member churches by two. Only a few weeks before the
Dallas plenary the General Assembly of the Presbyterian Church in the
United States, by a surprise vote, became a participating church. The
African Methodist Episcopal Church became the seventh participating
church at Dallas.

Principles of Church Union, in COCU parlance the "Blue Book," gave
the occasion for intensive debate and reflection among the official delegates. For the first time the whole range of consensus was seen in relationship to all the parts, and the dim shape of a united church began
to emerge. The *Principles* document included a preamble; four chapters
dealing with the faith, the worship, the sacraments, and the ministry of
the church; and three appendices entitled "An Open Letter to the
Churches," "The Structure of the Church," and "Stages and Steps Toward
a United Church." All three appendices, while not a part of the main
body of material, have ecclesiological significance and reveal insights into
the posture of the Consultation. Both the preamble and "An Open Letter
to the Churches" (one of the classic documents in ecumenical history)
defined the calling and character of a united church as involving our faith
in God, our obedience to his will, and the desire for the one Church of
Christ to be a light to the world which God loves.

The document on stages and steps outlined the various phases and
decisions that would be required as the churches moved from the approval of *Principles* all the way to a shared life in a united church. Unfortunately, this document soon became obscured; but in view of current
discussions about church union as "process," it should be identified as
the first attempt to convey this point to the churches. Particularly unique
to this strategy is the decision to wait until after union to prepare a

constitution. Until that time a Plan of Union will be sufficient basis for
the inauguration of the united church and guidance during the transitional period. "The writing of a final, formal constitution is, in our view,
of much less critical a character than the process of mutual discovery and
sharing which should characterize this stage." [11] The paper on structure
did not receive official approval at Dallas. However, it identified structure
as an issue which needed careful consideration. This paper proposed two
local church units: the parish-congregation and the task group, both of
which became central proposals in A Plan of Union. The Dallas plenary
was a moment of exhilaration and accomplishment. Its final action was
to commend Principles to the churches for study and comment.

The next two plenaries, Cambridge, Massachusetts (1967), and Dayton, Ohio (1968), focused primarily on structural issues in a united
church. These discussions were complicated and strewn with pain and
frustration, and with obvious reasons. There was no ecumenical consensus
on this issue which the Consultation could call upon, as it did on authority, sacraments, and ministry. Likewise, there surfaced the resistances
which come when the functions and polity of our churches are brought
under scrutiny. The deepest sensitivities seem to be related to the structures of the church. At any rate, Cambridge and Dayton revealed that
American Christians, long acknowledged experts in management and organization, are by and large severely handicapped by their emotions for
any creative discussion about ecumenical structures.

At Cambridge COCU also received clues about a shift in the ecumenical emphasis, particularly at the relation between the church and the
world. From addresses by John Dillenberger and Colin Williams, known
as "radical renewalists" by the typology of that time, came the first out-
cries of secular ecumenists who brought warnings to the Consultation.
First, church union would have to offer radical surgery, not medication,
to selfish, declining institutions; second, ecumenism must develop a sensitivity to the world and a desire to come to terms with the processes of
secularism and revolution; third, some would claim the possibility of
Christians of all traditions sharing koionia through common social involvement without the rigors of union negotiations. Actually, the Cambridge and Dayton discussions did not come through this systematized
or forceful, but the evidence was clear. COCU would have to face a
radically different theological climate, and would have to come to terms
with those whose interest is less in maintaining the ecumenical consensus
and more in confronting the concrete problems of mankind. Significantly,
such voices came from those who were within the Consultation and who
had given a major portion of their interest and time to the Consultation.

Between Dallas and Cambridge two other black Methodist churches,
the African Methodist Episcopal Zion and the Christian Methodist Epis-

copal churches, entered the COCU pilgrimage. The active presence now of three black churches changed the character and goal of the Consultation in a very fruitful way, and gave the Consultation the capacity and the necessity to deal with one of the life-and-death issues of the twentieth century.

The seventh plenary at Dayton, Ohio, in 1968, was the occasion for a number of practical developments which have had effective long-range influence: the delegations of the participating churches were enlarged from nine to ten persons with the provision that one delegate be a youth under twenty-eight years of age; an experimental liturgy, *An Order of Worship for the Proclamation of the Word of God and the Celebration of the Lord's Supper,* produced by the Commission on Worship, was used for the eucharistic service at the plenary, was received and recommended to the churches; authorization was given for the calling of a full-time Secretariat with permanent offices (later established at Princeton, New Jersey). In September, 1968, Paul A. Crow, Jr., became the first General Secretary. The most significant decision at Dayton, however, was the authorization of a Plan of Union Commission with a two-year mandate to bring a draft before the plenary not later than 1970.

The Dayton meeting received reports on church membership and discipline, the unification of ministry, and the provisional structure of the united church, and responses to the study of *Principles of Church Union.* The structure report provided the most heated debate. The key issue revolved around how the churches would be represented in the provisional assembly which would guide the united church from the time of inauguration until the permanent structures of the church were set up. The Dayton debate centered on whether there would be an equal number of delegates (twenty-five) to the provisional assembly from each uniting church, or whether delegates would be proportionate to the total membership of each church. Equal representation won by one vote, though that vote did not settle this structural issue.

The Plan of Union Commission was appointed by the participating churches shortly thereafter, and began what up to this point was to be considered the most productive task in the COCU process. There is not space to trace the work and dynamics of this Commission, chaired by William A. Benfield, Jr., minister of the First Presbyterian Church (PCUS), Charleston, West Virginia. It is enough to say that this Commission of seventeen working members handled its assignment with herculean commitment (often in the two-year period meeting one week each month, not including travel!) and became an effective community where intense debate, anger, joy, prayer, honesty, made the fulfillment of the assignment possible. The result of the members' work was more

than the production of a document; they experienced a foretaste of the
Church of Christ Uniting which they proposed.

The Atlanta, Georgia, plenary in 1969 convened in order to consider
three reports: "An Outline of a Plan of Union," "An Interim Report on
the Unification (Mingling) of Ministries," and "Guidelines for Local
Interchurch Action." The latter represented a new development for the
Consultation and an attempt to deal with a new situation in local communities with which it had to come to terms. There was already in existence and a growing number emerging of experimental relationships of
cooperation and union among congregations at the local level. These
guidelines were prepared to lay out the various options which this experimentation had identified and to offer constructive counsel as congregations engaged in various forms of cooperative and joint effort. Here
was a sign that mission and unity, two commitments of the Consultation,
were being actively sought in local situations.

Atlanta saw the Consultation broadening its perspective both by its
agenda and by the program participants. Two particular portions of the
wider Christian fellowship were dramatically and forcefully presented
and listened to. One of the main speakers was Bishop (now Cardinal)
Jan G. M. Willebrands of the Secretariat for Promoting Christian Unity
of the Roman Catholic Church. With warmth and graciousness, but with
theological astuteness, he discussed major issues and problems within the
Roman Catholic Church which parallel those in the Consultation. Cardinal Willebrands' address was very helpful; the event was historic. Furthermore, Atlanta represented a new moment when the black agenda, which
was reaching a peak in the American society, came squarely on the working agenda of the Consultation. It came to the agenda not in the terms
or the way the white man would have dealt with the problem but in
terms of the way the black man feels it has to be dealt with. A charismatic address by Frederick D. Jordan, Bishop of the African Methodist
Episcopal Church, candid and impassioned discussions on the plenary
floor about racial equity, and an unofficial late-evening session with black
leaders in the Atlanta area gave clear evidence of the Consultation's
commitment to racial inclusiveness. Of course, the sensitivity of the
churches had been primed, and to some degree they were still reeling
from, the impact of black militant James Foreman and the Black Manifesto, the riots at Watts, and other landmarks in the recent history of black
liberation.

At Atlanta the Consultation gained glimpses of the fact that the relation of blacks and whites in the Consultation and any eventual reconciliation of black and white Christians in a united church can be worked
out only as black and white Christians are able to establish trust relations
with each other and their institutions of power and wealth are led to be

responsive to a common future. Among some at Atlanta the option of black separatism was seen, romantically or necessarily, as a live option. Others, like Bishop Jordan, said that, despite the racism that exists in society and churches, the black churches are participating in COCU because they believe in its purpose.

> We know that sometime in God's good grace church union must happen. We do not think it is only enough to have almost happened. We are determined that if it fails to happen it should not fail because we do not join you in trying to make it happen.[12]

The joint commitment to reconciliation between blacks and whites was symbolized when the plenary participants—in an unplanned event—went together one rainy afternoon to lay a wreath at the grave of the martyred Martin Luther King, Jr.

After the Atlanta meeting the Plan of Union Commission went back to the drawing board and its unprecedented itinerary. In the fall of 1969 a National Conference on Program was convened in Cincinnati which brought together several hundred persons, staff and board members, who are responsible for educational and missional programs in the nine COCU churches. The announced objectives were (1) to identify several areas of mission where the COCU churches might engage in united planning and action, and (2) to secure commitment from these denominational boards and agencies to such common action and planning leading toward a united church.[13] It was also assumed that these key leaders, many of whom knew little or nothing about COCU, might be informed and involved in the process. The Cincinnati conference's success in these goals was only minimal. The conference's scheme to carry on the discussions in groups other than according to specialties (Christian education, national ministries, overseas mission, etc.) proved too severe a methodology for those present. Again, those engaged in current structures and programs, which in 1969 were beginning to feel the pulsations of a survival crisis, found it difficult to take seriously the possibilities of joint action as a stage toward a united church when their present operations were in jeopardy. It is also safe to say that many of those present thought that the church's mission might be fulfilled without actual church union.

At the ninth plenary, March, 1970, at St. Louis, the main bill of fare was the draft text of *A Plan of Union for the Church of Christ Uniting*. The bulk of this ten-chapter, 104-page document was a recasting and expanding of the earlier consensus, using *Principles* as a catalyst. New material was included on the nature of the church (Chapter III), church membership (Chapter IV), organization and government (Chapter VIII) including the transitional period (Chapter X), and two appendices composed of an imaginative Service of Inauguration and an ordinal to be used in the ordination of presbyters, bishops, and deacons. Certain issues which had been discussed at Atlanta—bishops, parish, inclusiveness, and others—received fuller, more mature treatment in the draft plan. The one-page Chapter I, "To Begin Anew," says a great deal not only about the content of the Plan but about the posture of the Consultation in a changing world. The idea of covenant among these nine churches, "a company of the people of God," is affirmed. Other distinctive birthmarks for the Church of Christ Uniting—the provisional name proposed in the Plan— are the acceptance of renewal from the Holy Spirit, the willingness to minister to "the deep yearnings of the human spirit for fullness of life," struggling against racism, poverty, pollution, war, and "other problems of the family of man," and the mutual sharing of the gifts of different traditions.

The climatic moment at St. Louis, as well as the fruition of a decade of hard dialogue and debate, came when *A Plan of Union* was approved for transmittal to "the member churches and to all Christians for study and response, seeking their assistance in the further development and completion of this Plan of Union." [14] Note again the intentions of this action: the Plan is sent "to all Christians"; this draft is commended for "study and response," not decision; the responses and evaluations of the congregations and churches will be the primary resource in the further perfection of the Plan. These rubrics denote an open process, not only for the two-year period ending June 1, 1972, but throughout the whole pilgrimage.

Apathy and Ardor: Dynamics of the Future

The eighteen months between the St. Louis (March, 1970) and Denver (September, 1971) plenaries brought two dilemmas to center stage: (1) the need to engage the churches at all levels in the study of the Plan and participation in the COCU process, and (2) the necessity of coming to terms with a changing situation both in the church and in the world.

It had long been understood that bringing the Consultation—its issues and goals—alive for local pastors and lay people in order that union might be seen as a response to faith and mission had to become a priority for the COCU churches. As early as the first plenary at Washington, Dr. Blake acknowledged that the task of informing and educating members of the participating churches presented an essential but immense responsibility.[15] Resolutions at different plenaries intermittently called this fact to the attention of the churches. After St. Louis it was seen with even more clarity, however, that the success of the Consultation depends not only on information and education; Christians from all walks of life must be involved, church union must be translated and legitimized within the context of how they view the church and its mission. Church union cannot be imagined as an exercise of national bureaucrats merging national boards and agencies; its implications run deep into the stream of local church life where Christians meet each other. Only such involvement and participation by a sizable portion of the 25,000,000 Christians represented will, therefore, bring credibility to the church union process. Only such widespread involvement will make a responsible, mature revision of *A Plan of Union* possible.

Once this need was identified, procedures were activated to enable local and regional participation. An Interpretation Commission was appointed to plan a strategy for local study and response to the Plan and to enable the COCU process to be effectively shared in by the participating churches. Along this line a series of conferences was held with the regional leaders (bishops, synod executives, regional ministers, *et al.*); a network of state coordinators was identified; communication resources were developed.

Another factor which confronted the Consultation in its post-St. Louis period was a radical, unanticipated shift in the ecclesiological climate. To illustrate, the Consultation was born in a period of relative peace and prosperity among the churches. The normal assumption was that unity and union would be realized by resolving the issues of faith and order. The decade which followed, however, turned out to be "one of the most disquieting and difficult in the history of the American churches." The fundamental crisis is a crisis of culture, but the church enacts its own version. The analyses of the crisis are as many and varied as the number of critics. Nevertheless, certain dominant traits characterize the new mood among Christians: a crisis of faith, a polarization over the church's involvement in social action, an anti-institution, anti-Establshment spirit, declining membership rolls and finances. These shifting sands have not been without their influence on ecumenism and church union. The most pronounced by-product has been attitudes toward church union which range from apathy to disenchantment. This gives support to the opinion that ecumenism is stalled and COCU is dead!

The tenth plenary at Denver, Colorado, in September, 1971, convened in a tentatively skeptical vein, though the aura of crisis was nothing new for the veterans of COCU campaigns. Above all, there was determination to be realistic about the present and frank about the prospects of the future. All who came to Denver realized that COCU had to come to terms with a new situation; it had to convey the capacity of a new style. Hence, Denver was a very different plenary in format. The design set forth four questions to be explored, all of which contained deep implications for the Consultation:

1. What does the church have to say to modern man?
2. How has the past decade affected the presuppositions for church union?
3. How do the understandings of some of the contemporary movements (black liberation, women's liberation, youth, and counterculture) relate to the goals and purposes of the Consultation on Church Union?
4. What commitments are necessary as we face the immediate next steps in the Consultation's process?

So designed and enacted, with input from sociologist of religion Peter L. Berger, black theologian Preston N. Williams, and biblical scholar James A. Sanders, the Denver plenary represented something far from a dodge into irrelevancy. It was an exciting encounter which strengthened the Consultation and broadened its potential.

While Denver's achievements reside primarily in its impact on the COCU process, two documents of importance did emerge. The first, "A Word to the Churches," reaffirmed the churches' commitment to "a united church faithful to our Lord's intention for a reconciled and reconciling community ministering to a divided humanity," then called upon the participating churches to take action in two interim possibilities —namely, serious promotion of "programs leading to the achievement of racial justice and compensatory treatment for minorities in the churches and the nation" and the practice of "an interim eucharistic fellowship on some regular basis." A second Denver paper was composed of ten recommendations urging, at the national, regional, and local levels, joint planning and programs related to Christian witness and service.

III

From this survey of the Consultation's brief life one can sense something of the agony and ecstasy of a new church in process of formation. COCU involves ordinary and extraordinary persons. It has faced and resolved a host of divisive issues; it now confronts an agenda filled with new polarities and schisms. Its plenaries portray a rhythm of giant steps toward union, punctuated with times of little momentum or interest. Breakthroughs and near breakdowns, crises and charismatic moments of the Spirit have blessed its history. It is assaulted by defenders of parochialism, ignored by the bored, damned with faint praise by the uncommitted, and affirmed by those who yearn for a church that is becoming. Its proposals partake of the new and the old, but never with the right proportion to satisfy the Right or the Left. It makes company with the traditionalists and visionaries, believing both are brothers and should be encompassed by the community of God's love. Daily it reminds itself and others that church union is not the merging of existing ecclesiastical structures but a search for new community, "unlike the churches any of us have known in our past separateness," which visibly expresses the oneness of Christ and his church for a broken world. Such a history carries the potential of rebirth.

NOTES

1. Quoted in Braaten, Carl E., "Ecumenism and Theological Education in the United States," *Œcumenica 1969*, edited by F. W. Kantzenbach and V. Vajta (Minneapolis: Augsburg Publishing House, 1969), p. 199.
2. Outler, Albert C., "COCU: Test Case for Ecumenism in America. Lecture I: Brave New Beginnings," p. 15 (mimeographed). Delivered as the McFadin Lectures, Texas Christian University, February, 1970.
3. *Digest of the Proceedings of the Consultation on Church Union*, Vol. IV (1965), p. 24.
4. Blake, Eugene Carson, "An Interim Report on the Proposal Toward the Reunion of Christ's Church in the United States," *The Ecumenical Review*, Vol. XIV, No. 1 (October, 1961), p. 85.
5. *Digest*, Vol. III (1964), p. 22.
6. *COCU: The Official Reports of the First Four Meetings of the Consultation* (Cincinnati: Forward Movement Publications, 1966), p. 24.
7. *Digest*, Vol. III (1964), p. 27.
8. *Consultation on Church Union, 1967: Principles of Church Union, Guidelines for Structure, and A Study Guide* (Cincinnati: Forward Movement Publications, 1967), p. 41.
9. *Ibid.*, p. 42.
10. *COCU: The Official Reports of the First Four Meetings of the Consultation, op. cit.*, p. 55.
11. *Consultation on Church Union, 1967: Principles of Church Union, op. cit.*, p. 87.
12. *Digest*, Vol. VIII (1969), p. 153. See chapter 8, "COCU and the Black Churches."
13. See Wilson, Donald, ed., *The National Conference on Program* (Princeton: COCU, 1969).
14. *Digest*, Vol. IX (1970), p. 89.
15. See Marty, Martin E., "Consultation on Union," *The Christian Century*, Vol. LXXIX, No. 17 (April 25, 1962), p. 515.

II

THE PRESENT SITUATION:
PROBLEMS AND CHALLENGES

3

The COCU Parish:
Plan and Perspective

THEODORE H. ERICKSON, JR.

Throughout its history the ecumenical movement has produced a number of compelling plans for church unity. One of the most ingenious was put forward by Roger Babson in 1938. Babson, then moderator of the Congregational Christian General Council, suggested the following as a version of the E. Stanley Jones plan:

> In view of world conditions and the attitude of our young people, I am sure that the different church denominations must take more active steps to eliminate unnecessary differences.
> Of all the suggestions, I believe the most practical would be for all of the Protestant denominations to adopt the same name. I care not what the name will be; but most of those with whom I have talked suggest "United Church." There will be no consolidation of organizations, headquarters or officers. No secretary would need to lose his position and no invested funds would be disturbed. *The denominations would be known, however, by numbers instead of by name.* For instance, the denomination having the largest membership would be designated as *Group One*. This number would appear on the signboard of the church and all literature issued by the denomination. Although everything else would remain as is, yet this would be a great step forward in the eyes of the nation.[1]

Church leaders have long yearned for a simple and speedy way to bring about unity in this world. By contrast, the Consultation on Church Union's parish plan is a thoughtful and comprehensive design for a sophisticated religious organization at the local level. It properly takes account of pluralism, diversity, organizational control, and emerging social

41

needs. This may be part of the problem. Its very adequacy could also be its liability.

As presently projected, the parish would be the basic local unit of the church and would include a number of existing congregations as well as new groups, task forces, and house churches. It may or may not be confined to a single geographic area. Its professional leaders would work as a team under the direction of "The Minister of the Parish." A parish council would become the responsible representative body, maintaining a ratio of two lay persons for each of the ordained staff in the parish. All church property would be held in the name of the entire parish, the council acting as trustees of the parish corporation. Membership would be held in the parish, although active participation may typically be limited to one or two smaller units. For example, a member of a parish may regularly participate in a congregation for worship and education, and in a smaller, more mobile task group organized to accomplish a specific goal on behalf of the entire parish.

Recent experience in organizing local groups analogous to COCU parishes suggests several arguments in favor of the parish plan. The parish size is probably the most effective local unit for dealing with change, since it is large enough to allow maneuverability but small enough for participants to comprehend their situation easily. Moreover, the parish is a critical unit for engendering mutual support and role differentiation among professional leaders. It is a rich context within which new forms of church life and action can develop and grow, although, as we shall see, it has limitations in this area. It offers the possibility for area-wide coordination of other agencies and organizations within the voluntary sector. It projects an image of a united and cooperative church. Finally, it provides a context for new kinds of association among lay-level members across present lines of separation.

But somewhere, something is wrong. "It's beautiful," remarked a judicatory executive, "but it won't fly." What causes this not atypical reaction? How can we get the parish off the ground?

Church leaders today are caught in a curious position. They want to implement the COCU parish plan, but they know intuitively the kind of resistance it will meet, as well as some of the reasons for that resistance. Thus, it is important that we distinguish between criticisms of the Plan itself and those reasons why the Plan may not be accepted and achieved. We may then be in a position to suggest how the important goals outlined in the Plan may be put into effect.

Theology and Intuition

Theological training has a tendency to impel thinking from the abstract to the concrete, from general principles to specific actions. However, ecclesiastical practice tends to be more pragmatic, moving from assorted givens to general norms. The typical process of a congregation "breaking in a pastor" is in large part helping him to reorient his thought and action from the former to the latter. This resocialization process focuses on helping the pastor become aware of what will work and what won't. Thus, while ministers continue to verbalize theologically, they also learn to operate intuitively.

Successful church development in America has been carried out by men whose intuitions were finely honed. For example, H. Paul Douglass, writing in 1914, recounts the differences between success and failure on the western frontier as the difference between leaders who understood the character and needs of the settlers and organized around those needs, and those who relied solely on doctrine as an organizing principle.[2]

In concept, the Plan is largely theological. It moves from general principles of unity and mission to specific roles, structures, and operating procedures. At a formal level, church leaders are trained to accept this direction. At an operational level, they are not. Hence the confusion.

Much resistance to the COCU parish plan is also largely intuitive, and this is difficult to articulate. Sifting through reactions to the parish, we see three levels of objections. The first level, most frequently stated by clergy and lay leaders, is that of personal relationship to the church. Local congregations encourage personal identity on the part of their members. No matter how small or how large, the congregation one has chosen and grown with provides an element of the social frame within which he understands himself. The parish, on the other hand, is still theory, an unknown social entity. Personal identity with the parish may be diminished or enhanced or merely changed. When a person joins or drops out of a church, he decides to do so for reasons relating to other aspects of his life-style: occupation, place in life cycle, or social expectations. However, when the church changes around him, he is forced to examine his whole life in light of that change. While we all can benefit from this kind of examination, wholesale changing of church structures may be a questionable and uneconomic way to confront people.

The second level of resistance is found in the unmistakable change of national mood at this point in history. The Plan is highly rational at a time when introspection is on the rise. The Plan is complex in a time when many seek a return to a simple faith. The Plan is institutional at a time of growing distrust of our established institutions. The Plan emphasizes structures and social action at a time when many look for deeper insights into the individual. The Plan depends on committed and talented professional leadership when many of our leaders have lost their visions and doubt that their skills are any more effective.

The widely heralded "new localism" in the church may or may not contribute to parish development. It may be a move away from all entangling alliances, or it may be a serious reconsideration of local needs and mission. While this dynamic has some organizational potential, it is often highly overrated.

The third level of reaction is the most subtle. What is the meaning of the Plan? Can the parish succeed in incorporating a link between the transcendent and the mundane for me and my neighbor? Does it have an existential reality that draws people into its life? The heart of church life is its ability to interrelate the subjective impulses toward the ultimate on behalf of many persons, and to give this interrelationship socially visible form. At this level we experience the church as history and possibility for the world. Everyday life is given a focus and particular meaning. No plan can promise to be ultimately meaningful. Yet, this is an intuitive demand on the part of those who would be its participants and supporters.

Unity, Diversity, and Creative Tension

Apart from the operational difficulties of the COCU parish plan, there are several formal contradictions within the plan itself that bear careful scrutiny (A Plan of Union, VIII, 1–140, pp. 56–72). Some of these contradictions are deliberate, introduced in the name of creative tension. However, tension always promotes unintended consequences. It is thus risky to plan for tensions before an organization is developed and before responsible persons are on the scene.

One of the contradictions in the COCU Plan is between the concepts of economy—consolidating structures, conserving resources, and saving money—and inclusion—incorporating diverse groups, structures, and professional roles into a single organization. An optimum organization in which the necessary goals are reached with a minimum of bureaucratic and structural overhead can be hypothesized, but in practice, voluntary organizations of this type are rare. Personal idiosyncrasies of the leaders, vested interests on the part of many participants, and the lack of a control mechanism, such as a profit orientation, by which operations can be evaluated and streamlined, all contribute to a questionable ecnomic operation.

A second, and related, tension lies between the emphasis on a consensus method of decision-making and the inclusion of many special-interest groups in the decision-making process. It has not been sufficiently demonstrated that the values of cooperation, wholeness, and mutuality are compatible with the conflicts inherent in decision-making which involves minorities, youth, and other groups whch are insured fair representation within the Plan. The typical church meeting format does not allow effective decision-making in such a diverse situation. Therefore it is necessary to invent procedures by which a conflict of interests can result in a unified but differentiated program operation.

The third contradiction lies in the relation between structure and person. The way the Plan is presently phrased, congregations and task groups are structured *to provide for* the needs of persons. Traditionally, American church organizations have developed as persons become aware of their own needs and join with each other to reach solutions. Structures which are designed at the top to meet presumed needs usually lack a certain vitality that attends a bottom-up approach, and thereby diminish their chances for success.

The fourth contradiction is between mission at the national and local levels. Reading through the Plan, mission seems to be concentrated within the parish area, or at best in the region. There is mention made of overseas mission. However, the Plan does not take account of the need for local participation in issues of national import. Today, national policies affect whatever happens in local communities. As a result, mission needs to be seen at many levels, requiring paraparochial structures both locally and nationally.

This leads to a fundamental question. Does the Plan assume unity in diversity, or diversity in unity? Put differently, is the Plan likely to attract those main-line Protestant-oriented persons who share similar life-styles, values, and social expectations, and within this framework to organize diverse church structures? Or does it intend to attract a wide range of persons within particular areas who themselves begin to design those structures which seem most appropriate? While the latter is the stated goal, there is much in the Plan to assure the former.

The other question is the level at which unity is expected. Our society has legitimized religious pluralism. Thus it is inappropriate to hope that a single, totally adequate church can or should become an institutional reality in our time. The value of organizational diversity was recognized by the church historian Phillip Schaff. In 1855 Schaff contrasted denominationalism with sectarianism, commenting that a true spirit of catholicity can be found among various denominations, while sectarianism is marked by a pervading self-interest. A variety of denominations can project a common understanding of unity. Sectarian groups, even under the guise of ecumenicity, detract from that understanding and thereby detract from the very values which they seek to promote.[3]

These questions are not raised to invalidate the intent or the serious consideration of the Plan. They are raised in the spirit of asking what assumptions are in the minds of the planners, and what assumptions are in the minds of those who read the Plan. Are these assumptions the same or are they different? If they are different, which is likely, we need to be aware of their possible results, and of alternative ways of proceeding.

Intuitive Ecumenicity

At the same time that the parish plan is under discussion, efforts at local ecumenical development persist across the nation. These efforts are commonly, although not universally, called clusters.

> Clustering can be described as a *process* which creates new, multi-level relationships, goals and structures among existing churches, persons and community organizations. Without citing here the distinctions between types of clusters, three distinct thrusts within this process can be noted.
> At one level, clustering resembles two familiar streams of traditional Church organization. One stream is the larger, or yoked, parish. These units were created to maintain the presence of congregations in given areas, usually in a rural setting and to consolidate resources in the face of a declining support base. The other stream is the contemporary arena of specialized congregations. This kind of developmental ministry seeks to identify social needs requiring attention beyond the capacities of many congregations, and to draw support from church agencies for concentrated mission action. Clustering combines these two streams in an effort to 1) *maintain* those existing activities and organizations which are useful and necessary for corporate activity, 2) *consolidate* those activities and organizations that duplicate one another and 3) *diversify* the Church's ministry and mission with new activities and organizations created around community identified needs and resources.[4]

There is a growing body of experience among church leaders who regularly observe or participate in cluster activity. While distillation of this experience is still meager, several generalizations are important for understanding and further work. These generalizations are not indisputable. However, they deserve analysis and testing in order to determine their usefulness to cluster initiators.

One generalization is that ecumenical clusters are seen both by pastors and by judicatory executives as competitive with traditional denominational loyalties. Where there is no corresponding judicatory interrelationship, the competition is seen as threatening and potentially disruptive. Where judicatory relations exist, the problem of competition is seldom dealt with adequately. Thus the judicatory is often caught between new local expectations and persisting national-agency expectations, on the one hand, and persisting local expectations from other quarters and new denominational expectation *vis-à-vis* clusters on the other. At the present time, cluster activity has put judicatories in an untenable position.

Another generalization from experience is that within each cluster there appears to be a cyclic process of participation, identification of needs, decision-making, and action. Usually, every completed action leads to a modification of involvement. New participants appear, some drop out or spin off into new, related activity. New participants define new needs, new action, and so forth. The cycle may continue. However, it may not. The prospect of change may so threaten the initial leaders that no action is taken. In fact, many clusters talk a far bigger program than they actually produce. That in itself is some kind of action, for it tends to discourage the impatient. Hence, the short life span of many clusters. On the other hand, extended discussion may, in the long run, lay a more solid foundation for multipurpose activity.

A final generalization follows from the cyclical process. Those clusters that complete a number of cycles also pass through several stages of development. The intitial stage is informal. Several leaders meet to discuss cooperative activity. Their motives may differ, but they agree on a general method. They begin to involve others and further explore and refine their ideas. Programs are begun, usually *ad hoc,* around the primary interest of the initiators. At this stage, action is carried out apart from regular church programming.

The second stage is more formal. Cluster leaders are elected or chosen. There is a written rationale or covenant. Program activity becomes routinized. Congregations become organizationally related to the clusters. Spin-off activity develops and new community relationships form. A small constituency meets regularly to legitimize and plan action.

In the third stage, a cluster becomes semi-autonomous. A part-time or full-time staff takes the lead. Multifaceted programming evolves. A self-administered budget draws from several kinds of funding sources. The constituency grows and differentiates among various programs. While churches participate in the cluster, they maintain their particular individualities.

A host of factors play a part in each cluster's process and development. However, two major factors stand out as being probably most influential. One is environmental change. Where there is no change or where there is very radical change in the church's environment, clustering is unlikely. Where environmental change is perceptible but incremental, the possibility of clustering increases. Whether or not the possibility is realized depends on a second factor, leadership. The quality of leadership response, specifically professional leadership, to environmental change substantially affects the results of clustering. Such factors as trust, perception, sensitivity, imagination, and commitment are decisive qualities which rarely come to light in broad-scale research of cluster activity.

From Intuition to Analysis

One major difficulty with many recent cluster efforts has been their inability to move beyond certain levels of growth. Clustering, even though it relies on the intuitions of local leaders and the support of those who are being served, has seldom solved the problems of personal identity with the church, correlation with national mood, and embodiment of a dynamic relationship between transcendence and immanence. We need to go beyond contemporary definitions of ecumenical development.

Both the intuitive and the theological approaches to church organizations are seriously limited by a lack of realistic social analysis. A theological approach appears correct, but engenders intuitive reaction. Clustering may give the appearance of relevance while perpetuating collectively the inadequacies of the individual congregations. Reflections on four areas of church life—community, economics, connectionalism, and consciousness—will serve to illustrate the need for sound analysis.

A basic kind of community organization was understood on the American frontier. In analyzing early church development, H. Paul Douglass emphasizes the values of communal action.

> The most constructive application of the ideal of permanence was in the group-apostolate or Band. Such home missionary groups went out from Eastern theological seminaries to successive frontiers—Illinois, Iowa, the Dakotas, Washington—all in the spirit of the famous eleven of the Iowa Band, "Each to found a church and all together a college." Such bringing of highly trained men to the task of institution building, in the plastic period of the West, constituted a social technique of the highest order. No method could be more effective if applied now to complex social situations.[5]

Today's church lives in, through, and for its community. Because they are voluntary associations, most churches are effective to the extent that they meet the needs of some people in the community. Moreover, most churches tend to draw the majority of their members from a fairly unified social-economic or ethnic group within which a manageable range of needs can be addressed.

Recent studies in two denominations indicate that within each denomination there are between ten and twelve different kinds of local churches based on factors of environment and organization. These studies indicate that each type of church will respond differently to particular renewal policies and techniques. What may be useful and helpful in situation A may actually be harmful in situation B.

The major question today, however, is not simply one of proper community study. It is, more profoundly, the locus of communal reality. There are an estimated 1,000 local church clusters in the United States today. There are more than that number of known communes in New York City alone. The character of communal life may be a clue to contemporary church organizing efforts. The following dialogue between a commune consultant and a potential client sounds strangely familiar to anyone who has engaged in church consultation.

A boy in an Army shirt stood up and asked, "What's your commune going to do?"
Brent said, "We're not here to set up a commune. Our purpose is to encourage you to say what kind of a commune you want."
The boy in the Army shirt said, "Jesus has already told us what the perfect commune is, like, in Acts."
"O.K.," said Brent. "Dig it."
"How can you set up a perfect commune if you're not free in spirit?" the boy wanted to know.
"We're trying to be free in spirit," said Brent.
Someone else said he wanted to hear about failures.
Brent said, "I'd like to say some more about failure. . . . If a commune breaks up, it doesn't mean it hasn't been a success because it's an added experience to your life you wouldn't otherwise have had." [6]

In this interchange the tone is contemporary, but the problem is ancient. How can prevailing interpersonal and social dynamics become creatively empowered by the infusion of a transcendent awareness? The answer which continues to emerge is that of sensitive and committed leadership. The parson is the person among people. It is he who shares common experiences while also hearing the sound of a different drummer. Successful communes depend on such leadership. Successful communities of Christian life are no less dependent on persons of insight and vigor. Perhaps COCU parish development should emphasize leadership training instead of structural planning.

Since Max Weber's *The Protestant Ethic and the Spirit of Capitalism*, we have been aware of the intimate connection between religious organization and general economic norms. For example, at the local level, church growth and vitality appear to be related to a high degree of home ownership. The failure of apartment-house ministries and other new forms which ignore this relation is not merely a failure of will, but a failure to comprehend the economic overtones of church life. Moreover, the internal model that describes many congregations today is that of a family business. Program activity is traditional. Decisions are made on the basis of interpersonal relationships and economic considerations.

Leadership tends toward paternalism, and power is concentrated in the hands of relatively few participants. Success is measured in growth of members and dollars. This kind of model has the qualities of stability, prudence, and high visibility. It lacks, however, the ability to engage in self-analysis, to make rapid adjustment to environmental changes, or to hold together a range of people with diverse goals and life-styles.

Thus, the questions of personal property and church property are intertwined. Today's life-styles include both those who are entering the middle class and enjoying the fruits of private ownership, and those who have already participated in a certain amount of worldly success and who now look beyond personal gain. The Plan's proposal for ownership of property reflects a certain depersonalization of property which speaks to neither group. It is a technical approach to a very intricate situation. Perhaps it is best to let questions of economic propriety be guided by emerging communal and ethical values.

Who is ecclesiastically related to whom and why includes elements of politics, accident, and church strategy. The limitations of congregational autonomy were long ago recognized, even among the most congregationally oriented.

> Thus in 1825 a senior in Andover Theological Seminary, Andover, Massachusetts, reading an essay before the student Society of Inquiry, said: "We want a system that shall be *one*—one in purpose and one in action—a system aiming, not at itinerant missionaries alone, but at planting, in every little community that is rising up, men of learning and influence, to impress their character upon these communities—a system, in short, that shall gather the resources of philanthropy, patriotism, and Christian sympathy throughout our country into one vast reservoir from which a stream shall flow to Georgia and to Louisiana, to Missouri and to Maine." [7]

The concept of a network is in vogue again today. Electronic media offer unprecedented methods of intercommunication and decision-making. Special-interest groups ranging from the areas of peace, women's rights, and national policies to chess-playing and disease control have nationally organized systems of information and contact. The question is: on what terms are effective ecumenical relationships established?

This leads us to a fourth consideration. Is there a qualitative change in consciousness which will profoundly affect the nature of religious thought and form? William Irwin Thompson has written recently of a new planetary consciousness:

> What the new planetary consciousness indicates is that something has already happened in the collective unconsciousness of mankind. The movement of humanism that began with the Renaissance is at an end and a new

ideology is being created in advance of its social need. What particular institutional form this consciousness will take no one can say.

. . . I would guess that the new planetary consciousness means that we are building up a larger model of reality in which religious myth and scientific fact are both simultaneously true. Clearly this will amount to a scientific revolution as large as that of the sixteenth century. In "The Structure of Scientific Revolutions," T. S. Kuhn says that ". . . at times of revolution, when the normal-scientific tradition changes, the scientist's perception of his environment must be re-educated—in some familiar situations he must learn to see a new *gestalt*." To see a *gestalt* is not to analyze things visually in pieces, but to have a vision.[8]

True ecumenicity must become preoccupied with the possibility of a global vision if it is to be real at the local level.

From Plan to Perspective

For many people, the organized church is the major block to Christian witness and celebration. This view has historical roots and shows no signs of diminishing. For others, organization is a necessary evil, to be put up with but not encouraged.

The most important aspect of the COCU Plan of Union is that it takes seriously the need for institutions in maintaining human life and aspiration. While it is doubtful that the parish plan will see the light of day in its present conception, it is necessary that ecumenicity be structured into our society and internalized by persons around the world. The incarnation continues to release its power through social institutions.

Thus, COCU's contribution to local church formation is more profound than a new organizational arrangement. It is a new perspective on life, death, and the future around which men and women can find confidence and hope. How that perspective is embodied is a question which plumbs the depths of human experience. We await new missionaries, new organizers whose vision and talents can spark the fires of the Holy Spirit. Then will we have the base for an engaging, enduring, and effective institution. Then we can plan the details and procedures. Until then, we need a continuing Consultation on Church Union to scan the horizon, sharpen the vision, and analyze the territory. And we need to follow the advice of the bronco riders: Sit loose and hold on tight!

NOTES

1. Douglass, H. Paul, *Five Kindred Proposals for Uniting the American Denominations* (New York: Commission for the Study of Christian Unity, Federal Council of Churches of Christ in America, mimeo., 1937), pp. 29–30.

2. Douglass, H. Paul, *The New Home Missions* (New York: Missionary Education Movement of the United States and Canada, 1914), *passim*.
3. See Mead, Sidney, "The Fact of Pluralism and the Persistence of Sectarianism," in Smith, Elwyn A. (ed.), *The Religion of the Republic* (Philadelphia: Fortress Press, 1971), pp. 247–266.
4. *Clusters: Guidelines for the Development of Local Church Clusters* (New York: United Church Board for Homeland Ministries and the United Presbyterian Church Board of National Missions, 1970), p. 4.
5. Douglass, *The New Home Missions, op. cit.,* p. 37.
6. "Talk of the Town," *The New Yorker,* October 16, 1971.
7. Douglass, *The New Home Missions, op. cit.,* pp. 14–15.
8. Thompson, William Irwin, "Beyond Contemporary Consciousness," *New York Times,* May 11, 1971, p. 39.

4

Parsimony, Pluralism, and the COCU Parish

GABRIEL FACKRE

After ten years of solid theological work, and much public rhetoric from all sides on the need to "bring us together," *A Plan of Union* is being offered for review by nine national church constituencies. But at this very moment *The Christian Century* notes a strange "ghoulishness" abroad which specializes in obituaries of religious ideas and institutions, the latest being the announcement that "COCU is dead." [1]

Hesitations and even brickbats do indeed daily proliferate. The sources are varied. Along with a predictable protest that comes from church power structures whose vested interests would be imperiled by any new arrangement, there are many in the renewal movement who interpret institutional melding as at best a low priority, and at worst a diversion from the real mission of the church in the world. And to the long-standing fears by some of a "superchurch" have been added recently the suspicion of all "elites" and "big daddies" by a new populism (ranging from students and blacks to middle Americans), and a corollary reaffirmation of grass-roots action and empowerment. On top of this, the present financial pressures upon, and survival quandaries of, religious institutions have made it hard for COCU even to squeeze itself into the psyche, let alone onto the program agendas of the churches.

If COCU is to be legitimated, ideologically as well as politically, it will have to demonstrate its viability in the face of this wave of skepticism and torpor. Specifically, it must move the level of debate from doctrines and sacraments to the addressment of what was called at one time the "nontheological factors," the social, economic, and psychological under-

---

Portions of this essay appeared earlier in the *Andover Newton Quarterly*, Vol. 12, No. 1 (September, 1971), pp. 34–41.

side of the church. Here is where the impediments lie, especially so on the American scene where the practical and earthy have always provided ballast for stratospheric theological speculation.

Ironically, nontheological factors are themselves profoundly theological. The messianic servant images have massive implications for "big daddy" conceptions of God, bishop, or minister and "big mommy" understandings of the church, as do Bonhoeffer's coming-of-age theses. And the secular grace of God at work in raising up children of Abraham from stones may also be at work in the erosion of ecclesiastical brick and mortar. But we make our way into the theological depths through the more horizontal agonies, especially the grass-roots survival instincts and empowerment thrusts so high on the agenda of the seventies.

The significance of COCU is to be found not only in its hard-won creedal agreements, but in its remarkable fitness for these agendas. We shall attempt to make its case at these points, locating first the processes at work at the ground levels of church life, and the tacks that seem most natural to take in response to them.

Secularization

Religious, sociological, and historical studies in the sixties underline the rise of modern secularization. In spite of the neomysticism currently popular in some quarters of the youth counterculture (itself an expression of secular factors), the secular momentum underscored by Dietrich Bonhoeffer in his *Letters and Papers from Prison* continues to define the future for religious ideas and institutions. Secularization is a historical process with two dimensions: this-worldliness and coming-of-age.[2]

This-worldliness. Horst Symanowski captured one characteristic of secularization in his comparison of sixteenth- and twentieth-century sensibilities. He noted that in an earlier time Luther's question "How can I find a gracious God?" launched a cultural revolution, political upheaval, and the profound wrestling of society's most sensitive spirits. Today, he says, few lie awake at night agonizing over such a "religious" quandary. What causes forehead veins to distend now is the question "How can I find a gracious neighbor?" To the foreground is not the problem of estrangement between man and God, but alienation between black and white, young and old, male and female, East and West, nature and man. The possibilities and perils generated by modern technology, and the increasing interdependence of the races have had their share in riveting our attention on issues of this world and this time. And so the questions that hurtle across page one of the newspaper rather than page one of the Bible become the preoccupation of our society.

Coming-of-age. Interlaced with our attention to earthly matters is our changing relationship to the symbols, rituals, and institutions of organized religion. "Religion," in these expressions, was sought out in former times as the solver of problems. If men could not cope with disease, death, mental distress, or social disorder, they found solace and support in the resources of religion. But increasingly Western society disengages itself from this dependence (and accompanying autocracy) and moves toward taking responsibility for its own future, just as a child grows toward the age of discretion and finally self-determination. While Bonhoeffer has helped us to view this coming-of-age as the providential work of a Father who wills the adulthood of his offspring, it nevertheless means the severe dislocation of traditional religious systems and institutions.

Polarization

The tremors of this earthquake of secularization were felt in the church life of the sixties. In fact, a gaping ecclesiastical fissure opened up. On the one side were those who had monitored the shock waves and devised a strategy to deal with them. They wanted to build highly flexible structures that rolled with the seismic tremblings. A new breed of churchmen, lay and clergy, emerged that sought to relate the church to the secular process by engaging in secular mission. If justice for the poor, the young, and the black was an overwhelming reality of our time, then let the church "get with it." If the world was one vast Jericho road, then let the church take seriously its commitments to its Good Samaritan neighbor love. Further, if the world was coming of age, then the church should cease playing paternalist with the culture and instead adapt its teachings and methods to the new secular time by casting away its crutches and clubs. Encourage the world to stand on its own feet and let the church live out the role of resource and servant with modest language, tools, and ecclesiastical claims.

While "mission in the world" came to be written on the banners of churchmen who plunged deeper and deeper into the social struggle of the decade, a "silent majority" was growing restless in the church. While others cried "mission," they muttered "tradition." With the much talk of "letting the world write the agenda," this group still wanted the church to write the agenda for the world. While some of the new breed were saying that action is prayer, they continued to make the distinction and stressed the latter. When it became popular to start coffeehouses, have dialogue discussing the existential depths or relevance of the latest play or film, they asked for Bible study and sent angry letters to denominational magazines for getting too worldly. When new ministers urged them to go to Selma or tutor a child in the ghetto, they instead turned on the radio to hear Billy Graham, or started a campaign to get rid of the world-drenched preacher.

The growing dissonance began to have its institutional effects. Clergy disillusioned with the negative responses they received to their calls to secular mission began to leave the profession. Laity with like-minded clergy formed "underground churches," or drifted out of the ecclesiastical orbit altogether, affirming that "to join the world was to join the church."

There were realignments also among clergy and laity of more traditional perspective, as conservative denominations drew in main-line drop-outs. But more often the reaction of the tradition-oriented churchmen was a boycott of the institution. And the withdrawal included monies that had formerly gone to support the church-in-world thrust of earlier days. "Polarization" became a familiar word in the church lexicon.

Where do we go from here? Any fresh direction must surely take into account the hard facts of both secularization and polarization. It entails as well some reevaluation of the simplistic moralism and novelism to which visionaries were prone and a letting go of the rigidities and irrelevancies to which traditionalists were wedded. And it will include sounding notes muted too long by both churchly and worldly Christianity, one of them being telling the Christian story. In the context of structural issues raised by COCU, we look primarily at the question of strategies, drawing implicitly on theological premises. We find two commitments of great importance to a church geared to the context of the seventies: parsimony and pluralism.

Parsimony

A growing ecological consciousness has made us aware again of the ancient wisdom of carefully husbanding limited natural resources and learning to live with less. A new life-style of parsimony is good counsel as well for the church. It has nothing to do with penny-pinching at the church collection plate or miserliness in mission. Secularization means that a small town, city, or suburb once prolific with congregations, their buildings and real estate, is no longer a hospitable matrix for such expansive church life. Simple survival of what is valuable in Christian ministration means the fusion of resources and the consequent elimination of acres of overextension. Similarly, the effective deployment of leadership, clergy and lay, points to the same kind of careful reallocation of personnel.

Pluralism

Very early in Christian history, one of the church's organizers delivered himself of a passionate plea for people of God with many ministries. St. Paul's letter to the Corinthians agonized over the same kind of polarization we currently experience, and sketched both a model and a spirit as timely as last Thursday's squabble at the deacons' meeting. A church is a body with many parts (I Corinthians 12). The eye cannot say to the hand that it has no purpose, and vice versa. So there must be mutual accreditation of the many gifts God has lavished on his covenant community. Further, no part must isolate itself from the others, but must instead interact and interpenetrate in love (I Corinthians 13). While it may well be that some of the parts are more important than others (I Corinthians 14), even the least is not to be disdained.

The church of the seventies desperately requires this kind of affirmation of pluralism. It no more needs the self-righteous sectarian spirit that sends visionaries into the isolation of their underground churches and traditionalists into esoteric enclaves than the church in Corinth profited by clans that proudly declared, "I belong to Paul," "I belong to Apollos," "I belong to Cephas." Action-oriented renewers must admit the ease with which they ignore the more tender and intimate dimensions that are indeed part of a full-orbed faith. And those who find the Gospel meaningful in personal terms cannot deny that the prophetic tradition is indeed a vital part of the Bible they so ardently affirm, and the history of the church to which they continually point back. Innovators must learn that it is continuity and stability that provide a base for innovation itself, and institutionalists must learn the lesson of even the most conservative secular structure—namely, that the research and development division (whose job is to brainstorm totally new directions and call into question all going policies) is the most valuable part of an institution that must prepare itself for times of rapid change.

Let us take the next logical step and attempt to sketch a model that might catch up these motifs.

A Model

"Futurology" found its way into the churches in the same decade that worldly mission moved to the fore. It was natural, therefore, for renewers in the sixties to spin out scenarios for tomorrow's church. Among them were some that began to include a sensitivity to secularization and polarization. Stephen Rose proposed a three-point model with Central House and associated launching pads for education and social action.[3] Harvey Cox playfully postulated a loose-jointed community with two poles, small groups, and "the big show." [4] I speculated about a "theological park" (similar to the educational park of the public school system) with satellite task forces and house churches.[5] With a little more data now in our computers, let us try another model that builds on some of these earlier designs and works with the motifs of parsimony and pluralism.

We begin with the assumption that secularization will have taken its toll in local communities in the years ahead, forcing congregations with greatly reduced memberships and income to consider the options of dissolution, conventional merger, or imaginative realignment of resources. A responsible (and likely) version of the last would be constituted by a design with three foci. The ministries undertaken at these points—or in relation to them—could be housed in buildings formerly occupied by the covenanting congregations.

1. A center for "world-oriented ministries." Here would be based the Jericho road ministrations. Constituted in the main by task forces addressed to specific issues, the center would address itself to matters of social action and social service called for by the times in which the church lived and the place it served. Today it is the issues of race, peace, poverty, the needs and rights of the aged, women, children, and the natural environment in which they live, that command attention. Tomorrow it will be a new set of challenges. Whatever the needs, there must be a place in the design of the church where visionaries who dream dreams of a human world are free to exercise that ministry, and are fully accredited by the whole company of faith to carry out that mandate.

2. A center for "church-oriented ministries." Here is the home for the ministries of nurture—educational, personal, spiritual. The troops are fed, the "saints are equipped" for work in the world. All kinds of nourishment are available: theological and biblical mind-stretching, Christian story-telling, dialogue with the cultural issues, psychological and social support groups for the wounded and growing, opportunities for the cultivation of prayer and the mystical life, experiments in new and old life-styles. The forms these ministries might take would be short-term seminars, happenings, and encounter groups, long-term communal life together, counseling, spiritual sustenance, and educational training. The center would host some of these occasions, but would carry on its work far beyond the building by way of a network of house churches, intentional communities, and retreats.

3. A "new cathedral." This central house would be the unity symbol and gathering point for a constituency otherwise engrossed in the various world-oriented and church-oriented ministries. But baptism into the body of Christ happens here, membership is held in the community of which this central house is the embracing home, and the celebrations of all of the people of this place would take place under this roof. Such celebra-

tions will include weekly worship that ranges on a Sunday morning (or other times) from a 7:00 A.M. high liturgy, through an 8:00 A.M. Quaker meeting to a 9:00 A.M. preaching service, 10:00 A.M. "black worship," and 11:00 A.M. banner, guitar, and rock festivity. But at appointed times, perhaps in the great seasons or once a month, all of the people of the community would gather for the Great Celebration together.

Coordinating the "people of God with many ministries" would also go on at this place of cross-fertilization, and planning for the Not Yet would be centered also in the cathedral of tomorrow.

The Ministry

Part and parcel of this design is the centrality of the ministry of the laity. The variety of components gives opportunity for the cultivation of the many talents to be found in a typical Christian community, and a chance also for leadership in those areas. In the conception of clergy style and portfolio, the gifts and calling of the whole *laos* are especially affirmed.

The professional minister is seen as an enabler. He is a resource (not source) that seeks to release the Corinthian gifts. Reinforcing this alongsideness is the modesty of his competence that is built into the threefold design. He is not expected to be a jack-of-all-trades whose omnipresence tends to discourage lay initiative. Rather he is called to steward his special training and experience in one of three directions: [6]

1. A center for world-oriented ministries requires staffing that includes at least one person trained in the overall understanding of Christian mission but with expertise in, and commitment to, social action and social service.

2. A center for church-oriented ministries requires staffing that includes at least one person trained in the overall understanding of Christian mission but with expertise in, and commitment to, Christian nurture in its broadest sense.

3. A central house needs a coordinator.

There is an intriguing similarity between the functionally necessary roles so described and the classic threefold office of the ministry. This is no accident, as the latter rose out of the sociological demands and faith claims of historic Christianity. If the three traditional forms of professional ministry are updated and translated into the enabling, alongsided style and coequal partnership team of tomorrow, they mesh very well with the resource roles of leadership in our three-pronged design. Thus the diaconate, devoted as it was in the early church to the service of human needs, could be embodied in the diaconal resource person related to the center for world-oriented service. The presbyter, understood historically as the one responsible for telling the Christian story, is represented by the steward of nurture ministries at the commensurate center. And the bishop, responsible for "oversight" of area ministry and stewardship of lateral and historic continuities (described significantly in some traditions as "the metropolitan"), is represented by the coordinator who, in a new alongsided rather than top-down style, facilitates the overall planning and interrelationship of ministry in that sector of society (probably a metropolitan one in an increasingly urban society).

The New Model and COCU

By examining the cultural ferment, and considering what meaningful church response might mean to it, we have arrived at a design for local mission that is fully consonant with the parish proposed by A Plan of Union, (VIII, 1–42, pp. 56–63). And the threefold ministry as enabler of the laity is virtually the same as the ordained office put forward by COCU (A Plan of Union, VII, 1–92, pp. 38–55).

The parish in the COCU Plan is pluralistic, consisting of "those traditional emphases essential to the mission of the church, and new emphases to be developed in new forms" (A Plan of Union, VIII, 20, p. 59). While a general "congregation" is still viewed in the Plan as a unit within the parish—a concession to the political realities of new merger—this entity might easily evolve into a congregation with special interests and portfolio and finally into the world-oriented, church-oriented, or coordinating centers described in our model. The Plan takes seriously the ad hoc methodology used at points of both mission and tradition, recommending the concept of a "task force . . . focusing the efforts of action and prayer on specific ministries and projects" (A Plan of Union, VIII, 28, p. 60). It envisages the possibility of multiple centers for the parish's varied work: "The parish program may be conducted in several different places as may be most expedient for mission and for providing opportunities for the members to experience face to face relationships" (A Plan of Union, VIII, 31, p. 60). Within this variety there is a place for and celebration of unity by common membership in the parish, governance through a parish council, and service by a common professional ministry.

The fresh thinking COCU has done on the ministry of deacons (A Plan of Union, VIII, 81–92, pp. 53–55) and its definition of presbyters (A Plan of Union, VII, 42–80, pp. 46–53) makes possible the kind of meaningful pluriform ministry to a secular society attempted in the model. While the model's concept of bishop relates the office more directly to grass-roots church life, and presupposes a more radical secularization and disappearance of institutional apparatus than envisaged by COCU,

the coordinating and continuity role definition is essentially the same
(*A Plan of Union*, VII, 57–80, pp. 49–53).

Denominations are destined to disappear. Local churches will have to
face hard survival choices. The richness and variety of perspectives and
gifts within the Christian community will persist, as well as the multifaceted needs of human beings. The facts of secularization and polarization surely press toward a church model of parsimony and pluralism.
If COCU did not exist, we would have to invent it. But it does exist—as
a plan and possibility. The next few years will tell whether possibility
becomes reality, or whether COCU will have to be re-invented by another generation.

Testing The Design

As theology is best done in the context of involvement, so these fore-
going theses have taken shape in the writer's experience in church renewal efforts in the congregation and community (Pennsylvania and
Hawaii) and participation in a denomination-wide program, "The Local
Church in God's Mission." More recently, as a member of a "united
parish" committee struggling to form a three-church union, I have had
a chance to see up close the possibilities and problems of the model
sketched above. These concluding observations attempt to bring the
dream in range of the realities of the latter.

The conventional wisdom on the COCU Plan declares that resistance
can be anticipated from congregations unwilling to "give up" their traditions and buildings. The sounds made by the more cautious components
of the union in question appear to indicate just that. But on closer examination it is clear that something more is involved than self-centeredness,
nostalgia, and the edifice complex.

One congregation has a strong visionary commitment, with a history of
participation in the human-rights struggle and the peace movement in
particular, and has developed innovative and controversial worship patterns. Another congregation, with a large number of older members, has
focused on a ministry to senior citizens. The third congregation, with a
strong educational program and an imposing building, has a membership
equal to the other two congregations put together and is more affluent.
The first two constituencies entered gingerly into the union, displaying
no little caution and armed with a certain political sensitivity. This is
interpreted by the third partner as preoccupation with the past, lack of
trust, and fixation upon such secondary matters as buildings and personnel. But what appears as foot-dragging toward the vision of unity is in
fact commitment to the genuine pluralism that must be part of any future
ecclesiastical life together. That means at the parish level at least two

things: honoring different, even jarring, life-styles and perceptions on the one hand, and people and ministries on the other.

The real test of that willingness to affirm the variety of parts in the body of Christ comes at the pedestrian level of bylaws, physical space, distribution of monies, and selection of professional staff. Do these resources together make possible turf on which each varying set of commitments and perceptions with their attendant communities can "do their thing"? While the full trinity of staff and centers suggested in a threefold model (one, incidentally, being actively explored by this particular three-church fusion) cannot be insisted upon in every cluster and union when financial resources are prohibitive, it remains the lure of all and a judge of anything less. What must be faced realistically is the preservation of the parts of the body even while we move toward its wholeness.

The other side of the manyness is, of course, the oneness. The will to enter into relationships with other congregations for a united parish is the first sign of good faith in the goal of unity. The second sign is the readiness to build into the plan of union the kind of cross-fertilization, mutual ministry, and accountability which anything worthy of the name *unity* requires. At the level of structures, this means a parish in which ultimate membership is held not in the centers or working groups but in the parish as a whole. Baptism and confession of faith take place in the midst of the whole people of God in this place. Fullness also means that each center reports in to the whole Christian community, and gets feedback from it; the staff with its variety of expertise and responsibilities works as a team; overall purposes are hammered out by the whole community; the life together of the parish is celebrated regularly by the eucharist; while the center of gravity of one's commitments may be in one or another working group, exposure to other perspectives and activities is built into the membership covenant.

The temptation that must be fought by those struggling for pluralism (the two congregations mentioned heretofore) is the "sect mentality." Thus, between those eager to assure continuity of their witness (in this case, the world-oriented constituency of one congregation) and those concerned about ministry to the aged in another congregation, there is a danger of destroying the dream of larger unity and a fuller Gospel. Here there must be a willingness to acknowledge the limits of one's own perceptions, and to risk new relationships and openness to other styles. All this can indeed happen when the whole gives reliable assurances to the parts fearful of the loss of their own identity. It is yet unclear in the union in question whether the double goal of pluralism and unity can be achieved. Perhaps it is only when the erosion process so imperils each institution that God's secular grace will draw us together.

While the parish struggles with diversity-in-unity at the grass roots, similar pulls and pushes in COCU negotiation go on at the national level. Here the test is the readiness of the national entity and its constituencies to make a place in its delegations, committees, and programs for a variety of persons and perspectives—black, young, poor, women in the former case, and liberation movements and visionary thrusts in the latter. The floor debate and decisions at the Denver plenary in 1971—an occasion when such concerns vigorously appeared—did not fully allay the fears of visionaries that the pluralism of COCU was more in word than in deed. And it is not yet clear either whether the militancy of the same visionaries is so high that it short-circuits their willingness and capacity to enter into union.

St. Paul's counsel to the Corinthians is as fresh as yesterday's united parish committee or the 1971 Denver plenary. It is a good word for times of polarization and parsimony, pluralism and quest for unity: "The body does not consist of one member but of many . . . and all the members of the body, though many, are one body. . . ."

NOTES

1. "On Ghoulishness and COCU" (editorial), *The Christian Century*, Vol. LXXVIII, No. 19 (May 12, 1971), p. 579.
2. For a detailed exploration of these factors see Gabriel Fackre, *Humiliation and Celebration: Post-Radical Themes in Doctrine, Morals, and Mission* (New York: Sheed and Ward, 1969), pp. 15–27.
3. Rose, Stephen, *The Grass Roots Church* (New York: Holt, Rinehart and Winston, 1966), *passim*.
4. Cox, Harvey, comments made in an address before Conference on Religion and the Future, Philadelphia, November 23, 1969.
5. Fackre, Gabriel, "The Church in 1984," *Secular Impact* (Philadelphia: Pilgrim Press, 1968), pp. 118–125.
6. Theological students training for nonpreaching ministries, and church judicatories unsure of ordaining such students, will both be well served by this design, as will clergy who want to specialize in similar vocations. Such "secular" ministry is part of a grass-roots parish, and kept in touch with story-telling and story-celebrating as befits ordination, yet is freed to concentrate on the human issues that are confronted in the center for world-directed mission.

5

Theology in the Consultation: Commitment, Consensus, Integrity

RONALD E. OSBORN

The genius of the Consultation is its deliberately theological approach to the practical problems of church union and renewal.

COCU's commitment, from the beginning, to a corporate venture in doing ecclesiology distinguishes it from every other large-scale attempt in the twentieth century to bring the American churches together. Whoever fails to see this, whether critic or champion, will miss the avowed intent of the Consultation and will gain only a superficial understanding of *A Plan of Union.*

The Pragmatic Approach to Union

The casual onlooker tends to think of church union as a project in ecclesiastical engineering. He looks on it as a problem of combining a number of functional units (denominations) in the interest of greater efficiency. He understands the process as political and psychological, involving a measure of tit-for-tat compromise in which all parties concerned make appropriate concessions of sovereignty and of peculiar practices for the sake of the common goal, a united church.

If our onlooker knows anything of the Christian mentality, he recognizes a certain theological pressure toward reunion; after all, the notion does have a good deal of biblical admonition going for it. Nevertheless, a kind of pragmatic realism offers the most evident arguments in favor of church union to the mind of the average American. He understands that the denominations separated over doctrinal issues. He sees no indication that any one of the denominations has won, or is likely to win, the others to its own version of true dogma. He concludes, therefore, that any viable effort at union must play down theological concerns. If he is suspicious by nature, he wonders what kind of under-the-table deals must have been made in order to get a plan of union. If he is inclined toward Christian activism in meeting contemporary needs, he confidently declares, "Doctrine divides, service unites." That old watchword of the Life and Work movement a generation ago resounds again as a battle cry for Christian soldiers marching into the ghettos or storming the barricades at the Pentagon.

The pragmatic approach to church union, with theology confined largely to the areas of motivation and rationale, has indeed been tried. Twentieth-century America has seen three such ventures in broad-scale ecclesiastical engineering.

In 1918 nineteen denominations responded to an initiative from the Presbyterian Church in the United States of America, the product of their joint efforts being dubbed the Philadelphia Plan. It conceived of union as federation, leaving the internal life and the structures of the member denominations largely untouched. When the sponsors could rally little support, the plan was soon forgotten.[1]

A generation later, during World War II, E. Stanley Jones advanced his scheme for Federal Union. It would provide for union of the member denominations "at the top," with one national plenary body and appropriate state and local assemblies, at the same time leaving the denominations as continuing "branches" working side by side within a united church. Jones propagandized persuasively for his proposal in the religious press and in a series of mass meetings across the country. Even though no denomination formally endorsed the plan, the popular response indicated a good deal of grass-roots sentiment in favor of a united church which promised the advantages of union without threatening denominational mores or congregational life.[2]

About the same time nine churches joined together formally through their representatives in forming the Conference on Church Union, popularly known as the Greenwich movement after the town in Connecticut where its first meeting was held. Its genius was avowedly pragmatic. The notion originated among a group of ecumenical veterans who had long worked together in the conciliar movements. These friends discovered that, despite their peculiarities of doctrine, their churches actually functioned in pretty much the same way. Divided not by doctrine but by parallel institutions, they could be united by putting the institutions together. Acting on this proposition, the General Council of the Congregational-Christian Church in 1946 issued a general invitation to those churches which "recognize one another's ministries and sacraments"—the theological issue was already settled!—to work on a plan of union for uniting the structures.[3] The Greenwich Plan awakened a good deal of ecumenical hope, but, coming on stage in a new era of theological concern, its nontheological genius proved its undoing. John Mackay was widely quoted as observing that Greenwich had no doctrine of the church. When Eugene Carson Blake as stated clerk announced the withdrawal of the Presbyterian Church, the Greenwich movement was dead. It formally terminated in 1958.

This brief historical excursus on pragmatic attempts at union is not out of place in a chapter on theology. For it provides the context within which the genuis of COCU is to be understood. Greenwich and its precursors were theologically correct in their goal of a united church; they were theologically less than fully responsible in attempting to by-pass the hard doctrinal issues of reunion on the implicit assumption that the life of each member church was theologically adequate and compatible with that of all the others. Nevertheless, let it be remembered that up till that time theology done in denominational isolation had indeed divided the churches. But the "great new fact" of the ecumenical movement offered the promise that theology worked out together by heretofore separated Christians might point the way to a united church.

A Theological Approach to Union

The same stated clerk who had dashed the hopes of ecumenical enthusiasts committed to Greenwich caught the attention of the Christian world in his daring "Proposal Toward the Reunion of Christ's Church" advanced in his sermon at Grace Cathedral, San Francisco, in 1960.[4] In calling for a common exploration into the possibility of a united church "truly catholic and truly reformed," Eugene Carson Blake provided the formula which led to the Consultation on Church Union as a responsible venture in ecumenical theologizing. Skillfully he incorporated into his proposal the four elements of the Lambeth Quadrilateral, the most venerable, most responsible, and most widely known invitation to union hitherto offered the Christian world by any church, yet he dealt with these in such a way as to indicate their common appeal to all Christians in the current situation. Here was a call for reunion, not without its pragmatic implications to be sure, but founded on a solid and inclusive doctrine of the church.

Theological commitment marked the Consultation on Church Union from the start. Very early its members agreed to ban the use of the word *merger* in their discussions; they were not looking for ingenious means of bringing religious corporations together in one large institution, but rather they were exploring that *union* with integrity which they trusted would eventuate from a more adequate doctrine of the church than any of the denominations could produce by itself. They set themselves an awesome task, one far greater than the mere harmonizing, or compromising, of the ecclesiologies carried in their particular denominational traditions. They undertook a quest for a richer understanding of the church such as they believed would be given in studying together not simply the question of how to achieve union but the larger issue of how to conceive the church which God wills for today and tomorrow.

The Consultation began its work in the "fullness of time" for such a venture. Its members were not under the necessity of breaking open all the issues *de novo*. Rather their task was to work out the implications, both doctrinal and practical, of a long generation of theological creativity and constructive labor unparalleled since the Reformation.

COCU set itself the task of appropriating quite consciously the results of forty years of ecumenical theologizing in the work of Faith and Order (Geneva, Lausanne, Edinburgh, Lund, Oberlin, Montreal), a tradition which had explored the imperative to union, the theological issues which separated the churches, and common formulations offering breakthroughs to penetrate ancient misunderstandings. Indeed, COCU began its discussions in that kind of discourse which had come to be inexactly labeled as "official ecumenical theology"—a theology which, if now seen as less final than it appeared a decade ago, has not been repudiated, but subsequently amplified and pointed in new directions.[5]

The Consultation likewise stood in a position to appropriate a generation of biblical theology and critical study of the New Testament. The historical sophistication and precision of twentieth-century scholarship dealing with Scripture offered insights capable of freeing all the member churches from the presuppositions of that rigid biblicism which prevailed at the time their traditional ecclesiologies were formulated. On almost every issue where the denominational fathers had taken a hard dogmatic stand resulting in division, biblical study had brought a broader perspective, especially in its insights into the dynamism and the diversity which characterized the life of the apostolic church. At the same time, the interest in biblical theology which animated Christian thought at mid-century had resulted in a new awareness of the importance of unity in every aspect of New Testament ecclesiology (*A Plan of Union*, III, 11–20, pp. 17–19).[6] Evidence of COCU's commitment at this point has been its regular practice of devoting a major block of time at every plenary meeting to Bible study under the leadership of a ranking scholar.[7]

The Consultation began its work in a climate still largely dominated by the neo-Reformation theology which during the previous generation had awakened new excitement over the Gospel and the seriousness of its demands (*A Plan of Union*, II, 22, p. 13; III, 1–4, pp. 15–16).[8] The insights of this theology into the pervasiveness of human sin and the idolatrous pretensions of institutions had enabled churchmen to break out of the absolutism which had earlier characterized the ecclesiological assumptions of the denominations. This particular theological perspective combined with a new sophistication regarding social and cultural factors [9] to give religious leaders an objective understanding of the origins, witness, and history of their own separate traditions, and this new realization of the limitations of all the churches accentuated the longing for a more acceptable form of church, a church more in keeping with the nature of the Gospel and with the requirements of the mission laid upon it. COCU symbolized this vision in its oft-repeated slogan, "a church truly catholic, truly evangelical, truly reformed" (*A Plan of Union*, III, 21–28, pp. 19–21).[10]

Accompanying the theological renaissance with its ecumenical, biblical, and neo-Reformation emphases had come a new appreciation within the various denominations of the contemporary vitality of unique elements in the particular traditions. To a far more pronounced extent than had been true in the era of the old liberalism, responsible theologians among Presbyterians, Episcopalians, Methodists, United Churchmen, and Disciples saw elements within their particular heritages which they wished to emphasize anew for the health of the total church. In contrast with their fathers, however, they now found it possible to advocate these emphases from an ecumenical rather than a sectarian stance.[11]

The Consultation carried on its first four years of intensive work within a theological climate dominated by the influences just indicated. These theological trends had contributed to the forming of a common mind among the COCU delegates expressed in the remarkable consensus entitled *Principles of Church Union*, which the Dallas plenary unanimously adopted in 1966. These principles gave *A Plan of Union*, completed five years later, its theological shape.

Meanwhile two new theological emphases produced a large impact on American religious thought during the first decade of the Consultation's work, and each of these exerted decisive influence on *A Plan of Union*. These were the theology of mission, with its profound concern for the secular, and the theological reflection arising from the black consciousness.

The theology of mission gained wide currency as a result of studies conducted by the World Council of Churches and the National Council of Churches on the missionary structure of the congregation. It attempted to articulate the imperatives for service and social action implicit in the thought of Dietrich Bonhoeffer, which exerted such wide appeal in the 1950s and early sixties. It also undertook to respond constructively and radically to the spate of popular books critical of the traditional religious institution. It emphasized the Christian significance of the secular and the imperative for churchly involvement in secular concerns. (*A Plan of*

Union, II, 10–16, p. 11; III, 5–7, 10, pp. 16–17; IV, 10–11, 15, pp. 23–24; V, 15–18, pp. 28–29; VIII, 1–13, pp. 56–58; IX, 16–20, p. 75).[12] This theology largely determined the *Guidelines for the Structure of the Church*, adopted in 1967. It profoundly affected *A Plan of Union* in its conception of ministry: the ministry of the laity, and the definition of the work of presbyters, bishops, and deacons (*A Plan of Union*, VII, 1–23, 48, 69, 82, 89, pp. 38–55, *passim*).[13] It also determined in large measure the nature of the district and more particularly that of the parish (*A Plan of Union*, VIII, 20–73, pp. 59–66). Despite a wholehearted response to the theology of mission and the emphasis on secularity, COCU showed little inclination toward the romanticizing of the secular which characterized much popular advocacy of that point of view. Neither did the Consultation manifest much interest in death-of-God theology or other extreme forms of secular thought.

The theology associated with the rise of black consciousness and the self-awareness of other minority groups impressed itself upon COCU not so much theoretically as personally. Many members of the Consultation, despite the popular impression of theologians and denominational officials as disengaged, participated actively in the Freedom Movement of the early sixties and cherished a concept of the church as inclusive fellowship and advocate of the oppressed. Nevertheless, the entrance of the three predominantly black churches into the Consultation produced a radically new dynamic. A sudden disturbing awareness of the biblical dimensions of Christian union possessed the delegates in an entirely new way. A task far more radical demanded attention than the theological resolution of denominational differences in doctrine: a truly united church must demonstrate an inclusiveness of race and class, with equitable participation of minorities and other oppressed groups at all levels of its life and mission.[14] The realization of such a vision requires the transformation—indeed, the conversion—of all the member churches. It will enable the church to stand in redemptive judgment upon a pagan society, manifesting within its own life that wholeness of humanity—a truly evangelical catholicity—which demonstrates the divine hope and promise for mankind.

This kind of theologizing can be done only in anguish of spirit. The Consultation listened with pain and chagrin to voices from the black ghetto at Atlanta in 1969 and to Chicanos at Denver in 1971. The Executive Committee and the Plan of Union Commission spent numerous sessions with representatives of various minorities and radical groups. More particularly, the members of the Consultation itself—black, brown, and white; male and female; old and young—engaged in searching dialogue which convinced them all of the absolute necessity of conceiving a far more inclusive church as God's instrument of reconciliation than any one of the denominations had heretofore realized or even imagined.

The repeated stipulations in *A Plan of Union* concerning equitable representation of various groups and the obviously mechanical provisions for assuring positions of leadership to members of minority races reflect a newly sensitized conscience in these matters. The same is evident in the call from the Denver plenary for programs leading to racial justice and compensatory treatment for minorities. (*A Plan of Union*, II, 17, pp. 11–12; III, 2, p. 15; IV, 2, 15–17, pp. 22, 24; VII, 40, p. 46; VIII, 7, 14–19, 132, pp. 57–59, 71).[15]

The Church of Christ Uniting offers an opportunity for a radically Christian transformation of the American church not otherwise available to any of the denominations in its separateness. The realization of such a church will require a commensurate transformation of American popular theology in its doctrine of the church. The achievement of such a result will more than justify the incalculable expenditure of time and energy already committed to the work of the Consultation and yet to be put forth in the realization of the Church of Christ Uniting.

In summary, the Consultation has worked at every stage with a clear understanding of its task as a necessarily theological enterprise. With the release of *A Plan of Union* to the churches for study and response, it becomes evident that the process of achieving a united church, from this point on, requires not so much salesmanship or interpretation of the plan but a major involvement of American Christians in every community in common discussion and reflection on the nature of the church. In its quest for church union COCU has undertaken an approach which is forthrightly and inescapably theological.

A Mode of Theologizing: Commitment and Consensus

The theological work of the Consultation has moved because it began with a goal. The churches sent their delegates to COCU to explore the possibility of a united church—catholic, evangelical, reformed. The goal itself derived from theological considerations, from reflection on the will of Christ for the world and for his covenant community within the world. A commitment to that goal from the beginning gave to the theologizing of the Consultation a dynamic which is often lacking in ecumenical or academic discussion of doctrinal issues. In its commitment to discover a form of the church which will accord more nearly with both the divine intention and the contemporary mission, the Consultation cast theology in an enabling rather than a self-serving role.

The denominational dogmas of the past resulted from an uncritical tendency to make theological truth an end in itself; as a result, Christians were divided from one another by their varied apprehensions of Christian truth, partially apprehended and rigidly conceived. By contrast COCU has seen theology not as an end in itself but as an instrument in the service of an obedient church. If the theological enterprise has been classically defined as faith seeking understanding, we may properly conceive it within the context of the Consultation as faithfulness seeking a common way of obedience.

This servant role which the Consultation has called on theology to fulfill has brought realism and vitality to the discussions of a decade. As the churches have committed themselves to a quest for faithfulness in unity and mission, theology has interacted with pragmatic concerns, both giving and receiving judgment, to produce in *A Plan of Union* a vision of the church far more authentic and more exciting than the American Christian community has ever known. Commitment to a more faithful obedience on the part of the church, with the fullest possible understanding of what that obedience means for the form, self-understanding, and mission of the Christian community, produced in COCU theologizing with a purpose. How, then, did it go about its task?

The method of work is essentially that of theologizing toward consensus, employed throughout the history of the church in its various councils and brought to a high degree of effectiveness during the past half-century of ecumenical endeavor.

Besides its general and continuing Bible study in a broad perspective, designed to provide openness and insight in every aspect of its task, the Consultation has commissioned careful biblical studies on particular practical issues to which it addressed itself.[16] Whereas members of the Consultation carried memories of other days when their denominational fathers—or even they themselves—quoted Scripture against one another, they now found themselves engaged in a common search toward a common goal. This kind of Bible study, which we already tend to take for granted, is really something quite new within divided Christendom. It makes possible a kind of theologizing more irenic, more comprehensive, more constructive than our fathers could ever undertake in their isolation from one another and in each one's assumption of the correctness of his own position over against the errors of his rivals.

In a similar way the Consultation commissioned historical and sociological studies on various issues before it.[17] These included attention to that degree of consensus never lost in Christian history, to particular positions of various denominations within and without the Consultation, and to the theological work undertaken in other ventures toward church union throughout the world. One lesson of ecumenical history proved particularly helpful as discussants deliberately sought to avoid terms which have proved sterile or productive of hostility in past discussions, terms with exclusive overtones like *validity*, *esse*, and *apostolic succession*. Throughout its historical work the Consultation sought to state positive values while avoiding expressions which suggest a negative inference.

Much of the work of the Consultation has gone on in small groups, both the working sections into which each plenary has divided and interim committees assigned particular tasks between annual meetings. In these face-to-face encounters, delegates and observer-consultants from churches not in the Consultation explored issues in an atmosphere that led first to trust and then to mutual affection. The groups did not duck hard issues. Rather they faced them with openness, honesty, and a willingness to listen to disturbing points of view. Thus every member gained an understanding of practices and doctrines he had never taken seriously before. On matters which have long separated us, such as baptism or the ministry, members reached a positive appreciation for points of view which our fathers never considered, or considered only to deny.

All this work reached its consummation in the effort to achieve a comprehensive formulation acceptable both on theological and on practical grounds, a formulation which found expression first in the *Principles* and then in *A Plan*.[18]

Despite a popular misunderstanding of the nature of union negotiations, the COCU mode of theologizing has not led to reductionism. It is widely feared that any ecumenical solution must necessarily be thin because of the presumed inevitability of reducing theological differences to a least common denominator. The Consultation has sought to avoid any such impoverishment of the church's faith and life. Instead it has sought "more" rather than "less," endeavoring to comprehend within the life of the united church whatever any of its member churches regards as essential or even highly important, so long as a convincing case can be made for it in the present theological situation. Any such element must of course serve the unity of the church with doctrinal integrity. Thus *A Plan* provides for the conscientious practice of either adult baptism or infant baptism (*A Plan of Union*, VI, 16–22, pp. 33–35). It calls for diversity in liturgical practice even while emphasizing those elements which mark all proper Christian worship (*A Plan of Union*, VI, 6, 8–9, p. 31).

Two points must be noted against possible objections.

Perhaps no individual theologian will find the formulations of *A Plan* entirely to his own liking. One might wish for a higher doctrine of episcopacy specifically spelled out, another for a tighter doctrine or ordination, another, by contrast, for less insistence on church order in favor of views prevalent in the "underground church," another for requirement of a weekly Eucharist. In most such instances, however, the critic will find that the COCU formulation enables him to hold and to advocate his particular views within the united church even if it does not permit his enforcing these views on others. He will also discover that his situation in this regard parallels that in his own present denomination. Very likely the position he advocates so strongly is not official dogma of his own church but rather an opinion which his church embraces among others, just as the united church will do. It may be that certain "parties"—the term is not here used invidiously—will find themselves comparatively weaker in the Church of Christ Uniting, others comparatively stronger, than at present. In one's proper concern for any matter advocated by such a party, one must compare *A Plan of Union* not with one's own private theology but with the doctrinal standards of one's own present church and with the diversity which these permit.

Some persons with strong concerns at a particular point will discover in certain statements of *A Plan of Union* a greater flexibility than they might desire. The flexibility is intentional. In ecumenical circles it is sometimes whimsically referred to as "holy ambiguity," a mode of speech justified by the fact that it permits one to have his cake without requiring everyone else to eat it. It enables crucial affirmations to be made which some will wish to take maximally and others minimally. Thus, "The united church accepts the Apostles' and Nicene Creeds. . . . The united church will use these creeds as acts of praise or allegiance" (*A Plan of Union*, V, 9–10, pp. 26–27). The proponent of a tighter statement on the authority of creeds and the advocate of a looser statement or of no statement at all must each face with theological realism the implications of his own position. In any case, *A Plan* calls for a church where the creeds will be used as witnesses to the historic faith without imposing them as tests of orthodoxy. Is there really a better alternative?

The mode of seeking a consensus comprehensive rather than reductionist characterizes the work of the Consultation. To understand the theology of *A Plan of Union* one must seek to grasp the genius of this mode within the context of the theological movements of our century. He must also engage in the process of discussing the plan with persons of other traditions, for only thus can he begin to grasp the living reality of those concerns which it seeks to embody in a united church.[19]

An Integrity Achieved and Awaited

In the last analysis, the theological integrity of the Consultation must be sought not in its intention, its commitment, or its mode of work, but in the provisions of *A Plan of Union*. Does this product of a decade's labor on the part of COCU command theological respect?

The limitations of *A Plan* are obvious. Like most committee documents (aside from the Declaration of Independence), it lacks literary distinction. Because of the diverse authorship of various parts and the pressure of time on all who had part in shaping it, it is repetitive and overly long. Some of its theological statements are doubtless less precise than this or that scholar might have produced. The document, however, is a pragmatic design, shaped by theological considerations but not a textbook in theology. It is offered to the member churches in the service of a great end. If it fails to state a particular point quite adequately, it needs amendment, not repudiation.

The conception of a united church which underlies the plan possesses obvious integrity. Accepting the unity given us in Christ, A Plan proposes a united church which seeks to manifest this oneness in witness, eucharistic fellowship, mission and service, integrity of structure, inclusiveness of human differences, comprehension of religious diversity, and receptivity to the new (A Plan of Union, II, 1–30, pp. 10–14). The union here conceived is open, not exclusive; beginning with a dramatically broad reconciliation of numerous diverse traditions, it looks hopefully toward further union and promises continued fraternal cooperation with all other Christians (A Plan of Union, II, 23–24, p. 13; IX, 1–20, pp. 73–75). It is ecumenical, not individualistic, formulated not by one charismatic leader, nor by a few, as our denominational positions were, but growing out of a common apprehension of the great Tradition of the church and of values in our particular traditions (A Plan of Union, II, 18, p. 12; V, 6–8, p. 26).[20] It is dynamic, not static, conceiving the church functionally in terms of its mission rather than absolutely in terms of some presumed eternal pattern (A Plan of Union, VIII, 1–3, p. 56). It is organic, not purely "spiritual" in its concept of union, believing that the oneness of the people of God requires expression in structures of relationship and service (A Plan of Union, II, 1–7, p. 10). It is horizontal, not hierarchical in organization, with heaviest stress falling on the local units of districts and parishes where mission is carried out (A Plan of Union, VIII, 4–9, pp. 56–57). It is historical, not absolute, in the claims it makes for itself, seeking without triumphalism to embody the best current understanding of the church in mission and to keep itself open to constant renewal and reform by the Spirit of God—an intention which no church can guarantee to fulfill but to which it must give itself in constant prayer (A Plan of Union, II, 22, p. 13; III, 1, 4, 8, pp. 15–17).

With respect to the faith of the church, A Plan advances an understanding of Scripture and Tradition and of obedient response to their witness which, taken seriously, would deepen rather than diminish the spiritual vitality of any Christian community (A Plan of Union, III, 1–28, pp. 15–21; IV, 1–17, pp. 22–24). With regard to worship and the sacraments, it sets forth profound interpretations of baptism and eucharist, including certain variant practices, out of the conviction that Christians dare no longer remain separated by their diverse interpretations of these reconciling gifts of grace and unity (*A Plan of Union*, VI, 15–32, pp. 33–37). In the matter of ministry, it sets forth a solid doctrine of the ministry of Jesus Christ expressed through all his people and through servants ordained for specific tasks (*A Plan of Union*, VII, 1–6, 12–25, 28–33, pp. 38–45); it emphasizes the missionary character of the work of presbyters, bishops, and deacons more clearly than the formulations of any of the present churches, even as it conceives these offices in a manner which makes them available for new types of ministry (*A Plan of Union*, VII, 7–11, 48, 69, 82, 89, pp. 39–40, 47, 51, 53, 55). In dealing with the church as community of the faithful, it provides through parish, district, and task group for capabilities in mission and service which the denominational system has not offered (*A Plan of Union*, VII, 28, 31, 35, 36, 43–51, 72, 73, pp. 60–63, 65–66); even though for valid reasons it organizes the church within the boundaries of the United States, it seeks to guard against an ecclesiastical nationalism or an accommodation of the church to a particular culture (*A Plan of Union*, III, 2, 28, pp. 15, 21; IX, 2, 4–6, 11, 14, pp. 73–74). If all these matters necessarily involve pragmatic considerations, they have all been informed with a theological concern at once honest and relevant.

The members of the Consultation have already traveled far enough together to discover that a pilgrimage of obedience constantly leads to divine surprises. If they had not previously realized the intensely eschatological character of New Testament faith, their experience in COCU has enabled them to understand it. For all along the way, just as a solution for one problem was found, a new problem emerged. Yet in that new difficulty members became conscious of the living Lord of the church calling on to a new stage of insight and obedience. Thus we have been led to a vision of his church far more vital, personal, free, and effective than any of us had been able to conceptualize a decade ago. The farther we go on this quest, the more intently we realize that the form of church we have described in *A Plan of Union* is not final but subject to continuing reform and renewal by the Spirit, even as we know that the vision already achieved must leave us increasingly dissatisfied with the partial expressions of church life now open to us in our separateness.

In a spirit of expectation we therefore await the responses to *A Plan of Union* yet to come from hundreds of study groups in every part of the nation. For we have had enough experience in the process to know that any authentic problem which may be presented, however difficult, may well become the means by which we are led to a larger understanding of the nature of a church truly catholic, evangelical, and reformed. Receptive to the past and sensitive to the present, we have learned to live in openness to the future.

Some commentators on *A Plan of Union* have suggested that the theol-

ogy which underlies it reflects views prevalent a decade or so ago but
not now. To this accurate observation, three replies may be in order. First,
any such enterprise in corporate theologizing must inevitably trail the
leading edge of constructive Christian thought in view of the time required for any new position to commend itself to the leadership of the
churches, and also of the lag between theoretical appropriation of an
idea and the attainment of a consensus concerning its practical applica-
tion. The criticism would have compelling force if the Consultation
showed itself a generation or more behind the times, but such a charge
can scarcely carry credibility. Second, COCU has demonstrated a measure of common sense in not responding frantically to the evident faddism
of the past decade, with its rapid succession of theologies which went
"out" almost as soon as they appeared to be "in." Third, such a venture
as COCU must work from a substantial breadth of doctrinal consensus in
the member churches. Responsible new work now being done by leading
theologians will inevitably reshape presently accepted formulations on a
broad scale, but it has not yet done so, particularly in the area of ecclesiology. The Consultation's track record so far indicates readiness to
respond to such emerging insights as promise to lead the churches into
greater faithfulness. There is every reason to believe that in its future
work such responsiveness will continue.

One earnest request we address to the theological critics of A Plan.
Remember the servant role of the queen of the sciences in this enterprise.
In other words, do not think that Christian intellect can discharge its
obligation merely by pointing out some difficulty or flaw in the present
proposal. Go on from there to suggest how theology acting in ecumenical
responsibility can open a way for the people of God into larger faithfulness and more serviceable mission through such a form of church as the
Lord wills for today and tomorrow.

NOTES

1. Douglass, H. Paul, *Church Unity Movements in the United States* (New
   York: Institute of Social Research, 1934), pp. 243–245.
2. *An Outline for a Constitution of a United Church in America* (Newton
   Centre, Massachusetts: Association for a United Church of America, n.d.).
3. *A Plan of Union for a United Church in the United States* (Proposed for
   Study by the Greenwich Conference on Church Union), cf. *Ecumenical
   Studies Series,* Vol. III, No. 2 (Indianapolis: Council on Christian Unity,
   July, 1957).
4. Blake, Eugene Carson, "A Proposal Toward the Reunion of Christ's
   Church," *Christian Century,* Vol. LXXVII, No. 51 (December 21, 1960),
   pp. 1508–1511.
5. See particularly Tomkins, Oliver S. (ed.), *The Third World Conference*

on *Faith and Order* (London: SCM Press, 1953); Minear, Paul S. (ed.), *The Nature of the Unity We Seek* (St. Louis: The Bethany Press,, 1958); Rodger, P. C., and Vischer, Lukas (ed.), *The Fourth World Conference on Faith and Order* (New York: Association Press, 1964). For developments in directions suggested by Faith and Order, see Wedel, Theodore O., "The Body-Spirit Paradox of the Church," *Digest of the Proceedings of the Consultation on Church Union*, Vol. I–II (1962–1963), pp. 69–82; Outler, Albert C., "Scripture, Tradition and the Guardians of Tradition," *ibid.*, pp. 83–95; Shepherd, Massey H., Jr., "Toward a Definition of the Church's Liturgy," *ibid.*, pp. 120–134; "Reports of the Study Commission as Adopted in Plenary Sessions by the Consultation," *ibid.*, pp. 44–49; "Reports of the Consultation," *Digest*, Vol. III (1964), pp. 20–32; Mollegen, A. T., "The Relationship Between the Ministry of the Whole People of God and the Ordained Ministry," *Digest*, Vol. IV (1965), pp. 133–142; Filson, Floyd V., "Freedom Within Unity," *ibid.*, pp. 143–157; Deschner, John, "Church Order as Continuity in the Church," *ibid.*, pp. 227–246; "Reports of the Consultation," *ibid.*, pp. 19–32; "Principles of Church Union," *Digest*, Vol. V (1966), pp. 38–66; Dillenberger, John, "Theological Givens as Theological Orientations," *Digest*, Vol. VI (1967), pp. 42–52; "Commission and Work Group Reports," *Digest*, Vol. VII (1968), pp. 55–111; Outler, Albert C., "The Mingling of Ministries," *Digest*, Vol. VIII (1969), pp. 106–118; Willebrands, The Most Rev. Jan G. M., "An Address," *ibid.*, pp. 139–147. The effect of discussions in the mode of Faith and Order is evident in *A Plan of Union for the Church of Christ Uniting* (Princeton: Consultation on Church Union, 1970), especially Chapters II–VII, IX, Appendices I, II.

6. A list of representative works in this vein might well include the following: Streeter, Burnett Hillman, *The Primitive Church Studied with Special Reference to the Origins of the Christian Ministry* (London: Macmillan and Co., Ltd., 1929); Scott, Ernest F., *The Varieties of New Testament Religion* (New York: Charles Scribner's Sons, 1947); Robinson, William, *The Biblical Doctrine of the Church* (St. Louis: The Bethany Press, 1948); Craig, Clarence Tucker, *The One Church in the Light of the New Testament* (New York: Abingdon-Cokesbury Press, 1951); Bultmann, Rudolf, *Theology of the New Testament*, 2 vols., translated by Kendrick Grobel (New York: Charles Scribner's Sons, 1954–1955); Knox, John, *The Early Church and the Coming Great Church* (New York: Abingdon Press, 1955); Minear, Paul S., *Images of the Church in the New Testament* (Philadelphia: Westminster Press, 1960). Cf. footnote 16.

7. Minear, Paul S., "The Promise of Christ Fulfilled," *Digest*, Vol. I–II (1962–63), pp. 135–159; Minear, Paul S., "Pictures of the Apostolic Church," *Digest*, Vol. IV (1965), pp. 247–272; Vischer, Lukas, "The Temple of God," *Digest*, Vol. V (1966), pp. 90–113; Fuller, Reginald H., "Bible Study," *Digest*, Vol. VI (1967), pp. 103–122; Johnson, Joseph A., Jr., "The Bible Study Based on Galations 1, 2," *Digest*, Vol. VII (1968), pp. 122–147; Keck, Leander, "Horizons of the Church's Life: The Sermon on

the Mount," *Digest*, Vol. VIII (1969), pp. 157–185; Newbigin, Lesslie, "The Bible Study Lectures," *Digest*, Vol. IX (1970), pp. 193–231.

8. A climate variously influenced by Barth, Brunner, Tillich, and the Niebuhrs produced some important excursions into ecclesiology, among them Tillich, Paul, *The Protestant Era* (Chicago: The University of Chicago Press, 1948); Tomkins, Oliver, *The Wholeness of the Church* (London: SCM Press, 1949); Flew, R. Newton, and Davies, Rupert E. (ed.), *The Catholicity of Protestantism* (London: Lutterworth Press, 1950); Nelson, J. Robert, *The Realm of Redemption: Studies in the Doctrine of the Nature of the Church in Contemporary Protestant Theology* (Greenwich, Connecticut: The Seabury Press, 1951); Morrison, Charles Clayton, *The Unfinished Reformation* (New York: Harper & Brothers, 1953); Newbigin, Lesslie, *The Household of God* (New York: Friendship Press, 1953); Outler, Albert C., *The Christian Tradition and the Unity We Seek* (London: Oxford University Press, 1957); Hooft, W. A. Visser't, *The Pressure of Our Common Calling* (Garden City, New York: Doubleday & Company, Inc., 1959). The mood of neo-Reformation theology pervaded the Consultation generally during much of its first decade.

9. Social and cultural factors in division received important notice at Lund in 1952; see footnote 5: Tomkins (ed.), *The Third World Conference on Faith and Order*, op. cit., *passim;* cf. Ehrenstrom, Nils, and Huelder, Walter G. (ed.), *Institutionalism and Church Unity* (New York: Association Press, 1963). COCU has also given attention to these factors: see footnote 17.

10. The adoption of this threefold slogan inspired a number of studies of the ideal it implies: Hunt, George L., and Crow, Paul A., Jr. (ed.), *Where We Are in Church Union* (New York: Association Press, 1965); Vassady, Bela, *Christ's Church: Evangelical, Catholic, and Reformed* (Grand Rapids, Michigan: Wm. B. Eerdmans Publishing Company, 1965); Osborn, Ronald E., *A Church for These Times* (New York: Abingdon Press, 1965); Day, Peter, *Tomorrow's Church: Catholic, Evangelical, Reformed* (New York: The Seabury Press, 1969).

11. For example, Horton, Douglas, *The United Church of Christ* (New York: Thomas Nelson & Sons, 1962); Trott, Norman L., "The Nature and Structure of the Methodist Church in Relation to the Consultation on Church Union," *Mid-Stream*, Vol. VI, No. 2 (Winter, 1967), pp. 67–73; Osborn, Ronald E., "The Eldership Among Disciples of Christ," *ibid.*, pp. 74–112; Mathews, James K., *A Church Truly Catholic* (Nashville: The Abingdon Press, 1969).

12. See Williams, Colin, *Where in the World? Changing Forms of the Church's Witness* (New York: National Council of Churches of Christ in the U.S.A., 1963); Williams, Colin, *What in the World?* (New York: NCCC, 1964); Williams, Colin, *For the World* (New York: NCCC, 1965); Department on Studies in Evangelism, *The Church for Others and the Church for the World: A Quest for Structures for Missionary Congregations* (Geneva: World Council of Churches, in 1967). This concern is reflected in COCU documents: Williams, Colin W., "The Structure of the Church," *Digest,*

Vol. VI (1967), pp. 53–74; Commission on Structure, "Presuppositions for Church Structure," *ibid.*, pp. 75–84; "Guidelines for the Structure of the Church," *ibid.*, pp. 87–93; Neigh, Kenneth G., "Cooperative Ventures in Mission," *Digest*, Vol. VII (1968), pp. 33–42; "Guidelines for Interchurch Action," *Digest*, Vol. VIII (1969), pp. 120–136.

13. Cf. Hazelton, Roger, "The Diaconate in a United Church," *Digest*, Vol. VIII (1969), pp. 74–87; Osborn, Ronald E., "The Meaning of Presbyter in the United Church," *ibid.*, pp. 88–105.

14. Jordan, Bishop Frederick D., "An Address," *Digest*, Vol. VIII (1969), pp. 148–153.

15. "A Word to the Churches," *Digest*, Vol. X (1971).

16. Nelson, J. Robert, "Some Aspects of the Christian Ministry in the Light of New Testament Study," *Digest*, Vol. III (1964), pp. 53–71; Gealy, Fred D., "Baptism in the Light of Contemporary New Testament Studies," *ibid.*, pp. 108–118; Young, Franklin W., "One Table in Contemporary New Testament Studies," *ibid.*, pp. 119–142; Best, Ernest, "Ministry and Ministries," *Digest*, Vol. IV (1965), pp. 206–226.

17. Historical studies include McNeill, John T., "The Ministry in Light of the Historical Situation," *Digest*, Vol. III (1964), pp. 35–52; Wilburn, Ralph S., "The One Baptism and the Many Baptisms," *ibid.*, pp. 72–107; Wolf, William J., "The Ordained Ministry in Uniting Churches," *Digest*, Vol. IV (1965), pp. 37–106; Handy, Robert T., "The Ministry in American History: A Reflection in the Light of Ecumenical Encounter," *ibid.*, pp. 107–132; Osborn, Ronald E., "Ministry or Ministries?", *ibid.*, pp. 158–205. For sociological interest, see Dillenberger, John," Theological-Cultural Factors Demanding Union of the Churches," *Digest*, Vol. I–II (1962–1963), pp. 58–68; Harrison, Paul M., "Sociological Analysis of Participating Communions," *ibid.*, pp. 96–119; "Report on Analysis of Partiicipating Communions," *ibid.*, pp. 46–47.

18. See Hazelton, Roger, "Consensus Theology: Reflections on the COCU Experience," *Andover Newton Quarterly*, Vol. XII, No. 1 (September, 1971), pp. 2–11.

19. "A Word to the Churches," *Digest*, Vol. X (1971).

20. Cf. "An Open Letter to the Churches," *Digest*, Vol. V (1966), especially pp. 70–71.

6

Catholicity and A "Plan of Union"

WILLIAM J. WOLF

Catholicity with respect to the Plan points to a quality of openness to further union with other Christian churches and even to a deepening concern for, as the preamble puts it, the whole "family of man." The word *catholic* has many meanings. Rooted in the Apostles' and Nicene Creeds as an adjective descriptive of the church, it meant for the Greek fathers "a wholeness, an orthodoxy, or fullness and integrity of life and thought" and came to mean additionally in the West, particularly with Augustine, "universal" in a geographical sense.

In a more specialized way, catholicity today means an openness to, and a desire to be reconciled with, the Eastern churches, the Roman Catholic Church, the Old Catholic Churches, as well as with the Anglo-Catholics within the Episcopal Church. One of the obvious problems is that these churches and people differ about what should be included in "catholicity." The Consultation on Church Union has consistently sought something far greater than pan-Protestant union.

> The uniting churches desire to form more than a new and more inclusive denomination. We seek full reconciliation with earlier and still separated Christian churches as we do with those of more recent divisions. The specific purpose of this union is not the merger of denominations, but the formation through union of a dynamic united and uniting church. This pilgrimage has as its ultimate goal the unity of the whole church [*A Plan of Union*, II, 24, p. 13].

This general goal becomes quite specific in its catholicity in Chapter IX:

> The Church of Christ Uniting will continue the efforts already begun by the various uniting churches to strengthen fraternal understanding, the-

ological dialogue, and cooperation in mission with the Roman Catholic Church, the Orthodox Churches, and various other Christian churches with which full communion has not yet been established. [*A Plan of Union*, IX, 10, p. 74].

One of the chief problems of catholicity, at least from a Western point of view, is that the Plan begins with a church union limited to the United States. Criticism of a merely national church by the Roman Catholic delegate-observers at Dallas resulted in a stronger statement in *Principles of Church Union* [1] than in the draft document. Cardinal Willebrands in his address at the Atlanta plenary of the Consultation returned to this problem.

> A national church, as a limit of Christian concern, is as unthinkable as a national god. If the Roman Catholic danger is the universal at the expense of the local, yours is the danger of the local or national at the expense of the universal. No matter how carefully the tension is formulated in the *Principles*, I suggest careful sensitivity must be given to the danger in practice. Here, in dialogue, we can help each other through mutual alertness and fraternal correction.[2]

This helpful criticism has contributed to the reworking of this section of *Principles* in the Plan with an even more definite commitment to catholicity in a supranational dimension.

> *The Church of Christ Uniting intends to be in fact a uniting as well as a united church.* This means emphasizing the united church's incomplete and provisional character and our desire to press steadily forward toward wider unity both within this nation and beyond its borders. We recognize the dangers in a church organized solely on a national basis, as nationalistic attitudes may pervert or silence the prophetic voice of the church so that God's judgment on the nation's domestic and foreign policies may not be articulated clearly. Yet there must be meaningful identification with the nation if the church is to serve as a voice of conscience. The dangers are matched with opportunities [*A Plan of Union*, II, 23, p. 13].

Under the area of "nation" in the chapter on organization there is also a specific acknowledgment of "a special kinship with the movement toward uniting churches in Canada and the West Indies."

> The possibility, moreover, that the overall structure of the united church might through a future union or a new relationship encompass more than the political boundaries of a single nation is not to be forgotten [*A Plan of Union*, VIII, 12, p. 58].

Throughout the document there is a modesty about this first step of bringing the nine churches into union.

> Yet we believe that God who wills his church to be one also wills that its ordained ministry shall be one, with as much universality and authority as is possible in a still divided church. These are the presuppositions of the united church in providing for the acts of reconciliation and unification of the existing ministries of the uniting churches and for all future ordinations [*A Plan of Union,* II, 18, p. 12].

The Plan introduces a pioneering feature unique among the many plans of union abroad in its expressed willingness to study, for example, the documents of Vatican II and those of other churches such as the Lutheran confessions.

> There are churches, not yet included in the united church, to which we are bound in "one Lord, one faith, one baptism." These churches have expressed their stewardship of the gospel in their own symbols, statements, and creeds. The united church intends to study these confessions, and where possible to join in them, thus enhancing the strength and richness of our common faith and expressing the fuller unity of the Body of Christ [*A Plan of Union,* V, 13, pp. 27–28].

This principle already expressed in *Principles of Church Union* has been extended in the Plan to include openness to other polities than those reconciled in the united church. The reference to the supranational office of papacy is unmistakable in this context.

> Our understanding of the ordained ministry, enhanced by our unification, will not be closed to new insights; for, just as the united church will study the confessions of churches not yet included in this united church, so it will study the polity and offices of the ordained ministry in these same churches in the interest of still wider reconciliation [*A Plan of Union,* VII, 30, p. 44].

A chapter assigned to analyze the catholicity of the Plan has the danger of becoming merely an exercise in a backward-oriented ecumenism to the extent that the exciting orientation toward renewal in the present and future is lost. The aim of the Church of Christ Uniting is no mere ecclesiastical ecumenism, but a secular one as well, responsive to the whole human situation. The Plan addresses itself to churches separated because of racism. To express its seriousness very concretely on this issue, it provides, in addition to committees on equitable representation at all levels of the church's life, that the presiding bishop shall always be followed by one of different racial background. "Catholocity" expressly requires racial inclusiveness. But even this constantly recurring theme is related to a wider secular ecumenism.

As we go forward in the Church of Christ Uniting, such a re-forming, re-fashioning, re-creating process will make new and unfamiliar demands upon us of assimilation and of receptiveness to the Spirit's guidance in mission and renewal. . . .

To the renewed church the need of men for enough food, for meaningful work, for adequate housing and healthy environment, for acceptance as human beings without prejudice and discrimination, for the creation of beauty, for peace, for human love in a dehumanized world, and for an inward experience of the knowledge of God presents the call to mission. In faithfulness we seek to demonstrate the power of "one Lord, one faith, one baptism" not only in our own life but in the service of all men [A Plan of Union, II, 25, 27, pp. 13–14].

It would be unfair to proceed to the ordained ministry in the Plan, probably the most difficult issue of catholicity, without first seeking to understand the view of the church and the definitions of *catholic* and *apostolic* which supply the needed theological context. It had been a proper criticism of the section on the ministry in *Principles of Church Union* that it had not first rooted the topic in an ecclesiology.

Firstly, the church is one, made so by the act of God in Christ, not by what planners do for it. The given unity of the church as a reality of God's doing through the Holy Spirit is basic to the Plan.

The church is described in the third chapter along the lines of the· New Delhi statement with special emphases upon its mission, its role in a secular society, its servant stance, and its eschatological nature. Then follows, as in Vatican II, a list of scriptural images—the church as the new creation, as the people of God, as the body of Christ, as the community of the Holy Spirit. An interesting definition of the "indefectibility" of the church concludes the chapter:

No claim is made that the Church of Christ Uniting is the whole church. What is sought is that it be a representative of the whole people of God in this place and participate with Christians in this nation and other nations in the upbuilding of the whole body, in faithfulness to the Gospel, and in the fulfillment of our Lord's total mission. As long as the church is responsive to the commission, it will lead men to faith and salvation and "the powers of death shall not prevail against it" [A Plan of Union, III, 28, p. 21].

The sacramental character of the church is described in language that suggests the positions of Vatican II.

A sacrament, therefore, is an effective sign, symbol, or seal; it not only signifies, but also, by God's gift, conveys that which it signifies. Christ may be called the fundamental sacrament of God's gracious encounter with mankind, and the church, as the body of Christ, may be considered a sacrament of the Kingdom of God [A Plan of Union, VI, 15, p. 33].

This strongly sacramental quality in the Plan has commended itself to many Roman Catholics. Bishop William Baum, one of the two official Roman Catholic observers to the Consultation, has written:

In Chapter VI, "This People at Worship," once again Catholics will recognize themselves in the description of the Church's life of worship. COCU's treatment of sacraments and liturgy illustrates the amazing degree of convergence which has already been achieved thanks to contemporary biblical-theological development and to the Liturgical Movement. It is especially hoped that Catholics will become familiar with the COCU statements on Baptism and the Eucharist.[3]

To Principles of Church Union's additional designations for the service of the Lord's Supper as the "Eucharist" and the "Holy Communion," the Plan, enlarging its catholicity, adds the "Divine Liturgy" and the "Mass." The Plan also includes a strong statement on eucharistic sacrifice.

The Lord's Supper is an act of sacrifice in which we are united with Christ in his self-offering to the Father; with him, we offer ourselves in praise, thanksgiving, and service. The church corporate and its members are renewed in the covenant of grace, receive the forgiveness of sins, participate in the divine life, and receive eternal life. In the Holy Communion, the church is built up ever anew and its unity is both signified and brought about through the Holy Spirit [A Plan of Union, VI, 27, p. 36].

Bishop Baum comments specifically on this passage. "If the Church of Christ Uniting can be truly united in accepting this text, then a great step has been taken in the reconciliation of Catholics and Protestants." [4]

The offering of "spiritual sacrifices" is mentioned again in the service of inauguration and in the ordinal. What is perhaps even more surprising than the references to eucharistic sacrifice, considering the Reformation polemic about "the other five sacraments," is to find the traditional ones listed along with other Gospel actions as having sacramental character "from the records of the Gospel and from the Tradition of the church" [A Plan of Union, VI, 32, p. 37].

The sacramental character of ordination is clarified further in Chapter VII:

In ordination, the united church recognizes that the call to the individual man or woman is of God, prays that the one to be ordained will continue to receive the gifts of the Spirit, believes that God gives grace appropriate to the office, accepts and authorizes this ministry in and for his church [A Plan of Union, VII, 32, p. 44].

The service of ordination to a particular office in the united church shall not be repeated for any individual [A Plan of Union, VII, 33, p. 45].

A deliberate linking together in ordination of catholic tradition ("the bishop acting as the presiding minister") with a reformed and evangelical addition of representative participation by all offices, ordained and lay, will be certain to arouse much discussion in catholic circles, although the practice was described in Principles of Church Union and became a consultation agreement as early as Lexington.

In all ordination rites, including particularly the laying-on of hands, representatives of all offices and orders or ordained ministry in the church and representatives of the laity, shall participate. This participation signifies that ordination is an act of the whole church [A Plan of Union, VII, 33, pp. 44–45].

The Plan contains a specific reference to monastic vocation.

As part of its internal diversity, the united church will recognize a call to some of its members to associate together in a common life under a rule for growth in the ways of prayer, and in order to serve God and men [A Plan of Union, IV, 16, p. 24].

Principles presented a statement on Scripture and Tradition that was widely greeted by many Protestant, Orthodox, and Roman Catholic scholars as an important ecumenical breakthrough. Three interrelationships between Scripture and Tradition have been carefully refined and more consistently defined in the Plan. The section on Scripture has been strengthened, but the old battle cry of sola Scriptura has been dropped. The definition of Tradition (with capital "T") is more carefully drawn to avoid a certain romanticism in the Dallas document that conceivably could be interpreted as the sola Traditione theory. The need for change in Tradition is clearer than in Principles and now appears in the sentence: "Living Tradition is a continually flexible reality" (A Plan of Union, V, 6, p. 26). One cannot overstate the degree to which this resolution of the battle between Scripture and Tradition has liberated the Consultation from the "hang-ups" of old polemics. When it is realized that not everything that is said about bishops, presbyters, sacraments, etc., must be found solely in Scripture, but may be admitted as developments in Traditon, there is available both a considerable therapy and a theological method of reconciliation with very great potential for the future.

Bishop Baum hails this "achievement" of relating Scripture and Tradition: "this statement and the teaching of Vatican II on the same question seem to be in accord. Thus hope is offered that the old debate over Scripture vs. Tradition may be resolved." [5]

An important section in Chapter III defines the special adjectives of the Consultation—*catholic, evangelical,* and *reformed*—stating that all three must be held together, each balancing and interpreting the other two.

> The word *catholic* has three significant senses. First, it literally means whole, universal, and comprehensive. Thus it points to the continuity of the Church across centuries and links us to Christ's mission from the beginning and on into the future. Likewise, it points to the unity of the church on earth with the cloud of witnesses from past generations who are united with us in the communion of saints. A church catholic seeks to teach those essentials always and everywhere accepted by Christians. Secondly, the catholic emphasis has consistently witnessed to man in his totality, relating all of secular life to the God whose will is our peace. Thirdly, catholicity represents a rich diversity, like a prism through which light from one source issues in many colors. It reminds us today that the church can never be separated by cultural, racial, economic, or social divisions. Exclusiveness based on race, sex, class, education, or place of origin sins against catholicity. A catholic church is always bigger than the horizons which we see [*A Plan of Union,* III, 23, p. 20].

Bishop Baum is obviously in agreement over the definition of *catholic:* "Catholics should read Chapter III with great attention and in so doing will come to a deeper understanding of what it means to be a Catholic." [6]

In one context the word *apostolic* is used to describe the faith which "is continuously believed and expressed anew by the church" (*A Plan of Union,* V, 3, p. 25). More specifically, it refers to the creeds as "witnesses of Tradition to the mighty acts of God recorded in Scripture" (*A Plan of Union,* V, 9, p. 26).

> The united church will use these creeds as acts of praise and allegiance that bind it to the apostolic faith of the one Church in all centuries and continents [*A Plan of Union,* V, 10, p. 27].

Bishop Baum comments as follows: "Room is also found for creedal formulations and thus makes possible a new kind of dialogue between Catholics and Protestants on the meaning and value of dogma." [7]

A transition in the use of *apostolic* from primary reference to the message to include also the quality of continuity in the community is to be observed in Chapter VI:

> A church truly catholic, evangelical, and reformed must constantly keep itself apostolic, both through education in the apostles' message and through the apostolic commission which is ours as well as theirs [*A Plan of Union*, VI, 11, p. 32].

"Apostolic continuity," which is a synonym for "apostolic succession" of the episcopacy, is described as a "gift" in Chapter VII, paragraph 68 (*A Plan of Union*, p. 51).

It needs for its fuller understanding the statement made at the beginning of the section on ordained ministries:

> Within the ministry of the whole people of God there is and has been from the beginning a particular ministry representative of God who calls and of the church which ordains. This ministry is derived from Christ's action through his apostles and, under the guidance of the Holy Spirit, continues to derive its authority from the living Christ [*A Plan of Union*, VII, 28, p. 44].

One of the features that distinguishes the Plan from related plans abroad is the lengthy section on the ministry of the whole people of God, the *laos*. It is made clear that ordained ministers do not cease to be members of this *laos* when they are ordained, nor does the reality of ordained ministries (orders, or offices—the words deliberately used as synonyms) excuse any layman from his basic responsibilities of ministry as part of God's priestly people. Much here emphasizes the solid contributions made over the last generation in "the theology of the laity" without the loss of the special vocation to ordination that haunts some priests and ministers today and makes them doubtful of their calling.

The introductory section on the ordained ministry has already been quoted. An important description follows on the nature of the church's continuity, the general tasks of the three orders, and a functional description of their special responsibilities which develops a sacramental view of the ordained ministers as "expressing," "representing," "serving" Christ in his church. This is a translation of the scholastic *in persona Christi* formulation.

> All ministerial ordination is grounded in the historic deed of God in Christ. Continuity in the church is maintained through Scripture ánd Tradition, through liturgy and creeds, through the life and witness of the whole people of God and through their representative ministries. The ordained

ministers of the church bear particular responsibility as guardians of the Gospel, Scripture and Tradition. It is their task to help equip God's people to share in the total service of the church, to proclaim and teach God's word responsibly and articulately, and to celebrate the sacraments with God's people. The ordained minister of the Word and Sacraments thus expresses, represents, and serves the redemptive work of Christ through his church in a particular, but not exclusive way.

The united church accepts and will continue the three ordained ministries (offices and orders) of presbyters, bishops and deacons [A *Plan of Union*, VII, 29-30, p. 44].

Bishop Baum's evaluation of the catholicity of the Plan at this point is extremely significant:

It is clearly the intention of the Plan thereby to bring the uniting church into the Catholic tradition and to embrace the "historic episcopate." Catholics will note that the vision of the ordained ministry is here much closer to their own point of view than that of the separate Protestant churches comprising COCU. The offices of presbyter, bishop and deacon are described functionally, and in the description of these offices as far as this description goes, Catholics will recognize their own view of the ordained ministry.[8]

There was some dissatisfaction that *Principles of Church Union* did not use the word *priest* for *presbyter*, although many who made the complaint seem not to have seen the phrase "the single priesthood which embraces every form of the presbyterate." The Plan makes it clear that *presbyter* and *priest* are synonymous terms, as they are in catholic tradition.

There has been almost universal criticism from Catholic quarters of the decision of the Consultation to list the ordained offices in the sequence "presbyters, bishops, deacons" rather than in the traditionally catholic order of "bishops, presbyters, deacons." It is to be hoped that a revision of the Plan will restore the more traditional order or, at very least, mix up the order in different places so as to remove what is clearly an offense to many catholic-minded persons. Even as kindly a critic as Bishop Baum calls this "a cause of some dismay" and further expresses his misgivings:

One fears that the Consultation may falter in its effort to embrace the episcopacy because of its fear of episcopacy. In any event, the hesitancy and ambiguity of the Plan illustrated by the choice of the sequence "presbyters, bishops and deacons" regarding the episcopacy will make recognition of its bishops difficult for Catholics and Orthodox Christians.[9]

Since Protestant sensibilities are often aroused here on the other side, it may be well to analyze how and why the Consultation moved to this novel sequence. For many there just is no theological problem here, but obviously for others there are important theological investments at stake.

One of the reasons was to break the sequence of services in the Anglican ordinal—deacons, priests, bishops—in which the diaconate is unfortunately called an "inferior office."

This reason has been highlighted by the Committee on the Ministry, which introduced the unusual sequence in the ordinal it prepared for the Plan of Union Commission by inserting into the preface the following statement:

> This is done with a definite intention to avoid the implication that the different offices are simply ascending steps in a hierarchy. This sequence seeks to convey the authenticity of each office of the ordained ministry and to allow creative insights into the interrelationships among these offices within the total ministry of the church [A Plan of Union, Appendix II, A, p. 90].

Another, more pragmatic consideration was simply that presbyters are more visible in the life of the church as seen by the average layman than bishops or deacons. It would be a serious mistake, however, to claim that this ordering of services or the one reason given for this as "a definite intention to avoid the implication that the different offices are simply ascending steps in a hierarchy" is meant to deny that there is any such reality as a hierarchy. The ordained orders are defined functionally; but the traditional functions ascribed to the bishop are certainly hierarchical functions. The attempt is to avoid a hierarchy of status, of absolute power, of career ascent. This acceptance of a hierarchy of function in order to serve the whole church rather than to dominate it is well illustrated in the question addressed to the bishop-elect in the ordinal: "Will you exercise the fullness of your priestly ministry so that the people of God may offer themselves in union with Christ's perfect offering of Himself to God?" [A Plan of Union, Appendix II, 16, p. 98.]

The bishop is understood sacramentally here as having "a fullness of priestly ministry." That is hierarchical. The thrust of the language in the preface to the ordinal is directed against "simply ascending steps." This concern has led to putting the diaconate at the end of the list, leaving the episcopate in the middle position where it often indeed finds itself. People have been too tense to see the humor in this. Because of the protests from the Catholic side, the sequence ought, however, to be restored to the traditional one which also characterizes the union churches of Asia. This break with tradition is needless. Protestant sensitivities are guarded elsewhere.

Another conceivable reason for the sequence, hinted at in the preface to the ordinal, is made explicit in the text. Historical studies about the origins of episcopacy and the presbyterate are often prejudged by super-imposed theories that tend either to oversimplify a very confusing picture or to inhibit full historical inquiry or theological dialogue.

From the section on presbyters two very carefully drawn sentences describe this issue:

> There have been in history many interpretations of the presbyterate and of its relationship with other ordained offices. The united church welcomes the diversity of these interpretations, but seeks to encourage new insights and understanding [A Plan of Union, VII, 43, p. 46].

The parallel sentences about bishops were beaten out in motions and amendments on the floor at the St. Louis plenary and are much more satisfactory than the previous *Principles of Church Union* statement, al-though they may unintentionally suggest a somewhat negative attitude rather than an open one. Here a distinction is made between the official view of episcopacy as set forth in the Plan and the freedom of the indi-vidual to continue dialogue about the historical origins and development of episcopacy and its theological significance:

> In accepting and maintaining the historic episcopate, the Church of Christ Uniting neither implies, excludes, nor requires any theory or doctrine of the episcopate which goes beyond what is stated in this plan [A Plan of Union, VII, 57, p. 49].

It might increase the catholicity of this statement on the episcopate if the sentences about presbyters were added here with appropriate changes:

"There have been in history many interpretations of the episcopate and of its relationships with other ordained offices. The United Church welcomes these diverse interpretations as it seeks new insights and under-standing in association with all Christian churches."

The Plan includes a rich definition of the functions of presbyters or priests. Only the section on the sacraments will be quoted here because questions have been raised as to its catholicity.

Celebrants of the Sacraments

The presbyter baptizes and celebrates the eucharist as a representative of the church, offering with all the people spiritual sacrifices acceptable in God's sight. Also he performs certain acts of sacramental character such as confirmation, marriage, ordination, declaration of the forgiveness of sin and announcement of God's blessing. He performs or makes provision for the performance of marriages, burials, and other rites of the church [A Plan of Union, VII, 46, p. 47].

The sense in which the presbyter "performs" confirmation has been so worded in Chapter VI, paragraph 22 (p. 35), "the laying on of hands by the bishop or presbyter in representation of the whole church," as to give priority to the bishop in administering this rite but also to allow the presbyter to do so. This breaks the Anglican barrier that forbids anyone other than a bishop to administer confirmation and does so by the principle recognized in other churches of catholic order in which the priest may administer confirmation at the delegation of the bishop.

The sense in which the presbyter "performs" ordination is guarded elsewhere and in the Ordinal, in which it is clear that only the bishop can preside at an ordination. The verb here should, however, be changed to "participates in" to clear up the ambiguity.

A major question about the catholicity of the Plan will be whether the episcopate of the Church of Christ Uniting can be recognized as a "catholic" episcopate. This section of the Plan needs to be read in its entirety, for it is too long to quote fully in this chapter. It spells out concretely the somewhat problematic acceptance in *Principles* "of the historic episcopate constitutionally defined."

> As part of the one ministry of Jesus Christ, the Church of Christ Uniting accepts and will maintain the historic office or order of bishops. This office has been a principal symbol and agent of unity and continuity in the church, unifying its doctrine and ordered ministry from apostolic times. The Church of Christ Uniting will thus have visible historic continuity with the church of all ages, before and after the Reformation, so that its ordinations may be recognized as widely as possible by all other Christian churches. The bishops together personify the continuity of the church's trusteeship of tradition and pastoral oversight. Therefore, in the Church of Christ Uniting the bishop—together with presbyters, deacons, and the people—will authorize the church's ministry of Word and sacrament and will act in all possible ways as the "servant of the servants of God" [*A Plan of Union*, VII, 59, p. 49].

The corporate character of episcopacy is next described. Just as Vatican II sought to relate the papacy to the episcopate rather than to set it over against the episcopate as was the tendency of Vatican I, so the attempt is made here to integrate the episcopate with the life of the whole church rather than to describe it as over against the rest of the church. It is this reformed or evangelical perspective (really a truly catholic one) which accounts later in the Plan for the following description of the organization of the united church:

> The organizational structures of the united church shall reflect, in so far as can be, the church's continuity with the past—with the great company of

faithful people who from apostolic times until now were witnesses to God's grace in Christ to all men. Thus, the united church accepts elements of polity previously identified as congregational, presbyterian, connectional, or episcopal, but it does not characterize its government by any one of these designations to the exclusion of the others" [A Plan of Union, VIII, 2, p. 56].

We return to the definition of the corporate character of episcopacy:

Corporately, bishops are called to lead the church in the fulfillment of Christ's universal commission given to the whole church. Oversight is exercised corporately by the church in its parishes and other organizational and programmatic areas as well as by the bishops especially consecrated for the task. . . . The episcopacy functions within the life of the whole church, is integrated with it, and exercised within it in a creative, connectional relationship [A Plan of Union, VII, 61, pp. 49–50].

The personal character of episcopacy is then spelled out:

This office personifies the unity and the continuity of the church. Within his primary concern for the whole church, the bishop personally exercises a ministry for specific individuals or portions of the people of God. He is a servant of Christ and of men, and thus brings his share of the pastoral office of the Good Shepherd directly to persons [A Plan of Union, VII, 62, p. 50].

The section on collegiality of bishops is a much longer one and often recalls positions expressed in the documents of Vatican II.

The episcopacy is collegial in the sense that the apostolic calling and responsibility of the whole church are especially an obligation of the body, or—to use the traditional term—the college, of bishops. The bishop does not function as an independent or isolated individual, though he is individually responsible and accountable. No bishop can be completely autonomous in function.

The bishop becomes a member of the episcopal college by election, by ordination (consecration), and by continued communion with its members. With openness to the Holy Spirit and with awareness of the conciliar principle as the consensus of all the faithful people of God, the episcopal body constantly works to strengthen the inner harmony of the church, to safeguard its unity of faith and discipline, and to maintain the distinctive and interrelated roles of presbyter, deacon, and parish.

The collegial role of bishops may well take shape in specific pastoral and prophetic leadership, but no statement of the bishops as a college shall have official force as a rule of the united church unless it is approved by the Transitional or National Assembly.

The college of bishops, operating on the national or regional levels, is thus a specific expression of the collegiality that applies to all offices of the church. It finds expression in conciliar assemblies and in world, national, and regional conferences. Thus, the collegiality of bishops aids in manifesting the supra-national ecumenical character of the church [A Plan of Union, VII, 64–67, p. 50].

In a summary statement, the special insights into the episcopal office received from the four uniting Methodist churches and from the Episcopal Church are listed, but pointed toward the future in which "the united church seeks to move toward a creative, new flexibility in the exercise of this office."

We receive as gifts of the episcopacy and thus as resources for episcopal functions within the united church as defined in this Plan of Union, many characteristics of the episcopacy existing in the uniting churches. Among these are collegiality, apostolic continuity, general superintendency, and equality of office [A Plan of Union, VII, 68, p. 51].

The catholicity of the episcopate collectively is stated in terms far more "catholic" than in the official documents of any of the member churches. It remains to examine the functions and responsibilities of bishops. This section should be read in its entirety together with the constitutional procedures spelled out in Chapter VIII on organization. Here only a collection of the most significantly "catholic" statements can be made for reasons of space.

(a) *Pioneers in Mission.* To keep the apostolic mission of God in Christ to the whole world before the members and parishes of the united church is an essential task of the bishop. . . .

(b) *Pastoral Overseers.* The bishop has the general pastoral oversight of all the people of the district to which he has been called, with particular responsibilities as shepherd for the ordained ministers and their families. He is responsible for furthering the true spiritual unity of the district. . . .

(c) *Teachers and Prophets.* The bishop shall do all that is in his power to preach and to teach creatively the Christian faith as expressed in the Scriptures and in Tradition and to interpret prophetically what God is doing in the world. He bears responsibility for evoking creative thinking and action by his people. He should concern himself with such public issues as race relations, peace, poverty, housing, urban development, conservation and environmental control, population problems, justice, the rule of law in society, and the other contemporary problems of human relations to which Christ's mission is to be directed. . . .

(d) *Administrative Leaders.* Bishops have responsibility for the supervision and administration of the church's organized work and life. As chief shepherds, they serve, either directly or by delegation, as participants in the development of administrative policy and as the church's principal executive officers for the effecting of policy. . . .

(e) *Liturgical Leaders.* Bishops have primary responsibility for the worship and sacramental life of the united church. . . .

(f) *Responsibility for Ordination.* The bishop is a chief symbol and means of ministerial continuity in the church and is responsible for the orderly transfer of ministerial authority. He presides at all services of ordination, along with representatives of other offices of the ordained ministry and of the ministry of lay persons. Thus, within the whole people of God, the bishop personifies the fullness of the priestly ministry of Christ. . . .

(g) *Ecumenical Leaders.* As an expression of the given unity of the church, bishops have a special responsibility to further ecumenical relationships. . . . The bishops, particularly in their collegiality, should seek the union of all Christ's Church and reach out in service to the life of the human community as a whole [*A Plan of Union,* VII, 69–79, pp. 51–53].

The way in which the bishops exercise their special responsibility with respect to issues of faith and order is developed by the method of necessary concurrence of orders under the description of the National Assembly:

On matters of faith and order, the members of the Transitional National Assembly shall vote separately as (a) bishops, (b) presbyters and deacons, and (c) lay persons. Such a proposal regarding faith and order may be enacted only upon the concurrence of these three groups each by a majority vote. Any particular matter shall be designated a "matter of faith and order" upon the request of a majority of any one of these three groups [*A Plan of Union,* X, 59, p. 82].

It may be helpful to see the way in which these constitutional sections are translated liturgically in the ordinal near the beginning of the service of ordination for the bishop-elect:

In the name of the Lord Jesus Christ, the head of the church, we are met together here to consecrate you to the office of Bishop. As a Bishop in the Church of God you are called to manifest and set forward the unity and continuity of the church at all times and places. The title of Bishop derives not from his rank but from his duty, and it is the part of the Bishop to serve rather than to rule. A Bishop is called to be a pioneer in mission, a healer of divisions among christians, a guardian of the truth of faith and the purity of worship, a pastor to pastors, and a wise administrator of the church's organized work and life. A Bishop is called to lead God's people in worship, in celebration of the sacraments, in the ordination of ministers, and in the mission of the church, to be a preacher and teacher of the Gospel, and a guide and overseer of the church's common life. We believe that it is God who gives you grace and authority for the office to which you are called [A Plan of Union, Appendix II, 16, p. 97].

There can be no question of the catholicity in terms of form and matter of the Ordinal of the Church of Christ Uniting and therefore of its adequacy to convey the threefold orders as they have been received in Anglicanism, unless one objects to the ordination of women as somehow invalidating it. In ordaining women the united church will have a deeper "catholicity" than the churches of historic catholic order in their present practice. As was remarked at Lambeth 1958 about the ordination of women, there is nothing in the New Testament to encourage the point of view that nothing should be done for the first time.

The services of ordination have been drawn from the South India Ordinal, from the proposed British Methodist–Church of England Ordinal, from revisions taking place in the participating churches, and from the new ordinal of the Roman Catholic Church. From this last source a direct quotation has been made: "The title of bishop derives not from his rank but from his duty, and it is the part of a bishop to serve rather then to rule" [A Plan of Union, Appendix II, 16, p. 97]. Bishop Baum asks Catholics to read this Ordinal with care: "The rites for ordaining presbyters, bishops and deacons are strikingly similar to the new rites of Ordination of the Roman Catholic Church. Catholics should be deeply appreciative of this development." [10]

There is no need here to analyze further the Ordinal, which needs to be read and judged as a whole. It is important in any consideration of catholicity not to miss the solemn intention in the preface:

> . . . the united church intends to continue the historic ministry of those ordained offices—Presbyters, Bishops, and Deacons—which has been given to the church from earliest times and which has come down to us through the uniting churches [A Plan of Union, Appendix II, 3, p. 90].

Many "catholic"-minded Christians have expressed concern about the service of inauguration, doubting whether it can be reconciled with "catholic" tradition. Some have protested what they feel to be "ambiguity" in the service. A careful study of the service, however, reveals no ambiguity. There is nothing ambiguous about prayer to God that he will unify the ministries of the member churches.

While it incorporates some unique features in the American religious situation and history, the service follows the general pattern worked out ecumenically abroad and recommended by the Lambeth conferences as an alternative to the South India Plan. This type of service has already been used to inaugurate in the fall of 1970 both the Church of North India and the Church of Pakistan. It is no longer a theory but a reality. This type of service of inauguration characterizes at least seven other plans involving churches of the Anglican communion with various Protestant churches.

The following rationale is quoted from the preface, but the service should be carefully studied as a whole.

They [the acts of unification] bring the members and ordained ministers of the uniting churches together in mutual acceptance of one another, and they express the hope that the membership and ordained ministry of the united church will be acceptable henceforth to all churches with which any of the uniting churches was in full communion prior to union. These purposes will be achieved for the members as representatives of the people of God in the uniting churches' covenant with one another to be one people and will be achieved for the ordained ministers as their representatives offer prayers to God and lay hands on one another. The prayers ask that each ordained minister may be so blessed by God as to receive the graces and gifts available to the ordained ministers in all of the uniting churches, together with such further enrichment as he may need for servanthood and mission in the united church. The laying on of hands is to be done in silence [A Plan of Union, Appendix I, 6, pp. 83–84].

Because there has been so much misunderstanding about this service, with some criticizing it as "an ordination free-for-all" or a "subtle or ambiguous form of ordination," the Plan of Union Commission added some description by way of further clarification.

This service inaugurates the Church of Christ Uniting. Since the uniting churches recognize that the ministers of all these churches have already been ordained, this service is not regarded as an act of ordination or of re-ordination. The intention of the service is clearly and unambiguously set forth in the prayers to God for his help, together with the initial declaration of each ordained minister, and the concluding acceptance by the people of the ordained ministers as presbyters, bishops, and deacons in the Church of Christ Uniting [A Plan of Union, Appendix I, 9, p. 84].

A number of questions have been raised about the role of the bishop in this service and whether he really expresses the "catholicity" defined for him in the other parts of the Plan. The service definitely will bring the Methodist episcopate in the four churches of Methodist tradition into reconciliation with the Anglican episcopate in the tradition of the Episcopal Church through prayer to God that he will unify these ministries and with the silent and mutual laying on of hands. The Plan requires those uniting churches which have bishops to present at least one bishop for the initial and representative act of unification in the mutual laying on of hands. In other words, as the services proceed from the national level into other locales even to special services for those who are ill, every ordained minister of the uniting churches will have had episcopal hands in the apostolic succession, along with those of other traditions, laid upon him. This unifying role of the bishop is particularly significant in that the Plan itself states that the bishop personifies the unity and continuity of the church. He, with the other participants in the mutual laying on of hands, will pray in silence as he places his hands upon another: "Lord of all ministries, help us to receive any gifts of ministry which you desire to bestow upon us. Amen" (*A Plan of Union*, Appendix I, 38, p. 89).

While the liturgical act of the revolving circle implies a general mingling of the ordained ministries of nine previously separated churches, there is no confusion of the three special orders of the ordained ministry in this act. This distinction between presbyter, bishop, and deacon is clearly recognized at three points: (1) in the initial declaration, (2) in the central prayer of the ordained ministers, and (3) in the acceptance and welcoming by the people of the "presbyters, bishops, and deacons in the Church of Christ Uniting."

There are other concerns for a renewed church of Christ than "catholicity," as necessary as this quality must be, but they are articulated elsewhere in the Plan and in this book. Every "catholic-minded" person, whether he be Orthodox, Roman Catholic, Old Catholic, or Anglo-Catholic, can rejoice that the Church of Christ Uniting will have a greater "catholicity" than any one of its uniting churches and that even this achievement is seen as only a step toward a still greater catholicity. What is needed in the future evaluation and criticism of the catholicity of the Plan is both the honest realism and the ecumenical openness of this statement from Cardinal Willebrands of the Vatican Secretariat for Promoting Christian Unity:

> We Catholics believe that the one church of Christ subsists in the Roman Catholic Church but cannot be perfectly identified with it, because other Christian communions have developed and manifested church-building elements which are Christian means of salvation. In meeting with these churches, the Catholic Church can also receive the authentic Christian heritage which they have treasured and fostered in separation. Catholic ecumenical life, then, does not look to a return to the past but searches for a reconciliation in the future."

NOTES

1. *Consultation on Church Union 1967: Principles of Church Union, Guidelines for Structure, and a Study Guide* (Cincinnati: Forward Movement Publications, 1967).
2. Willebrands, John Cardinal, "An Address," *Consultation on Church Union: A Catholic Perspective* (Washington: U.S. Catholic Conference Publications Office, 1970), p. 18.
3. Baum, Bishop William W., "A Catholic Perspective," *Consultation on Church Union: A Catholic Perspective, op. cit.*, p. 23.
4. *Ibid.*
5. *Ibid.*
6. *Ibid.*
7. *Ibid.*
8. *Ibid*, p. 24.
9. *Ibid*, p. 25.
10. *Ibid*, p. 26.
11. Willebrands, *op. cit.*, p. 19.

7

The Vision of the Church in "A Plan of Union"

JOHN T. FORD

A fundamental question implicit in efforts at church union is: what is the church? The very fact that this question is so obvious may be the reason why its importance is frequently overlooked. For example, at an ecumenical gathering, discussion about the church may leap almost immediately to such problems as the nature of the clerical ministry or the role of bishops. Such issues are ready-made for debate, unless some participant is thoughtless enough to remind the group that the overwhelming majority of church members are not clergymen and the overwhelming majority of clergy, personal aspirations aside, are not bishops.

In contrast, the starting point for an ecumenical ecclesiology might well be the vision of the church which Christians share in common, not the specific ecclesiological issues which divide Christians. This premise is a matter of logic: the answers to specific questions should be determined, whenever possible, in accord with the basic viewpoint on which they depend. This premise is also prompted by ecumenical strategy: by beginning with areas of basic agreement, one can hopefully place divisive issues in proper perspective, or at least in a less distorted perspective. If a basic commonality is present, divisive issues should prove less abrasive and perhaps even tolerable, if not resolvable. Yet the emphasis on commonality is not simply a matter of logic or strategy, it implies that a basis for unity already exists and so envisions ecumenical effort as an attempt to broaden this basis, as a challenge to further growth in unity.

Some may be puzzled by the statement that an ecumenical ecclesiology should begin with the vision of the church which Christians share in common. This, of course, presumes that every Christian has a vision of the church. Is such the case? An affirmative answer seems warranted insofar as the church has any meaningfulness for a church member. If the church is meaningless to a person, his church membership seems little more than a social convention, a matter of political expediency, or even a tax deduction.

To say that every Christian has a vision of the church does not imply, however, that each person's vision is clear-cut and well defined. On the contrary, this vision may be vague and unarticulated, more a matter of unthematized convictions than a set of specific positions. Indeed, everyone knows what the church is, until asked to define it. Furthermore, one person's vision of the church may vary from that of his neighbor in the same pew. For example, one person's vision may be restricted to his experience in his local congregation, with scant reference to a wider community. Another person's vision may be comprehensive, transcending the confines of his parish and encompassing all Christians of every time and place.

While a person's *view* of the church refers merely to the perspective from which he sees the church, a person's *vision* of the chuch implies the additional dimension of personal commitment. Thus, a person's *vision* of the church includes both the viewpoint from which he sees the church and also the meaning the church has in his personal life. One's vision of the church, then, is not simply an intellectual category which can be analyzed according to the rules of logic. One's vision of the church reaches to the root of a person's existence as he stands in the sight of God; it involves a person's participation in the "community of all those men and women of all ages and places, of all races and tribes, who have been reconciled to God in Jesus Christ" (*A Plan of Union*, III, 2, p. 15).[1]

Complementing this human need for vision is the fact that the church is a mystery. To describe the church as a mystery is a humble but necessary acknowledgment that God's presence in the life of his people surpasses our ability at comprehension and expression. One must "acknowledge the limitations of the languages of men to express the mystery of God's action in history except in symbols and images . . ." (*A Plan of Union*, III, 1, p. 15). Thus, no concept or set of concepts can ever completely delineate the church; our best efforts at describing the church are overpowered by what we are trying to describe; similarly, our attempts to understand God's design for his church as he leads us into the future are problematic.

If any vision is difficult to reduce to words, the task is compounded when it comes to our abilities to comprehend and to express our vision of the church as indicating God's action in the world. One may, of course, ignore the basic ecclesiological tension between our vision of the church and the actuality of the church, just as men almost instinctively tend to eradicate tension from their lives. Yet in ecclesiology this tendency is a temptation. For example, a theologian may be tempted to select one concept of the church and construct an ecclesiology that pretends to be definitive.

Ecumenists are working in vain if a definitive view of the church is expected of them. Ecumenical ecclesiologists can only hope to construct a partial view, a view subject to reformulation and correction. Consequently, those negotiating church union cannot legitimately expect any formula to describe the church totally, entirely, or completely.

The Plan of Union formulates its basic answer to the question—what is the church?—in its third chapter on "What It Means to Be God's People." To appreciate and assess the Plan's vision of the church, we must now turn to a consideration of the three perspectives—human, biblical, and theological—from which the Plan considers the church.

Human Perspective

"The church must be seen in historical perspective as a continuation of the apostolic church of the New Testament and as a contemporary body of believers that is also open to the future" (*A Plan of Union*, III, 1, p. 15). To maintain a healthy balance between past, present, and future may require "a constant struggle" (*A Plan of Union*, III, 4, p. 16), for it is frequently tempting to overemphasize one historical dimension while minimizing the other two. For example, those who prefer the "old-time religion" assume that the doctrines and practices of the past are completely sufficient for the present, even when these are no longer creative or evocative for many. Others, in a praiseworthy but overly pragmatic attempt to make Christianity relevant, casually jettison the past as excess baggage, while cavalierly ignoring the problems they may be creating both in the present and for the future. Still others, in a spirit of quasi-millenaristic expectancy, focus their sights exclusively on the future, and are inevitably disappointed when their dreams are not promptly realized.

The overemphases and resulting distortions in these examples suggest that the church must be simultaneously respectful of the past, relevant in the present, and open toward the future. "The church lives in tension between the 'already' and the 'not yet'" (*A Plan of Union*, III, 4, p. 16).

The church is confronted with another type of tension or "duality": "the church is divine and human, holy and sinful, faithful and unfaithful" (*A Plan of Union*, III, 4, p. 15); the church is visible and invisible, organizational and organic, institutional and charismatic. Here again it is important to maintain the appropriate balance, the necessary tension between potential polarizations. Yet, as the history of the church amply demonstrates, it is all too easy to overfocus on one aspect while neglecting others; for example, "Christians have long debated the essential life of the church in terms of the presence or absence of certain forms—canon, creeds, offices of ministry, baptismal practices, liturgy . . ." (*A Plan of Union*, III, 5, p. 16). Without implying that these or other forms are unimportant, one can insist that they possess a *relative* importance, but just that—an importance *related* to a broader vision of the church whose oneness is willed by Christ.

In general terms, what is at issue is the tension between a vision of the church and the actuality of the church. Reducing a vision to concrete terms is always somewhat disillusioning; conversely, few, if any, institutions completely exemplify the vision which prompted them. In particular, if the advocates of a structureless Christianity would presumably deny that there is any need to have formal organizations, church officials would presumably maintain that without organization nothing is going to get done. The structureless advocates are right in one respect: any attempt to put a vision into concrete terms is going to produce a deficient replica of the vision. Conversely, one must concede that the officials are right in insisting that some type of organization is necessary and inevitable in any group.

The persistent temptation when confronted with a vision and a structure purportedly actualizing that vision is to absolutize one or the other. The visionary opts for the vision and dispenses with organizational details. The organizer relegates the vision to the sidelines while striving to iron out kinks in the structural flow-chart. At this point, the ecclesiologist should remind both parties of the necessity to preserve the reciprocal tension between vision and structure in the church.

Given the tension between vision and actuality, it is hardly surprising that the Plan's proposals have occasioned a certain amount of dissatisfaction among Consultation participants. Part of this dissatisfaction stems from the fact that the Plan's proposed structures are not identical with those of any of the participant churches (*A Plan of Union*, II, 7, p. 10). This means that all the churches are called upon to accept structures that are somewhat strange and therefore somewhat suspect. For example, the Plan's proposed "parish," which is to be composed of a number of different local congregations and task groups, is different from anything presently in existence.

In addition to innovative proposals such as the parish, there are areas of compromise which have proved disconcerting to various participants. For example, "in accepting and maintaining the historic episcopate, the Church of Christ Uniting neither implies, excludes, nor requires any theory or doctrine of the episcopate which goes beyond what is stated in this plan" (*A Plan of Union*, VII, 57, p. 49). In effect, the problem of apostolic succession is bypassed. In spite of personal preference in favor of apostolic succession, one has to admit that this may be the only feasible solution. The idealized picture of apostolic succession—as an unbroken continuity of ministry through the imposition of hands from apostolic times to the present—faces a number of insurmountable difficulties if one attempts to verify it historically. In addition, if the ecclesial character of all churches is recognized, then the ministry of these churches must also be recognized, in spite of the theological difficulty of reconciling non-episcopal ministry with a historic episcopate.[2] Could the Plan, then, have done anything but what it did—sidestep a problem which is historically insoluble and theologically tendentious?

In any event, one should not expect a union proposal such as the Plan to be a duplicate of his own denominational formularies. If, on the surface, it might appear desirable that a union proposal resolve all difficulties in advance, appearances are deceptive. Should one assume that a united church must be a unanimous church? Such an assumption must face the fact that a spectrum of doctrinal positions, not unanimity, is presently found in most churches with the exception of those fundamentalistic denominations which demand a uniform interpretation of their confessions. In other words, if unanimity were really required, then most churches should separate into further denominations!

In fact, most denominational differences have little or no meaning for many church members. For example, many church members have with presumed good conscience changed denominations without apparent difficulty. Indeed, any individual who wants to become a church member would presumably be accepted by most churches. This factual evanescence of denominational differences raise some crucial questions: If doctrinal unanimity is a rarity in any denomination, can unanimity be demanded as a prerequisite for union? If most churches allow considerable doctrinal latitude in accepting persons for membership, should not the same degree of latitude suffice for a union of churches?

A pragmatic ecumenist finds the demand for doctrinal unanimity unrealistic. However, if a pragmatic answer is unsatisfactory to many theologians, one must also ask whether it is theologically justifiable to expect doctrinal unanimity as a prerequisite for union.

The answer to this question depends on the way "doctrine" is viewed. If doctrine is considered as a uniform view of truth, then a lack of doctrinal agreement would make union a sham: Christians would be uniting organizationally in an arranged marriage which would prove incompatible since their theological views were not identical. Thus, some seemingly feel that unless each specific issue can be resolved, no union should occur. A requirement of unanimity or uniformity would result in few church unions—or few marriages, for that matter; rather one would expect schism—or divorce.

An exit from this apparent impasse can be found by recognizing that doctrine is a historically conditioned perception of truth.[3] Just as no state-ment is meaningful without a context, no doctrinal formulary is intelli-gible outside the perspective in which it was formulated. Insofar as there are a variety of possible perspectives, doctrine can be stated in a plurality of ways and, at least to some extent, church structures can take a variety of forms. Instead of demanding doctrinal unanimity, it would seem bet-ter to consider doctrinal pluralism as a mutual acceptance of the many gifts which God has bestowed on his church.

Accordingly, the most that can and should be required in church union is a broad basis of agreement wherein not all specific issues are resolved, simply because they cannot be presently or possibly resolved. A similar proposal was advanced by Cardinal Willebrands in his address to the At-lanta meeting of the Consultation in 1969:

> What could be criteria for evaluating the Consultation on Church Union principles and commentaries? In my judgment, the central issue is not one particular point of doctrine (for example, the visibility of the Church, sacra-ments, ministry, and so forth) but the whole Christian life in faith, sacra-mental practice, organic structure, and missionary responsibility to the one world, home and afar. Once more, it is not a specific theological issue about which Christians are ultimately concerned but the full life of the whole united church, no matter how fragile and provisional its existence may be.[4]

In other words, if the Plan should be evaluated in terms of the life of Christians and not simply and solely in terms of particular doctrinal is-sues, then the factual church situation, which includes doctrinal plural-ism, can and should be employed as a theological criterion.

A similar conclusion emerges if one takes seriously the self-identifica-tion of the Church of Christ Uniting as *"a uniting as well as a united church"* (*A Plan of Union*, II, 23, p. 13). The purpose of the Plan is not a merger into a megadenomination. Rather, the Church of Christ Uniting is envisaged as a pilgrim church, whose "pilgrimage has as its ultimate goal the unity of the whole church" (*A Plan of Union*, II, 24, p. 13). This pilgrimage is more a camping trip into unexplored areas than a prepaid excursion with advance reservations. As any traveler knows, despite the best planning, a few tensions are part and parcel of traveling. Similarly, one should anticipate tension in pilgrimaging toward union.

From a psychological viewpoint, it can be argued that a person ma-tures and develops in response to tensions. While an excess of tension can obviously be harmful, the absence of tension may result not only in monotony and boredom but in a truncation of mutual enrichment and development.

This psychological view is instructive for ecumenical ecclesiology. Nearly all denominations are presently facing problems of adaptation, renewal, *aggiornamento*. Unfortunately, the concomitant tensions have frequently produced polarizations instead of being channeled productively into vigorous and creative forms of church life. A similar temptation has plagued Christianity in the past. The series of schisms which the church has experienced might well be considered as so many refusals to grow through tensions. It is always much easier to go separate ways than to balance competing tensions within a group. Similarly, it is easier to remain right where we are—in separation.

Thus, expecting a union proposal to manifest total agreement is not simply unrealistic but unbeneficial as well. The presence of tensions within a union proposal such as the Plan may well be a better index of its viability and validity than the pretense of unanimity.[5]

The Plan's tensions are a challenge first of all to Consultation participants: "as we go forward in the Church of Christ Uniting, such a re-forming, re-fashioning, re-creating process will make new and unfamiliar demands upon us of assimilation and receptiveness to the Spirit's guidance in mission and renewal" (*A Plan of Union*, II, 25, pp. 13–14). Furthermore, the Plan poses a challenge to all Christians: are church members ecumenically mature enough to employ the tensions that are necessarily involved in union in order to grow together? The response given this question will undoubtedly influence all ecumenical efforts in the foreseeable future.

Biblical Perspective

Basic to any human view of the church is the scriptural presentation. As the Plan points out, "the Scriptures speak about the church in many ways, but in none so appealingly as in the different images or figures of speech found there." Ecclesiology must take seriously the fact that these scriptural images or "pictures are so numerous and so diverse in their emphases that no one of them is adequate for a theology of the church, but a number of them must be looked at simultaneously" (*A Plan of Union*, III, 11, p. 17). Unfortunately, this principle has frequently gone unnoticed or unheeded. In the past, many treatises on the church have taken one image and developed its implications in a way that ignored or contradicted the implications of other images.

If no one image can be exclusively employed as the basis for ecclesiology, it would seemingly follow that no uniform ecclesiology can be demanded as the exclusive basis for church union. In other words, if Scripture evidences a variety of images of the church, church union must allow for a similar variety of ecclesiologies.

However, the diversity of scriptural imagery does pose a problem: given the plurality of images, is there an underlying unity? If this question is answered negatively and if the diversity in scriptural imagery is taken as a model or paradigm, then the diverse images may well be replicated by a diversity of denominations, though presumably without the evils associated with denominationalism. By such a view, which might consider denominations as necessary in efforts for renewal and mission, ecumenism would still be meaningful as an effort to further fellowship among Christians and to promote projects of common Christian concern.[6] But as an effort toward union, ecumenism would be pointless.

In sharp contrast, many theologians feel that such biblical texts as Christ's prayer for unity among his followers (John 17:21) and Paul's entreaties for unity of mind and purpose in the Christian community (I Corinthians 1:10) indicate that unity is a necessary dimension of the church.

> Yet the disunity of the visible companies of Christian people obscures this reality. In a world of repression and anarchy, a renewed church is called to a new unity. This oneness in the church is required for the credibility and effectiveness of Christ's mission. The characteristics that are God's gift to the church can be fully seen only as the church becomes visibly one. As the world looks at us now, it is unimpressed by our claim to love one another for it sees how we are fractured and divided by lesser loyalties [A Plan of Union, II, 3, p. 10].[7]

In effect, the superficial diversity of ecclesial images must be balanced by a premise of underlying unity.[8] Diversity and unity are not incompatible but complementary.

This compatibility can be illustrated in terms of human personality. A person may live with a great deal of diversity in his functions, attitudes, and interests. The same person may be variously teacher, faculty colleague, researcher, committee member, father, friend, and amateur photographer. In fact, a person's diversity usually enriches both his own life and those of others. Yet, despite this diversity, it would hardly be said, except metaphorically, that he is more than one normal person.

Similarly, the church not only can but should manifest a wide range of diversity. If the church is a mystery, then diverse images are necessary as a means of understanding and expressing what the church is. If the church is to witness Christ to all men of all times and places, then the church will have to adopt itself to the diversity of different men of different times and places. Diversity is no more alien to a vision of the church than diversity is foreign to man.

Yet insofar as the diverse facets of an individual's personality are somehow complementary, so too diverse understandings of the church should be envisaged as complementary. Just as men are confronted by modern communications with the demand to live compatibly in a "global village," so too Christians are summoned more urgently than ever to live in communion with each other. Thus, unity with diversity, diversity within unity, seem to be both a Christian obligation and a human responsibility.

As the Plan points out in discussing the implications of the biblical image of the church as the New Creation:

> Distinctions and divisions between races, cultures, economic classes, and religious convictions have been radically overcome. The church's unified life becomes a foretaste of the unity of all mankind [A Plan of Union, III, 13, p. 18].

A similar emphasis emerges from reflection on the church as the People of God:

> A people, a family, has an intrinsic tie of unity. They share a common origin from the same father; they share a common destiny. This unity generates love of the members for one another [A Plan of Union, III, 15, p. 18].

Christ's unity and identity with his people and their unity and identity with each other are eloquently manifested by the image of the church as the body of Christ:

> The relation between members and head, believers and Lord, is one of intimate communion, incorporated through baptism and sustained through participation in the Lord's Supper. Those who belong to his body share a common life in Christ, both in suffering and in rejoicing. Those who accept his gifts enjoy a unity in diversity [A Plan of Union, III, 18, pp. 18–19].

Christians then can find a basis for union in their common acceptance of the biblical images of the church.[9] In the past, this common heritage has not been accompanied by an awareness that "each image presupposes and points to the inherent unity of the church" (A Plan of Union, III, 20, p. 19). In addition, Christians possess a commonality in their profession of belief in Christ, celebration of baptism and the eucharist, and an active faith which seeks to live the Gospel in daily life.[10] Admittedly there are many divergences among Christians in regard to each of these observances. Separation, however, has clouded our awareness that by their very nature these observances presuppose and point to oneness among Christians.

This sharing of ecclesial imagery and commonality in faith, sacraments, and life are not simply matters for theological speculation. They pose a question: can any Christian be truly faithful to the biblical perspective of the church without wholeheartedly desiring and earnestly seeking union in order to witness what is professed?

Theological Perspective

The church can be viewed not only in a variety of biblical images but also in a number of theological perspectives. The Plan envisions the church as "truly *catholic,* truly *evangelical,* and truly *reformed*" (*A Plan of Union,* III, 21, p. 19).

Catholic is understood in three significant senses: (1) the church's continuity with Christ's mission across centuries and the communion of saints; (2) the relating of secular life to God; (3) a rich diversity that transcends exclusivistic separations (*A Plan of Union,* III, 23, p. 20). By *evangelical* the Plan envisions "a church with a passion for all the world to hear and respond to the Gospel" (*A Plan of Union,* III, 24, p. 20). As "radically Christ-centered," the church's "central mission is that men may receive God's gift of saving grace in Christ and learn to live in true communion with him and the Holy Spirit and one another" (*A Plan of Union,* III, 26, p. 20). As *reformed,* the church must live by Scripture and subject all its traditions and practices to the judgment and correction of the Holy Spirit. Reformation, however, is a continual responsibility: "Both old and new attitudes, institutions, and customs are constantly re-examined and reconstituted in order that they may be faithful and effective" (*A Plan of Union,* III, 27, p. 20).

Some denominational groups have traditionally identified themselves as "reformed," others have considered themselves "evangelical," while still others have classified themselves as "catholic," in ways which made these qualities or characteristics of the church seem antithetical. In a significant departure from ecclesiological polarizations, the Plan points out that "only when all three are affirmed and held together—each balancing and interpreting the other two—can we recognize their essential quality for the church we seek to be" (*A Plan of Union,* III, 22, p. 20).

By refusing to focus exclusively on any one of these qualities, the Plan favors an ecclesiology which reflects the tension and compatibility among the biblical images of the church. Can a church claim to be truly catholic unless it is faithful to the Gospel and opens itself to constant reform? Must not a genuinely catholic and reformed church always be evangelical, always responsive to the scriptural word? Shouldn't one recognize that "churches in the Reformed tradition have generally represented a concern for the catholicity of the church"? [11]

Whether or not this balance is preserved throughout the Plan is a further question. Some critics have protested that the Plan is insufficiently catholic, while, in an opposite vein, others are uneasy about its avowed catholicity. Similar reservations have been expressed about its evangelical and reformed character. In a sense, these opposite criticisms of the Plan —like a committee report which is acceptable to everyone, yet not completely appealing to anyone—may be an indication that it has been more successful in achieving balance than has been acknowledged.

Yet even if it is true that the balance between catholic, reformed, and evangelical elements is not preserved in every aspect of the Plan, must not one also grant that a balance which is accepted in principle is rarely, if ever, perfectly achieved in every detail? What seems most important is that this need for balance or tension is recognized and, one hopes, will be kept in mind not only in revising the Plan but in the church life of the participants.

This emphasis on balance may prove helpful as a criterion in evaluating the Plan. For instance, it is obvious that the Plan's doctrines and structures are not identical with those of any of the participant churches. The point at issue is whether church union requires identity or whether compatibility is sufficient.[12] If compatibility, not identity, is deemed acceptable, then one should not be surprised to find ambiguities or omissions in a proposed union formulary. Compatibility in principle admits non-identical elements. In other words, ambiguities and omissions, while admittedly somewhat disconcerting, are inevitable.

Does the Plan have to resolve all its present ambiguities and rectify all omissions? If the Plan represents a bureaucratic merger of the participating churches, and if the Plan is a legal contract, then it should presumably detail all structural specifications and provide for the resolution of all eventualities in advance. Yet to construe the Plan as essentially a legal instrument for an amalgamation seems to be a serious misrepresentation.[13] Rather, isn't the Plan a formula for union? If so, like any formula, it must be elastic enough to be employed viably according to the variable dimensions of the present and future. Shouldn't the Plan then be read as an attempt at responding to the renewal of the church demanded by God at this moment in history?

In pilgrimaging toward unity, omissions and ambiguities seem necessary as opportunities or open-ended possibilities for future growth. In terms of ecumenical strategy, omissions or ambiguities are much more desirable than provisions which could presently or subsequently hinder further union. From a theological viewpoint, omissions and ambiguities are inevitable in ecclesiology, which can never surmount the inherent tension between our vision of the church as mystery and its earthly actuality. In a futuristic perspective, one should at least be open to the possibility that union may require a restructuring more pervasive, more revolutionary than most of us presently foresee.

The Plan necessarily reflects the tensions, anomalies, and risks of the church pilgrimaging from past to present toward the future. Omissions and ambiguities may well be part of the cost of a pilgrimage guided by the Holy Spirit.[14] The challenge posed by the Plan may then be formulated: is our vision of the church worth the price of renewal and the tensions accompanying renewal? [15]

Reflections

Any attempt to answer the basic ecclesiological question—what is the church?—encounters an irresolvable series of tensions: tension between the church as mystery and the church as actuality; tension between past, present, and future; tension between unity and diversity; tension between congregational, presbyterian, connectional, and episcopal models of polity; and so on. It may be tempting to ignore or deny the existence of such tensions; likewise, it may be tempting to resolve ecclesiological tensions by one or another type of polarization. One may, for example, try to emphasize unity at the cost of diversity or, on the other hand, attempt to extol diversity by sacrificing unity. An authentic vision of the church, however, must be prepared to face tensions honestly, live with them humbly, and grow through them wholeheartedly.

> Christians are called to respond obediently to the new conditions God is now disclosing to us. In this spirit, we envisage a united church, embodying all that is indispensable to each of us, and bearing enough family resemblance to our separate traditions to verify their continuity in it, yet unlike the churches any of us has known in our past separateness [A Plan of Union, II, 7, p. 10].

In attempting to actualize a vision in concrete terms, the actuality will always be an imperfect replica of the vision. Specifically, the Plan can be improved and hopefully the ongoing critique will produce an improved Plan. Yet to postpone church union until the perfect formula of union is devised is to postpone union forever. Finally, the Plan is more than a scheme for amalgamating ecclesiastical bureaucracies. The Plan represents an urgent call to realize the oneness which Christ envisioned for his followers. It would be a tragic judgment on all churches if this call went unheeded.

NOTES

1. In regard to this specific text, Richard P. McBrien, "The COCU Plan of Union: A Catholic Critique," *The Andover Newton Quarterly*, Vol. LXIV, No. 1 (1971), p. 27, suggests that it read: "community of all those men

and women of all ages and all places, of all races and tribes, who acknowledge the reconciliation of God and man in Jesus Christ."

2. Specifically, Vatican II's recognition of the ecclesial character of non-Roman churches does not indicate the implications of this recognition *vis-à-vis* their ministry.

3. Cf. Crowe, Frederick E., "Dogma Versus the Self-Correcting Process of Learning," *Theological Studies,* Vol. XXXI, pp. 605–624; Dulles, Avery, *The Survival of Dogma* (Garden City, New York: Doubleday and Company, 1971), pp. 152–203; Rahner, K., "Pluralism in Theology and the Oneness of the Church's Profession of Faith," *Concilium,* Vol. XLVI, pp. 103–123.

4. *Digest of the Proceedings of the Consultation on Church Union,* Vol. VIII (1969), p. 141; reprinted in *Consultation on Church Union: A Catholic Perspective* (Washington: U.S. Catholic Conference Publications Office, 1970), p. 14.

5. In an opposite vein, George Peck, "Church Unity and the Future: Some Theological Tensions in the COCU Plan of Union," *The Andover Newton Quarterly, op. cit.,* p. 21, feels that the Plan postulates "a synthesis which conjoins ideas which would never have existed in separation if they had had actually been able to live and breathe together in the first place." Are these ideas incompatible in themselves or in the minds of their proponents? Is there a hermeneutical perspective in which presumably incompatible ideas can be seen as complementary?

6. Cf. Käsemann, Ernest, "Unity and Diversity in New Testament Ecclesiology," *Novum Testamentum,* Vol. VI (1963), pp. 290–297; Peck, *loc. cit.,* pp. 18–21.

7. A similar statement is made in Vatican II's *Decree on Ecumenism,* #1.

8. Cf. Brown, Raymond, "The Unity and Diversity in New Testament Ecclesiology," *Novum Testamentum, op. cit.,* pp. 298–308, reprinted in *New Testament Essays* (Milwaukee: Bruce Pub. Co., 1965).

9. The Plan's biblical perspective displays much in common with Vatican II's scriptural presentation in its *Constitution on the Church,* #6–17.

10. Cf. *Decree on Ecumenism, op. cit.,* #20–23.

11. Williams, J. Rodman, "The Plan of Union, Impressions—Theological and Otherwise," *Austin Seminary Bulletin,* Vol. LXXXVI, No. 4 (December, 1970), p. 24.

12. Tavard, George H., for example, "A Catholic Perspective," *COCU: A Catholic Perspective, op. cit.,* pp. 28–45, contrasts two ecumenical options: doctrinal and organizational; the contrast certainly exists, but does this mean that the two options are so irreconcilable that it is impossible to make both simultaneously?

13. To a certain extent, the Plan fosters this misrepresentation by placing its structural provisions (Chapters VIII–X) in the same context as its enunciation of doctrinal principles. Some difficulties might be clarified if polity provisions were placed in a separate section. In addition, the structural provisions seem overly detailed.

14. Some may object that omissions and ambiguities are tantamount to doc-

trinal indifferentism—an espousal of the least common doctrinal denominator with the implied surrender of essential doctrinal values. Hopefully, this objection is not a disguised demand for uniformity. Union efforts necessarily rely on a theological pluralism which attempts to navigate between the Scylla of uniformity and the Charybdis of indifferentism. Cf. Ford, John T., "Ecumenical Convergence and Theological Pluralism," *Thought*, Vol. XLIV (1969), pp. 531–545.

15. "There can be no ecumenism worthy of the name without a change of heart" (*A Plan of Union*, II, 7, p. 10); it is highly significant that this sentence appears in Vatican II's *Decree on Ecumenism*, #7.

8

COCU and the Black Churches

FREDERICK D. JORDAN

The black man's experience of the American church has been ambivalent, to say the least. It was the church which provided the material which informed the mind and set aflame the heart and spirit of those who led the movements for abolition and emancipation. Men like Frederick Douglass, Richard Allen, William Wilberforce, Phillips Brooks, Freeborn Garretson, William Lovejoy, and John Brown were inflamed by the message of the Christian church. This church furnished the blowtorch which burned the chains from the souls of the enslaved even while their bodies were yet bound. Yet it was this same American church which also blessed the auctioneer at the slave block as he turned the image of the eternal God into a commodity, as he twisted and distorted the truth of the Gospel concerning the nature and destiny of man, and as he found the infallible word of God upon the lips of drunken Noah. I say the experiences have been ambivalent. It was the American church that offered the black man a back seat in its sanctuary, a basement ward in its hospitals, a segregated corner in its cemeteries, and his own lonely heaven all to himself.

Recently, the visibility of the church as institution in the civil-rights revolution in the form of the ecumenical agencies, the staff heads of judicatories, the local pastors and members marching and laboring, testifying at congressional hearings, and even dying before the bullets of the assassin gave the American church a new opportunity in the black community.

This chance, however, is now threatened by the promises that have failed to materialize, the programs that have faltered, and the injured

---

This is a revision of an address delivered to the Eighth Plenary of the Consultation on Church Union, Atlanta, Georgia (March 19, 1969). The address appears in *Digest of the Proceedings of the Consultation on Church Union*, VIII, pp. 148–153.

paternalism exemplified in threats and the attempted intimidation which says if you do not stop your violence and be nice we will cut off your welfare and take our special courses out of your schools. This ambivalence and this opportunity form the background against which the Consultation has assembled.

Now let us look at the Consultation on Church Union itself, which is composed of nine denominations now that the merger of the Methodist Church and the Evangelical United Brethren is complete. Of these nine participating denominations, three represent the black Methodist churches which over the past nearly 200 years have come into existence in American life and today represent a constituency of approximately 3,000,000 persons. When these three churches joined the Consultation, although the other participating churches had a considerable representation of blacks in their membership, I believe there was no member of the black community on the Executive Committee and very few blacks in the delegations. One or two were included as visitors and observers.

This is said neither to accuse or embarrass anyone, but rather to point out the dynamics of decision-making in the American society—white people have been making the decisions so long and have already put each other so completely into the decision-making spots that *conscious* racism is unnecessary to produce a lily-white administrative structure.

I think there were those already at work in the Consultation who recognized this situation and were happy to welcome these black churches not only to speak for their immediate constituency but also to provide a voice for the black members in their own church who somehow, in the mechanics of representation and in the realities of power distribution, had found it impossible to have a voice.

Now the thing which faces you today in this Consultation is that its present shape does not include all of the churches and that it will not be the last development in church union in American life. When consummated, as now projected, the total black constituency will be proportionate to the total membership of the new church in somewhat the same ratio as of the, shall we say, "inclusive" churches today. Where, at that time, will the representatives on the policy boards of the Church of Christ Uniting come from? Who, at that time, will be there to remind the authorities that the normal channels of what may seem to them adequate representation actually do not represent? In short, you see, the problem is that if we had not had in American life today the three separated and independent black churches to answer to your invitation to come and participate as separate institutions, the black voice in your processes would be inadequate.

I want you today to face the question: what would you have done about the Consultation if these three black churches had not come in?

Would you have felt justified in going on to develop the Consultation as a suburban club? Would you have provided policy-making participation in the Consultation for the blacks now members of your churches? If the structure and processes of your churches as currently existing proved inadequate to provide a voice for significant black participation in policy-making, it is essential that you realize that these structures provide the model for the united church.

Some of your members see this clearly and are asking us, "What do you want?" I do not think, however, that is the way we should go about the issue. It is not the way we have gone about meeting and dealing with the other problems which have come before us. In this family circle, I think we can be specific without embarrassment. We have not said to the members of the Episcopal Church, "You write the ticket about apostolic succession, and we will take a look at it." We have not said to the Methodists, "Now you tell us what we can do about the settling of pastors, and we will take a look at it." And so, I could go down the list. Contrary to that and deeper than that for me is the realization that has come over many people in America, particularly the black community in recent years, that it does not make any difference how accurately you state the situation and how carefully you protect it with guidelines, rules, and regulations. The capacity of the human mind to devise evasions against the things people do not want to do will defeat any kind of structure you create. Therefore, the deepest concern to us is to know where *you* are going, what represents *your* idea of what the inclusive church in the life of America ought to be, and what guarantees *you* think there ought to be as a united church starts out. Now why do I say that?

A little while ago the Supreme Court made a decision about school desegregation. This action represented, we were told, the highest law in the land. And for fear everyone did not understand it all, Congress passed some additional laws supporting it. Then after that the Department of Justice wrote some regulations; the Department of Health, Education and Welfare did the same things, and a whole lot of people got some really good jobs. From these activities the black people of America were to be delivered from the deliberate emasculation and denial of opportunity which had been their lot in American education. But now reality is before us. You and I know that actually in many places, North and South, over these past fifteen years educational opportunities for blacks have deteriorated. We have poorer education, diminished professional opportunity, and heightened frustration. It is also clear that while the tactics to defeat public-school integration plans now center in opposition to "forced bussing" of school children out of their neighborhoods, bussing was not a major issue when it was being used to support *segregated* schools.

So we have to ask ourselves, how much conflict are we willing to have in the church, and between the church and society? When the church first faced race in America at the point of slavery, she denounced it vigorously; but her voice diminished as the trade increased and became more profitable until at last she was its ardent defender, although there was always a valiant minority within the church on the other side. It is from this history that she moves today. The most sober, responsible, and technically capable investigators of our society have described it as "white-racist." Do we contemplate a church willing to take on this monster and battle him to defeat, or do we anticipate some type of accommodation which perpetuates this unfortunate heresy?

This experience makes us afraid of laws. It makes us afraid of things on paper, and yet we know there have to be things on paper. You have seen the agonizing of the black Christian struggling in American life to maintain the integrity of his witness as a Christian, to believe God has only one family and that there are no stepchildren, and, in spite of all he has experienced, to remain open and ready in heart and fact for every approach toward the union which he knows is God's will for his people. We feel that you, having seen all of this agony, need to enunciate for us how this has affected you and to say to us how you feel you can remove this situation and create one which can be the fullest experience of Christian fellowship.

Some of the problems you will be thinking about when you draw up this proposal will be that most white Christians really find it difficult to believe in the authenticity of the black man's religious experience. It is still something curious to you, an inheritance from his precivilization status. But somehow this has to have acceptance. God speaks to us and we respond to his voice. The life-style of the Negro must have its recognition without in any degree being made to feel that it has to be a copy or an imitation of anybody else's life-style.

Then there is the problem of the relative poverty of the black churches and the affluence of the white churches. It is like marrying the boss's daughter. Can the Consultation on Church Union find a way toward equalization without embarrassment? Can there really be on the part of the wealthy parents the providing of additional resources and sharing with the oncoming family without at the same time the embarrassing, humiliating initiatives which have been expressed in the past? You know how real this can be. It is no less real for a group than for an individual.

Then there is the deeply ingrained expectation of the white churches to make all the decisions. This grows out of the fact that your churches are composed of persons in the dominant society where they have been making all of the decisions for that society, and who somehow really unconsciously believe they can make the best decisions. Where one has to deal with this type of prejudice, when many have not become aware of it and have not come to the place where they feel the importance of changing, we know an unhappy condition is bound to result. In our churches we have an experience of decision-making. Our followers do not always like all of our decisions. But they put us in that decision-making situation and for the most part they follow with a "glad mind." In short, we are accustomed to the fact that our constituency accepts the authority of our position. It would not be pleasant to have it any other way, and I am sure you do not want it any other way either.

May I illustrate what I mean? There was a congregation where the bishop thought he should send a pastor who was not of the same race as the members. Here was the white congregation with a black pastor, and the congregation did not like it. As a result, they decided to withhold funds. We in the Consultation certainly do not wish to be the occasion for disrupting the spiritual life of anybody like that! Representatives of the churches have to face this problem with the people they are representing. It is not so much what we blacks want; it is how much can you stand?

Now, finally, I suppose after a statement like this you might ask, "Why are you black churches here?" Well, for one reason, we were invited. But that is not enough. We accepted the invitation because we believe in the purpose. We know that sometime in God's good grace church union must happen. We do not think it enough that once it almost happened. We are determined that if it fails to happen it should not fail because we did not join you in trying to make it happen. But we do not want you to tell us to make it happen by ourselves.

I close with a little reminder from Sidney Poitier's participation in the movie *Lilies of the Field*. Sidney has the Roman Catholic sisters singing the song "Amen," and for the refrain they are talking about the chapel which he has built for the sisters. They sing, "He built the chapel" as the sisters point to him. Sidney replies, "I built the chapel, yes I did," then, "We built the chapel." Finally, they realize that the things that made this possible were beyond any one of them or all of them together. You will remember they close with the insight that "He [God] built the chapel." It is in his name that we labor in the Consultation on Church Union, and it is to him that we look for the success. He will build the Chapel.

9

COCU and the Cultural Revolution

PRESTON N. WILLIAMS

The church exists today in a world where all social institutions, including the church itself, participate in and are affected by revolutionary change. Revolutions are not only frequent, but they have almost become routine and commonplace. The concept and process called Consultation on Church Union is one attempt on the part of nine major American denominations to revolutionize themselves and to address themselves to the revolutions in their midst. Although COCU is only one response, it is unique and deserving of special attention because it seeks to capture and contain in one church much of American Protestant diversity. The radical nature of this effort is recognized when one considers that the changes envision a restructuring of the churches that reaches into local communities and merges into common parishes people who would not trust each other as neighbors even when they were members of the same denomination. COCU is one of the most revolutionary processes existent in the American churches today despite the attempt to conceal some of this radicalness by the usage of smooth sentences which speak of "a united church embodying all that is indispensable to each of us, and bearing enough family resemblances to our separate traditions to verify their continuity in it" (*A Plan of Union*, II, 7, p. 10). Underneath this reassuring phrase is the seed of revolutionary change. For our reflection the central question is not whether COCU is revolutionary; that it is should be obvious. The central question is whether it is sufficiently revolutionary and whether it seeks the proper type of revolution for our time and the days ahead. The answer given by the cultural revolution of our time is clear. COCU is not sufficiently revolutionary; COCU is not revolutionary about the issues that matter.

This was given as an address before the Tenth Plenary at Denver, Colo., in 1971, and will appear in the *Digest*, X (to be published).

When we seek to assess the sufficiency of the revolution envisioned by COCU we must remind ourselves that, no matter what may be considered the motives behind COCU, what has emerged thus far is described best as organizational restructuring. A scheme by which the churches can free themselves from some of the dysfunctional aspects of organizational life has emerged together with some elements of a common liturgy. The present plan does promise something concrete in the way of change. The overchurching of small communities by competing denominations can be corrected; the inability of denominations to keep up with the highly mobile character of their members can be ended; the unresponsiveness of individual Christians to what in a former age was considered "indispensable to each of us" can be better addressed; and the high cost of administration and services can be reduced. The tendency to solve the administrative and organizational problems of the church is predominant, however, even in matters of faith, worship, ministry, and mission.

I am not personally unhappy with this state of affairs. I have seen too many miserable little churches in the rural South, the middle Atlantic states, and New England not to want parish reorganization. As a Presbyterian in New England, I have felt too keenly the loss of Pittsburgh and Charlotte Presbyterianism not to take seriously the need for a national church and a more universal type of liturgy, piety, and social witness. Visits to 475 Riverside Drive and to the Witherspoon Building; conferences with the church's spiritual leaders and staff; participation in the life of a local congregation argue for taking seriously the administrative problems related to the religious life. This is essential if one is to carry the Good News to the poor, the despised, and the rejected. COCU's approach therefore is not so much wrong as it is inadequate. The cultural revolutionaries draw attention to these shortcomings.

Comparison of the structural revolution advocated by COCU, in fact if not in intent, with the revolutionary style of the blacks, women, and youth discloses the reasons why COCU, to these groups, appears to be almost irrelevant. The cultural revolutionaries differ in their views about organizations, action, and the nature of unity. The structure they seek conveys no aspect of the well-oiled bureaucratic machine. The cultural revolutionaries are movement-oriented, not institutionally oriented. They seek liberation from oppressive structures while COCU seeks liberation through greater rationalization of institutional structures. The cultural revolutionaries seek small local units responsive to the people. They are here at one with the conservatives and America's traditional distrust of centralized power. COCU revolutionaries, on the other hand, do seek a super-organization with, hopefully, relatively autonomous and responsive decentralized units. They are at one in this respect with the managers of General Motors and General Electric Corporations. Organizational efficiency, quality control of the product, is more important than consumer preferences. The present COCU documents, as I understand them, seek to persuade persons seeking community control to accept the limited freedom possible as a unit in a huge decentralized corporate structure. How realistic that expectation is I leave to you to judge. I want only to suggest that, except remotely and tangentially, neither attitude has anything to do with the Christian faith.

At the organizational level, then, the cultural revolutionaries and COCU revolutionaries have little in common—one seeking freedom from organization, the other freedom through organization. Since, however, it is COCU that seeks to build a rational organizational structure, it will have to make the sacrifices necessary to woo the blacks, the women, the youth. Since these groups do not see a unified church as an important prerequisite for their ends, they can afford the luxury of nonparticipation. I am not, of course, speaking of all blacks, all women, all youth. Some are to be found inside as well as outside the COCU delegation. Thus far COCU has, however, done very little to solicit the support of any of these groups, and because COCU leaders tend to be basically church politicians, what they have done smacks, perhaps falsely, of manipulation and patronage peddling. To the cultural revolutionaries this has meant one thing only: COCU is basically about business as usual and the crumbs of enticement will be swept away as soon as the bird is caged. Given the history of even the liberal Christian church toward blacks, women, and youth, the failure of COCU aggressively to court the cultural revolutionaries conveys the notion that COCU's phrases are just another set of church pronouncements to be more honored in breach than in fulfillment. A church group not willing to risk confrontation prior to merger on the scale envisioned by COCU is seen by cultural revolutionaries as a church which shall be unable after merger to enforce racial, sexual, and age equality.

For purposes of negotiation, I think, one could accept the integrity of the statements made by COCU personnel in respect to the "truly new church" and even accept the notion that the "truly new church" will have greater power for the achievement of true Christian brotherhood and sisterhood.

Agreement at the level of organizational structure raises another type of question, though. What latitude will be permitted the deviate? How shall dissent be handled? Will not a church "truly catholic, truly evangelical, truly reformed" take itself a bit too seriously? No advocate of COCU that I know of has made the claim that it will be the "Kingdom of God on earth as it is in heaven." The cultural revolutionaries can assume, therefore, the continued existence of white racism, male chauvinism, and Establishment-oriented control. How then shall blacks promote black theology, defend the Angela Davises and the Attica victims? Given white attitudes in the church, I am confident that racism will be present. I am not confident that genuine deviance will be tolerated. The restriction of dissent will mean that the problems of women and youth in the new church will also be extremely precarious. Will the male clergy, church officers, and bureaucrats fighting for the fewer positions of honor in the church really be willing to share them with women and youth? And if not with white women and youth—their wives, sons, and daughters —do you think they will share them with black women and black youth? What kind of deviant response, then, will white, black, and other minority women and youth be permitted to make in this church that is "truly catholic, truly evangelical, truly reformed"?

The style of the cultural revolutionaries has been and remains that of direct action, that of COCU education. COCU's present plan is one that asks the direct-action revolutionary to trust in education, but this is perhaps too much to ask of those outside of the institutional structures of power. It presupposes a trust in the righteousness and fairness of white male officeholders which perhaps is not warranted. COCU officials need once again to bend in such a way as to demonstrate the viability of deviance and dissent in the truly new church.

The Black Manifesto and the Angela Davis case have demonstrated for the cultural revolutionaries what conservatives already professed to know —namely, that liberals too can be absolutist, self-righteous, open to corruption by glory, gold, and power. Since bargaining by church officials has apparently succeeded well enough to convince the Establishment that what it considers most essential will be preserved in the new uniting church, it is now in order to launch an aggressive approach to the strangers outside the camp. The very nature of alienation experienced by blacks, women, and youth suggests this bargaining must be done in the fresh light of day and COCU must embody in action what is adumbrated in A Plan of Union. Deviance and dissent need to be more solidly embedded in A Plan of Union before blacks, women, and youth can be expected to come in fully.

This need underscores the fact that the nature and extent of unity differ among the COCU and cultural revolutionaries. Blacks, women, and youth are not separatist. Dissent and deviance are already dead if rejection of the majority consensus means that one is going to be labeled a separatist. The question is one not of separatism or nonseparatism but of the terms and conditions under which coalitions can be made and of the end and goal of the coalition. Here it seems to me the COCU officials have a conception of unity vintage 1948, and the cultural revolutionaries are still in the process of developing their understanding of unity. I do not think that their conceptions will be too much affected by what is called "the great scandal of Christianity." Unity for the cultural revolutionaries is to be found and sought in action. People are together when they are willing to risk their lives for a cause. Unity for them is not achieved through well-defined contractural relationships. If the real thing exists, they seem to believe, one does not need a contract; if it does not exist, a contract is just a piece of paper. Moreover, they are all concerned with neglected particulars which few think merit inclusion in any contract or know how to state in contractural terms. How does one guarantee the existence of soul, the elimination of male chauvinism, or the future acceptance of youthful idealism? More can be done than has been; nonetheless, the accomplishment of the task prior to life together is hard to contemplate. Yet there is no life together, licit or illicit, without courtship that is persuasive.

The first point I want, then, to suggest is that COCU is not sufficiently radical to persuade blacks, women, and youth who are cultural revolutionaries to join, and this despite the genuine revolutionary character of COCU. What is needed is a further demonstration by COCU of its appreciation of Christianity as a movement, its willingness to accept dissent and deviance, and its intention to include in the new uniting church particulars found outside the mainstream of religious life.

Secondly, it must be borne in mind that we are speaking about, at a minimum, three cultural revolutions and that three plans of action are necessary as well as some conception of priorities. Only the arrogance of leadership lumps blacks, women, and youth together. The very arrangement itself points to one of the difficulties endemic to COCU. It places the pseudopriestly above the genuinely prophetic. It suggests playing church rather than attempting to be church. It elicits images of bureaucratic centralism rather then pastoral care and concern.

We must never forget that there is not much hope for unity vintage 1948. Wendell Willkie's dream of One World is no longer an accurate conceptualization. When we speak of unity we must speak of three worlds, at least, not one world. Thus the World Council of Churches speaks of a dialogue with Jews and Muslims, and Catholics sit on its committees. So also the National Council of Churches opens itself to Catholics in a fashion not expected in 1948. Unity today includes group pursuit of self-interest and group giving of self to others. It is no longer fellowship among individuals or simply Europeans rediscovering their lost kin. Unity in 1970 requires full consideration of group interest; and blacks, women, and youth are distinct groups. As a consequence they require separate billing; each one's goals and aims should be stated by themselves—just as I imagine Presbyterians in COCU speak for Presbyterians and Methodists for Methodists without any one labeling them as separatist or despairing about how their differences shall be overcome.

Since I am neither woman nor youth, I shall not attempt to outline their aims or objectives. I shall limit my remarks to the stating of what I think compels one to separate their causes from that of the blacks. In the first instance, the women and youth movements are predominantly white. This means that they are part of the Establishment. They sleep in the bed of the possessors of power. They profit—even if not equally—from white supremacy. They are part of the primary group that motivates the white male to achieve even at the expense of the blacks. And they share the status, inherit the power, and participate in the oppression perpetrated upon black Americans. I do not deny that women and youth may suffer, but I do reject the notion that they are or can become niggers. Women and youth are like confessing German Christians talking to German Nazis. Blacks are the Jews in the basement. Now while it is true that the women and youth at the door may contribute something to the safety of the nigger in the basement, never should the two be confused. Women and youth can always leave the door and enter the world with only a slight accommodation. The nigger in the basement can enter the world only at the risk of death. Women and youth are white, therefore they have never as a group suffered as the blacks have, and they have always had available a means of escape not available to blacks. There are black women and black youth who may see matters differently. My observation is that they are very few in number and have almost no influence in the women's movement or the youth culture.

A second consideration that distinguishes blacks from women and youth is their cultural roots and their class. Winthrop S. Hudson, writing in the volume *Reinterpretation in American Church History*, raised the question, "How American Is Religion in America?" He answered it by saying:

> The fact that Asians and Africans have tended to call us European . . . should have reminded us that we are Europeans in almost all respects—not only in ancestry, but in language, religion, legal institutions, diet, clothing, and household furnishing, as well as in our most characteristic proverbs, our most familiar nursery rhymes, and most of our literature, music, art, philosophy, and science. We have been and are a part of Europe." [1]

Though the good doctor exaggerates a little, the overstatement should not obscure the fact that women and youth in the movements are European. Blacks may be European by adoption, but they are also African, and increasingly this shall make a difference.

So also with class. White women and youth in the movement tend to be upper- and middle-class. They have not only European culture but quite often the best of it together with the material advantages it will buy. Their goals and purpose tend therefore to be determined by what is needed to make influence and affluence even more enjoyable. Lady Bountiful does not distribute food baskets but ecology leaflets, her naturalness is no longer rosy cheeks but a thirst for orgasms, and her purpose in life is not to soften men by love but to defeat them by achievement. Both images are, of course, carricatures, but they contain a truth. Women have in the past and in the present contributed little to the solution of the problems of black men, even though they have been more sensitive to some social or personal ills of society than white males.

So, too, with youth. Indeed, with white youth and white women one could argue that what has been best in their protest style was adapted from SCLC, SNCC, and other black civil-rights organizations.

Women and youth speak to the upper- and middle-class. They seek to teach Americans how better to enjoy their affluence and the church how to celebrate its more worldly ethics. Black revolutionaries are simply unable to identify with such groups. That is why the Panthers now seek to join the black community and the black church.

COCU faces the task of relating itself to three, at a minimum, cultural revolutions, not one. I have here attempted only to indicate a few reasons why blacks cannot be lumped together with women and youth. What I have demonstrated from the black perspective can also be shown from the perspective of women and youth. The groups are different and COCU must, if it cares to succeed, learn to bend more. This is required because the issues of the seventies shall be defined by these groups. Attica is an illustration of what lies ahead if racism is not addressed. Job equality, abortion reform, population control are just some of the issues that women will bring to the fore. Drugs, participatory democracy, issues of war and peace, and radical politics are some of the causes upon which youth shall demand action. Unless the new uniting church has a message to address to these issues, no one will much care whether their local communities have one, three, five, or no churches.

Since I am a black churchman, I want to say a few special words about the black revolution and COCU. Bishop Joseph A. Johnson said in an address in Atlanta last May, "From now on, and through the remainder of this century, we will be in the Age of the New Black. What mission the church has, the nation has, or anybody else has, will be affected by what the New Black thinks, plans, and does." [2] I think the bishop is correct, and because COCU seeks to build a new church along what seem to be national lines, it needs to pay particular attention to the blacks. The women and youth are by and large already in the church—i.e., the local congregation, the hierarchy of denominations, and the ecumenical movements. If they are not present, all one needs to do is tell wife, son, and daughter to join in the work of the Lord. There are injustices, to be sure, but no greater injustice than exists already in the home. A relatively easy solution can be found for this problem. The blacks are, however, on the outside. Ask any white person and he'll tell you he cannot find any. If he finds one, he will inform you that he's not domesticated and suitable for tasks in the *oikoumene*. COCU's major problem, if it is not to continue furnishing the nation with models for inequality, is the problem of relating to the black church. What, then, shall it do?

The major task is the empowerment of the black church. The task is unavoidable because one-third of the churches in COCU are black. COCU must provide the black church with sufficient funds to do well its mission in its neighborhood. Because black people are the last hired and the first fired; because the black people when fired receive inadequate welfare payment and when working inadequate wages and inferior schools, houses, and neighborhood resources, the black church is underfinanced for its mission. It needs, therefore, help from the richer denominations. The black church, not idealistic white youth or white Christian ladies, needs to be empowered to do the task of mission to the black community. This is imperative because only black churches are in the ghetto and this shall remain true for some time to come. This task will have several dimensions, theological, social-ethical, and pastoral. There is need for more adequate images of black identity, more sophisticated understanding of the task of building community, political, economic, and cultural organizations, more vigorous pursuit of full equality, and more care and comfort in pastoral relations. Now, since there are few white churches in black neighborhoods and few blacks in the locale of white suburban churches, it makes good sense to me to empower the black churches to do the task of mission in the black community. Such a church structure would not be a form of apartheid because blacks would be free, if they chose, to join other churches or to move to non-black parishes. Moreover, on the basis of the United Presbyterian Church's contention that a congregation was integrated if it had six Negroes in it, there would probably be sufficient whites in the inner city and blacks in the suburbs to integrate all the parishes. There would, however, be strong black churches comparable statistically and programatically with the best white churches. This would result not only in a more adequate ministry, especially for blacks, but it would equip blacks to extend their ministry to the new city migrants.

The new migrant would also receive a different image of the Negro and when he moved to the suburb he would be better equipped for the ministry of racial reconciliation. As time passed and the fruits of integrated community and school programs became visible, these churches and communities could change their character while leaving in the "truly catholic, truly evangelical, truly reformed church" the proud legacy of racism overcome.

Another consequence of this program would be the providing of an adequate constitutive base for the black churchmen in the hierarchy and staff of the new uniting church. This is essential, I believe, if blacks are to be free to dissent from majority rulings or to exercise the provisions for flexibility present in A Plan of Union. The experience of the Black Presbyterians even after they themselves paid the church's contribution to Angela Davis' defense points to the absolute necessity of this constitutive base.[3] Predominantly black parishes would also enable blacks to preserve their preaching style, their notion of the church as a nation within a nation, as well as black church music. Given the integral link of the black church to its community, it would be the height of irresponsibility for the black churchman not to follow his people through their revolution for cultural and social liberation. It would be wise for COCU to encourage, not seek to undermine, the effort of blacks to be supportive of blacks. Hopefully, these strong black churches would also be able to spearhead the new united church's mission to Africa. Through black Americans speaking to Africans the new national church would more easily be de-Europeanized and open to the possibility of universality and transcendence.

Secondly, COCU must begin immediately not only to empower black churchmen, but also to be active in encouraging black churchmen to come together in a united black religious community prior to their merger into COCU. It is the black denominations and black churchmen in predominantly white denominations that need now to draw up the boundaries for the new parishes, decide about the nature of the ministry and mission, and make recommendations about staff. Blacks need not only bishops but executive directors of missions, editors of curriculum materials, and treasurers of boards and agencies. Since the National Committee of Black Churchmen is already in existence as a black ecumenical structure, it should be utilized in this process, but the major task is with the denominations themselves.

It is not my intention to campaign for my outline. I hope that it will ignite a real discussion about the nature of a church erected upon a conception of world unity that presupposes pluralism and not the 1948 One World theory. Most of us are willing to admit that the prayer for unity in John 17 was the prayer not of Jesus but of the early church. As the church of the new age, let us pray for a new conception of unity adequate to our times and not dig up ideas fit for a less complex and less differentiated world.

I do not consent to the notion of a certain United Methodist bishop that COCU is dead. It is at present still alive. Death, though, may come if the leadership does not recognize that 1948-style unity is dead. Blacks, women, and youth are leading a new revolution for a new age of space ships, of human- not nature-determined evolution, and electronic communication of cultural patterns and values. No matter what the nature of the frustration experienced, persist in your task because one thing is certain—there shall be a new church. No return to the old is possible. If COCU does not succeed, a new COCU shall arise from the ashes.

NOTES

1. Hudson, Winthrop S., "How American Is Religion in America?" in J. C. Brauer (ed.), *Essays in Divinity*, Vol. V, *Reinterpretation in American Church History* (Chicago: University of Chicago Press, 1968), p. 155.
2. Johnson, Bishop Joseph A., "The Mission of the Black Church Is Liberation" (unpublished manuscript), p. 1.
3. "Angela and the Presbyterians" (editorial), *The Christian Century*, Vol. LXXXVIII, No. 27 (July 7, 1971), p. 823.

10

The Role of Women in the Church Union Process

JANET HARBISON PENFIELD

The attention the Consultation on Church Union has paid to women in the church has been minimal since the beginnings of this union effort. By the same token, the role of women in the union process has been minimal.

That these things should be so is quite understandable. The problems of faith and order that have separated the several denominations involved in COCU from each other are great. The bulk of the attention and time of the COCU delegations had to be spent, at least in the first years, in attempts to solve these. The leaders of the churches had to be the ones to do the struggling, and these leaders generally do not include women. While many believe that the proposed *Plan of Union* transcends most of these faith and order differences, there seem to be numbers of people within each of the denominations who think that the Consultation proposals merely paper over the cracks and that much time and thought will have to be devoted to these questions in the future.

Some of the knottiest of the problems COCU has been facing lie in the area of the ordained ministry, its nature and meaning, its functioning and ordering. Since an original and highly important denominational participant in COCU is the Episcopal Church, which did not and does not admit women to its priesthood, the solution of these knotty problems of ministry—episcopacy, role of clergy and their placement—would have been made at least a bit stickier if the ordination of women had been dealt into the mix by COCU from the beginning.

Doubtless for this reason, no ordained woman minister was appointed to any denominational delegation to the Consultation in the first years of its life. This despite the fact that all the other early denominations in the

Consultation had admitted women to their ordained ministries by the time the Consultation began to be organized. At all events, it was rightly deemed far more important, for the solution of the faith and order difficulties, to have the right bishops and clergy actively engaged in the union process and sympathetic to it early on than to involve women ministers—who had, in any case, virtually no influence even in the denominations that had been ordaining women for many years. Thus it was that of the original four denominations (the Episcopal Church, the Methodist Church, the United Church of Christ, the United Presbyterian Church), each one but the Methodists appointed *one unordained* woman to its first COCU plenary delegation. The Methodist delegation was all male.

The Consultation denominations that did ordain women, however, were not about to throw their women ministers to the lions. It was assumed from the start that all ministers of COCU denominations in good standing in their respective churches at the time of union would by some means or other be accepted as ministers in good standing in the proposed united church. Ergo, the new church would have at least some women ministers. It was tacitly assumed also, at least by the non-Episcopalians, that with the passage of time, theological and biblical objections that had traditionally kept women from full participation in the church having generally ceased to be convincing, even the Episcopal Church would admit women to the full range of the ordained ministry. While this has not taken place as of this writing, women are now admitted to the Episcopal diaconate on an equal footing with men, and several have been so ordained.

Among the few women present at the early sessions of COCU, the hypothetical question was sometimes raised as to whether the right of women to be ordained to the ministry might indeed be sacrificed if this should ultimately prove necessary in order to preserve the union negotiations. We happy few tended to think that it might—though we surely did not expect this to happen. There being no ordained women ministers among us, we were relatively free to make a theoretical offering up of the ordinations and aspirations of our sisters. So far as I know, no poll was ever made of church women as to whether they would choose church union over full church rights for women.

The number of women who have gone as official delegates from denominations to the annual Consultation meeting has varied very little over the years. Most, though not all, denominations have felt that they should include one woman in the nine- (later ten-) person delegation. When Christian-education and worship representatives from denominations have been included, the situation as to numbers of women present has changed scarcely at all. Significant, in light of the fact that Christian education has traditionally been a female area of responsibility, is the fact that only one woman Christian-education expert has consistently represented her denomination and that she is an Episcopalian. The Episcopal Christian Education department has been headed for some years by Carman Hunter.

The relative strength or weakness of women's groups in the churches, whether they control their own money and institutions (as the United Methodist women do) or are more loosely organized and emphasize prayer groups and altar guilds, like the Episcopalians, seems to have had no relation to the presence or absence, strength or weakness of women officially participating in COCU. The Christian Churches (Disciples of Christ), to take an example, a group whose women have traditionally had great influence and much money, and a group in which lay participation has been very important, have often fielded delegations in which no woman was present. It must be said that laymen have, by and large, fared little better in COCU. Clergy have mainly dominated the proceedings. It would be interesting to chart the lay participation in plenary sessions and special commissions of COCU. Aside from laymen who are professionally employed by the church, one gets the impression that few lay people have been significantly involved in the union process up to the present moment of study by the churches of a proposed plan.

The COCU Executive Committee, which had no woman member until last year when United Presbyterian Lois Stair became second vice-chairman of the Consultation (mercifully not secretary), has treated the few women members of the delegations to the plenary with no condescension. Women delegates have been made chairmen of discussion groups quite as often as they have been asked to be recorders; women have served on all the major special committees of the Consultation. When it came to the special committee to draft a plan of union, on which each denomination was to have one representative, it was realized that bishops and top bureaucrats of the church were surely destined to be named. A provision for special additional members was invented in order that two women and a couple of laymen might bring their particular perspective to bear on the work of this very crucial committee. Male clergy who are participants in the drafting process report favorably on the contribution of these special nominees.

The Executive Committee seems to have made an effort to use such talents as the women delegates possessed. It must be said, however, that the single woman delegate on most delegations each year (never more than two in any denomination) has tended to be a "house woman," so to speak. Most of these women were pretty much part of the denominational structures when they were appointed. They have not tended to be radicals, or young, or even very much against the government—i.e., the hierarchies of their own denominations. By the same token, they have not pressed any case for the inclusion of more women or of women's concerns in the union process.

Perhaps oddly, the leaders of women's guilds and associations have not regularly been members of COCU denominational delegations. Women delegation members have tended rather to be professional, but not ordained, women in church-related fields. Sometimes they have been staff people who worked largely with women. Of late, the category of accredited visitors to the annual COCU gathering has been emphasized, and it has brought about increased female participation, if only on the fringes of the union process. Some accredited observers have been active leaders in women's organizations in the churches. There is, of course, the danger that the accredited-visitor status may become a sort of dumping-ground for women, young people, lay people, and other groups the COCU leadership would like to interest in union plans and prospects but considers of marginal importance to the actual functioning of the denominations. A look at the roster of the last COCU plenary shows that nine women were voting members of delegations, while fourteen were accredited visitors. The number of bishops in delegate status was twenty; the number of bishops who came as accredited observers was five. Not all the denominations have formal bishops, of course.

No woman theologian, save one, has presented a paper for the edification of a Consultation group. This has been because the tacit understanding that the issue of the ordination of women would be avoided pretty well precluded the presence of women theologians as delegates to plenaries. And the COCU executive did not borrow trouble by looking for women theologians, who constitute a commodity in short supply anyhow.

The Presbyterian Church in the United States had been invited to join the Consultation in 1963 when invitations were issued to the major denominations in the United States to become partners in the union discussions. The invitation, periodically extended thereafter, had not succeeded in finding majority acceptance in the annual gatherings of the Southern church. In 1966, however, the Presbyterian Church's General Assembly finished its meeting just as the annual COCU gathering was beginning in Dallas. A day or so later there arrived a slightly bewildered group of Southern Presbyterians, newly appointed as their denomination's delegation to COCU and instructed to hurry on down to the meeting. A member of the group was the Rev. Rachel Henderlite, professor at Austin Theological Seminary and the first woman ordained by the Southern Presbyterian Church. By this time the Episcopal Church was apparently no longer likely to be frightened by an ordained woman—or maybe Rachel Henderlite's appointment just happened in the suddenness of the Southern Presbyterian vote. In any event, Rachel Henderlite has contributed theologically and practically to a number of COCU studies and gatherings. In 1967 she prepared a paper on "Discipline in a United and Uniting Church" for the special Consultation Committee on Unification of Memberships. Other ordained women have occasionally attended Consultation meetings and been part of COCU groups in one capacity or another. The potential in the ordained women of the COCU churches has, on the whole, been disregarded, however.

The specific provisions of the proposed plan of union, which has lately been under discussion by church groups, suggest that in the new church women will hold theoretical equality with men. "In every area of the new structure, in both lay and ordained leadership the united church shall assure all races, various age groups, and both sexes the right of full participation," says A Plan of Union (VIII, 14, p. 58). No minority dissent to this paragraph is on the record. Seemingly, the delegates to COCU accept women bishops, at least in theory. Moreover, "the church will: . . . enlist women for all offices of the ordained and lay ministry and provide for full participation by women in all policy-making groups" (A Plan of Union, VIII, 14–16, p. 59). If leadership of the proposed new church chose to implement this provision, and if the verb "enlist" means some kind of recruiting, broad changes in the participation of women in the governance of the church could ensue.

Moreover, the proposed form of government for the parish (the smallest governing unit of the proposed new church) provides that "a ratio be maintained of at least two lay members for each ordained minister" and that the "principles of equitable representation of racial and ethnic minorities, women, and youth be applied" (A Plan of Union, VIII, 33, p. 61). What "equitable" means in this connection is, of course, purposely left vague. It would seem, however, that women might stand a better chance of being represented at levels all up and down the line of the government of the proposed new church than many of them do in the present structures of denominations. A general rule of two laymen for each ordained minister is set up in the proposed form of organization for the Church of Christ Uniting. Some of the present denominations provide for a one-to-one relationship between ordained ministers and lay people (or even, sometimes, more ministers than lay people) at the higher levels of governance. In these cases, of course, the practical effect is to restrict the participation of women to a token presence. Since women are often accustomed to remaining silent in the churches, in accordance with Paul's famous suggestion, this minority status in church legislative sessions has meant that women have had virtually no effect on the conduct of church affairs. At least in theory, the proposed new church might change this.

The drafters of the proposed Plan of Union made a considerable effort to avoid blatantly sexist language. Most often the plan speaks of "lay

persons" rather than "laymen." Sometimes "lay persons" are put in opposition to "clergymen." This seems almost forgivable, given the awk-
wardness of "clergy persons." Indeed, it is only when the peculiarities of
English trap the drafters into a paragraph that starts out, "Because the
Christian has been grafted by baptism . . . he worships both privately
and publicly," and goes on to tell what "he" does for several more sentences, that feminists might have cause to find fault (*A Plan of Union,*
VI, 2, p. 30).

A group of women leaders, lay and professional, from seven of the
nine COCU denominations studied the proposed *Plan of Union* in a two-
day meeting in the spring of 1971. The women were convened by Dr.
Evelyn Green, an ordained minister and a staff member of the Presbyterian Church in the U.S. This group made a thorough analysis of the
Plan from the points of view of content and language. They commended
such portions of the proposal as they found admirable, and criticized
very thoroughly those parts that seemed to them to reflect male chauvinism.

The group sent a report to the COCU executive, which has since appointed a subcommittee on these concerns of women. A meeting involving women from the various denominations is being convened for early
1972, with Dr. Green again acting as the convener, and a plan to meet
with the COCU Executive Committee. Some idea of the temper of the
group that analyzed the proposed *Plan of Union* may be gained from
quoting a few paragraphs of their summary:

> It was quite evident to this group that the document has been written
> primarily by male theologians.
> It is quite clear that women are not very much included in the current
> *Plan of Union,* with few exceptions.
> The Plan does not seem to be elastic enough to take in a cultural pattern
> of all groups (the hierarchy of the Plan may be disturbing to Indian Cul-
> ture).
> It seems to this group that this is a clerical uniting rather than a merging
> of the people. . . .

It appears that women are fully as active as men, locally, in study and
criticism of the union Plan and process. However, as far as this writer
has heard, Dr. Green's group is the only one actually analyzing the Plan
from the women's perspective.

Somewhat as an afterthought, and tacked onto a meeting between the
COCU Executive Committee and some Canadian church-union leaders
in Toronto in the fall of 1969, a group of women was convened, mostly
women's-association officers and staffs, representing eight of the nine
COCU churches. Most of the denominations sent their full quota of five

representatives, although the Presbyterian Church in the U.S., commenting that Toronto was pretty far from Atlanta, sent only one. The Christian Methodist Episcopal Church sent none.

The meeting was not a success. The idea seems to have been to get women church leaders interested in COCU so that, upon adoption by the Consultation of a proposed *Plan of Union* the following spring, they would bring their influence to bear in their denominations. The male-dominated Executive Committee raised hackles on the backs of many of the women by the patronizing attitudes some of its members manifested. Some of the women present, already well launched into women's-liberation attitudes, of which the COCU leaders had apparently not been much aware, felt as if they were being manipulated into buying something they had had no part in creating. There has thus far been no attempt to follow up this meeting, and it appears that without the initiative taken by Dr. Green the whole matter of women's role and attitudes with respect to COCU might have been disregarded in the press of other crucial problems.

There is no specific provision in the proposed *Plan of Union* for anything like the far-flung women's associations and guilds of our present denominations. There is plenty of room, however, at every level of the proposed church for the creation of almost any kind of task force, agency, mission arm one can think of. It is to be assumed, therefore, that unless somebody—maybe women—decides there should be no "church beside the church" in the new structures, the full panoply of women's organizations will not be long in coming after union. It is quite possible that the structures in our society are so fixed, and women's energies so tremendous, that even full participation in the total life of the church would not preclude the formation of special groups for women. Certain of the accomplishments of women's groups—their knowledge of and interest in the mission work of the church overseas and in remote and poor areas of this country; their capacity to raise large sums of money, often on short notice, for specific objects; their zeal and skill in coping with particular problems in their own communities—should not be lost in a new church. Whether or not they require the full range of one-sex organizations we now have for their accomplishment might be another question.

That a particular role for women—whether the traditional one or something entirely fresh and different—should be totally absent from COCU thinking and planning up to date is hardly surprising. Until quite recently, women in the churches have not attempted to organize or to exert any pressure on the denominations to achieve a particular place of responsibility for women or even a more equal status in existing structures. (The women's organizations, of course, are thought of and act as a supporting, subordinate wing of the church.) This is doubtless because the average woman in the church accepts its teachings about the normative role of males, teachings that have the sanction both of Holy Writ and of centuries of practice. There are surely women who feel quite unhappy with an organization in which, as Susan Copenhaver Barrabee puts it,

> The medium is undeniably male. The main characters of Christian theology: God, a father; Christ, his son; the Holy Spirit, an impregnator, among other more elusive things; and Man (as in "the nature of"), although purported to be a generic designation, are unmistakably male.[1]

Up to now, however, women critics have been mostly silent.

Some women in the past who have harbored questions about the church's total maleness did not stay very long in the institution. Many, doubtless, expended their energies in the Young Women's Christian Association, in which the thinking was generally biblical, but which women controlled and directed. Some most likely continued as card-carrying members of Christian churches while giving most of their time and talents to political parties, or leagues of women voters, or unions.

A few of those who have stayed active in the church have worked to change its rubrics and customs. But mostly the Protestant church woman has tended to be a person quite content with her status as an inferior to men. She has generally been middle-class, small-town at least in mentality, well cared for and not in any kind of physical need. It is perhaps significant that even in 1971 church women's meetings tend to occur on weekdays in the daytime, when employed women (now a third of the female populace) are on their jobs.

Church women, by and large, have been married women, living therefore very close to the men who constitute the establishment. These women are involved emotionally in the maintenance of things as they are. Leaders of women's-liberation groups point out a major handicap women have in trying to improve their status: since they have a lifetime investment in the present order, women naturally fear any change. Church women perhaps more than others tend to have this "house-slave" fear of any revolt. They see at first hand the ravages that real responsibility for running things, whether in church, government, or business, wreaks on men. And they are, at least unconsciously, unwilling to subject themselves to these strains. Thus, women are often more fiercely opposed to the assumption of responsibility by women in the church than men are.

Women's status is in many ways like that of blacks in this country: their share of the job market, wages, opportunities for training, chance to be President or a justice of the Supreme Court are indeed like unto those of blacks. A black woman, with the new assertiveness of black men, is at the bottom of this totem pole. Black women nowadays have feelings about women's liberation that are at the very least ambivalent, and often are quite negative. Eager to see black men take a place of leadership that is the equal of that held by white men, they are often reluctant to assert their claims as women. This complex psychological situation of blacks may account for a phenomenon some COCU leaders have observed whereby the black women delegated to represent black denominations in COCU are often the wives of bishops.

Although the opening up of job opportunities for women has given at least a few of them alternatives to marriage, and the possibility therefore of a different life-style, until recently women have been too fearful of independence to mount any kind of campaign to change the status quo. The bids for equality of other oppressed groups in the nation—blacks first, then Spanish-speaking people, Indians, young people—have probably been the catalyst that caused restlessness on the part of some women with their lot to coalesce into what is called women's liberation. The ready availability of birth-control methods women can use, the threat of overpopulation that seems to make the bearing of numbers of children out of the question for thinking women, the so-called "new morality" in sex—which in effect assumes that women should have open to them the same options to express their sexuality that men have traditionally enjoyed—these are some of the influences that have brought some women to the point of fighting for more equality in American society. According to Caroline Bird in a poll made of Vassar graduates on their preferred life-styles, the "classes of 1964–1966 voted for 'career with as little time out for family as possible.'" [2]

This is of course in total contrast with the attitude of young women twenty-five years ago when the average age at marriage was going steadily down and most women aimed at marriage, children, and a split-level house, with a sprinkling of community activity to fill in the chinks.

Thus far, the churches have not seen the same kind of revolt on the part of their women that they have experienced from blacks, Chicanos, and young people. Signs indicate, though, that the time may not be far off. The United Presbyterian Church in the U.S.A., for instance, now has seventy ordained women ministers. They will soon be joined by many more, since the ranks of women candidates for the ordained ministry are increasing. These women expect to be called to pastorates and to receive other job offers commensurate with their talents, which are said by seminary spokesmen to be great. Up to now, ordained women ministers in most denominations have received at best patronizing treatment on the part of the authorities of their denominations. Elsie Gibson, an ordained minister in the United Church of Christ, points out in a recent book that women ministers can scarcely expect congregations to hire them and pay money when they have been accustomed for years to hiring a man minister and getting his wife's services free.[3]

In the United Presbyterian Church, at least, women are starting to react to this treatment. They have organized a professional-women's caucus and even had a mild demonstration on behalf of the report of the church's Task Force on Women at the 1971 General Assembly of the denomination. The report of this task force called for equal representation for women on governing bodies of the church's agencies, and representation of women on all local governing bodies. The male-dominated General Assembly voted in favor of most of the proposed reforms, with modifications, but then failed to find any way to fund further work of the women's group. ("They couldn't vote against women in principle, but they got them in the pocketbook," said one male observer.) It seems likely that ordained women of some of the other denominations of COCU, tired of being the last hired at the lowest wages, will begin to mount revolts as well.

Thus in the years to come the Consultation on Church Union is going to find the role and status of women among its unresolved problems. Since women presumably constitute more than half of the members of the denominations in COCU, will it be assumed, by the time the Church of Christ Uniting comes into being, that half the bishops should be women? And is it conceivable that the total church union effort could break apart on this soft rock?

This may be a hypothesis too far out to credit. Most church women, both those in organized women's groups and the vast mass of women church members who take only a peripheral interest in church life, would be indifferent if not hostile to any such efforts. But it is not impossible that "traditionalist" and "revolutionary" groups of women will arise with contradictory aspirations and demands as to the status of women in a united and uniting church. The experience of COCU thus far with organized groups of blacks whose ideas differ suggests that this possibility is not too far-fetched.

I would hope that organized women's groups, whether lay or clergy or mixed, would not limit themselves to fighting the sexist terminology of the Consultation on Church Union or plugging for technical equality. They ought to work for these things, of course. But it does not make a lot of difference whether the Holy Spirit is described as a "he" or a "she," or even whether the presiding bishop is a male or a female. The kinds of things the proposed church is about do make a difference, however. So far the Consultation has talked mostly about doctrine and organization. There has been less definition of the way the church serves the world, finds community, transmits the message. These three traditional spheres of the Christian's interest are also areas in which the special qualities (inherent or learned, no matter) of women could play some part and make some difference. Drama, color, dance, even ritual and celebration—areas which tend to make many white American Protestant men uncomfortable—are all congenial to many women. Let us hope that as women assume more of a role in the union process, they will bring to it some of the things that need more emphasis. If they cannot do that, they might as well leave the institutional church to the men.

NOTES

1. Barrabee, Susan Copenhaver, in Doeley, S. B. (ed.), *Women's Liberation and the Church* (New York: Association Press, 1970), p. 48.
2. Bird, Caroline, *Born Female* (New York: Pocket Books, 1968), p. 148.
3. Gibson, Elsie, *When the Minister Is a Women* (New York: Holt, Rinehart and Winston, 1970).

III

COCU AND THE FUTURE OF ECUMENISM

11

The Critics and the Nature
of the Union We Seek

J. ROBERT NELSON

I

Why should men and women work for the termination of the church
structure to which they belong? Is it not remarkable that the leaders responsible for nine denominations send delegates to a consultation which
aims to bring the separate histories of each of the nine to an end? Is this
a kind of treason? Is it an ecclesial death-wish? Is there some hidden
strategy, known only to a few, by which the game of church union can
be played for a time, even while measures are taken to be sure that the
consequences for each participating church can be avoided at the last?
Or are they in fact pressing on toward denominational doom?

What must die before the rebirth of union takes place? Not the diversities of doctrine and theology; not the various ways of worship; not the
continuing identity of congregations and ministers; and not the valued
traditions which each denomination has remembered, appropriated, and
experienced since the time of its beginning. All these will be gathered
together in a more comprehensive united church. And it is strongly believed by informed advocates of union that the integrating of these elements will eventuate in a church which is not only different from its
several predecessors but also more faithful and vigorous in its total life
of corporate service.

If the main reason for seeking union were economic efficiency or even
financial gain, then, and only then, would the frequently cited mergers of
industrial corporations and cartels be properly analogous to church union.
But this is not the reason, valid as it may be, which impels COCU.

If wider union would bring a sudden increase of power and prestige for leaders of existing denominations, including those who take part in COCU meetings, their zeal could be readily understood. Then, and only then, could the enterprise be attacked as church politics and nothing more. But the truth is that most denominational leaders would find their prestige diminished and their power reduced by union.

If the United States government were of such a totalitarian nature that it decided to coerce the churches into union so as to make them more easily controllable, then the problem would be of an entirely different order. This actually happened in Japan during 1944, resulting in the forced formation of Kyodan, or the United Church of Christ. But the government of the United States plays no role in COCU.

Why, then, do the denominations keep supporting this plan which, if eventually realized, will cause them all to be displaced by a much larger and quite different church?

Because *God requires it.*

That is the most succinct statement of the motivating faith supporting COCU. The Ecumenical Movement of the twentieth century did not suddenly discover, much less invent, this expression of the divine mandate. It has been known, believed, violated, partially obeyed, but never rejected nor forgotten since the generation of the church of the New Testament.

There is an abundance—indeed, a surplus—of literature on the biblical and theological understanding of God's will for the unity of the church. But the translating of that understanding and faith into the institutional forms of the church in a particular society or nation involves human planning which, because it is not necessarily under divine inspiration, is vulnerable to many kinds of criticism. Indeed, the comprehensive and multifaceted *Plan of Union* may be said to boast (in a perverse sense) something for everyone—to criticize! Some of these specific criticisms which have major importance need to be examined herein. But fortunately there is one kind of polemical charge which is seldom leveled against COCU and which could not at all be sustained; namely, that it is a calculated scheme "to put one over on the churches" by subduing them within a single vast structure. The faithful Christian intentions of the planners and drafters must be respected. All charges of unworthy motivation must be dismissed as immaterial.

To be an impartial judge of the legitimacy of the criticisms of this Plan is scarcely possible. If one is so detached and objective that he feels no concern or even passion about any elements under attack, he is probably not sufficiently interested in the Plan to qualify as a judge. However, if he is committed by faith and reason to the defense of certain elements, he becomes a party to dispute rather than a judicious mediator. In dealing with the critics and their complaints, therefore, one must inevitably reveal his own sense of conviction about certain issues.

II

First to be considered is a cluster of five complaints against the Plan which are lodged by persons of all denominations and types of theological persuasion. Some so-called liberals discover themselves as bedfellows with virtual fundamentalists. Some Episcopalians express the same strong protests as do Disciples and Presbyterians. Furthermore, these five are considered applicable to church union plans in all the countries where such are in progress, and not only in the United States. And—strangely, perhaps—almost every interested Christian would agree with these five criticisms if they were indeed pertinent to the *Plan of Union*. But *are* they pertinent? The evidence indicates that they are not.

(1) *Monolithicity.* Typical is the statement of the widely respected British theologian Professor John Macquarrie, who is an Anglican.

> The gifts of the Spirit encourage diversity as well as unity, and perhaps a vast monolithic church-structure has very little to do with real Christian unity. A super-denomination of 25 million members is not a very exciting prospect.[1]

Certainly this is a telling indictment of any proposed church union which is intended to be, or likely to be, monolithic. What is a monolith? It is a single stone of massive dimensions, an Egyptian obelisk or a huge block of granite. It is heavy, uniform, cold, and dead. Such an analogy can hardly be admitted, much less desired, by any advocate of church union. Neither does anyone wish to construct a "superdenomination" or a "super-church"—whatever that might really be. Does great numerical strength imply a "superchurch"? Then present denominations may find comfort in their slow growth, or even their loss of members! It is the structural monopoly which is legitimately feared. But must there be a monopoly? The literature of the World Council of Churches, similar ecumenical councils, and individual writers is replete with statements explicitly rejecting the idea of a monolithic superchurch. So also do the COCU planners reject it.

(2) *Uniformity.* Closely related to this is the charge of uniformity in the theology, liturgy, organization, moral insights, and style of a united church. It is a curious thing that this complaint is sounded so frequently. The fact is that *A Plan of Union*, like most others, gratefully acknowledges the gifts of the Holy Spirit which encourage diversity [as in I Corinthians 12] and specifically promises wide latitude within which

congregations and individuals may exercise their freedom to use such gifts (*A Plan of Union*, II, 11, 20, 21, pp. 11–13; VI, 8, 9, p. 31; VIII, 3, p. 56). In every social institution or community, including the church, the affirmation of freedom and diversity also raises the issue of an optimum degree of order and integrity. The same apostle who extolled the diverse gifts of the Spirit and the varieties of ministries also insisted that these were intended to build up the whole church, as body of Christ, and that the life of the church should be maintained decently and in order (I Corinthians 14). There is no question, then, that a church body must have a certain consistency of organization and polity, as well as doctrine, even while these do not constitute a restrictive and stifling uniformity.

(3) *Central Control.* Within American society and also within the church denominations there are opposing forces, the centrifugal and the centripetal. The need for self-expression, inventiveness, and initiative of persons and groups drives them away from the centers of bureaucratic control. But the need for effective action and witness in a large and complicated society requires certain centers of governance and agencies for corporate accomplishment. This is the same basic problem of diversity and uniformity as it is manifested in church institutions. It is quite possible that the reason for the present anxiety of many church members about centralizing tendencies within the proposed united church is that they already are alarmed to discern these in their own denominations. No Protestant denomination has a counterpart in fact to the Vatican, however institutionalized it may have become. Neither does the *Plan of Union* envisage or provide for such a focal point of ecclesiastical power. On the contrary, particular care has been taken in the proposed Plan for the devolution of governance and responsibility to regional, district, and parish structures (*A Plan of Union*, VIII). Further refinements and revisions will be needed to define and safeguard these provisions. Those who voice strong criticism against church union because of fear of centralization are thus performing a service to the project, rather than undercutting it. The intent of the planners was expressed by former COCU chairman Bishop James K. Mathews when he wrote of the united church, "It could be less top-heavy, less bureaucratic and less hierarchical, more decentralized than any one of the present denominations." [2]

(4) *Narrow Protestantism.* All the church bodies participating in COCU are Protestant, in the broad sense of the term. There are some members of the Episcopal Church, of course, who are displeased with COCU precisely because they prefer to think of themselves and their church as belonging to the Catholic tradition. Only a slight acquaintance with the history of the Church of England and the whole Anglican Communion is needed to enable one to understand their view. The Anglo-Catholic Revival of the early nineteenth century was seen not as a repu-

diation, but as a corrective of the effects of the sixteenth-century Reformation in Britain. For a century and a half, then, the desired movement of many Anglicans has been in the direction of a reconciliation and reunion with Rome. And the accelerating increase of such possibilities since the Second Vatican Council has made it seem to some that the goal of such unity is just beyond their fingertips. Recent developments in bilateral conversations at global and regional levels, supported by converging movements in ecclesiological and sacramental theology, have narrowed the distance between Rome and Canterbury to an astonishing degree.

Episcopalians are not the only ones, however, who are sensitive to the problem raised by COCU with respect to the Roman Catholic Church. Many leaders of the other denominations have been deeply changed in their attitude toward Catholicism by the revolution in ecumenical relations effected by Pope John XXIII and Augustin Cardinal Bea, and carried onward by Pope Paul VI and Jan Cardinal Willebrands. So the following criticism of COCU is shared by many. It was written by a Methodist biblical scholar who became an Episcopalian, Professor John Knox.

> Only as we recover our identity as the Church in history can we be united; and this recovery involves what, for lack of a better term, we are calling a "return." But Anglicans and Protestants cannot make this "return" by by-passing the Roman Catholic Church. . . . We can make the "return" only as the Roman Church makes it, too, so that we make it together.

Then he admonishes the denominations not to abandon COCU,

> . . . for this might be tragic, but only that these denominations should severally refrain from committing themselves to any plan of actual union until the meaning and scope of the ecumenical movement within the Roman Catholic Church are more fully revealed.[3]

It is rather ironical, though, that some prominent Roman Catholic ecumenists are more positive and hopeful in their attitude toward COCU than certain Protestant critics. Although *A Plan of Union* anticipates a united church which will be "truly catholic," Catholic theologians who profess sympathy toward the Plan are not yet satisfied with certain formulations. The French-born theologian Father George Tavard, A.A., who has become a prominent American interpreter of ecumenism, expresses doubts about the adequacy of the Plan's treatment of doctrinal formulations, sacraments, and the ministry of priests and bishops.[4] Despite such doubts, which arise inevitably when the Plan is compared to prevailing Catholic doctrine, Father John T. Ford warns that the failure of COCU to win acceptance by its constituent denominations would mean an irreparable loss for ecumenism. Not for Protestants only, but for all churches, the Plan is an urgent matter. "At stake is the foreseeable ecumenical future of American Christianity." [5]

Clearly, the question is one of strategy and timing more than of substance. Since the Second Vatican Council the lines of convergence for Protestant and Catholic churches have become increasingly evident. The hope for *some form* of integral unity cannot any longer be regarded as illusory or futile. But when? How long would it take to effect, through the most complicated processes of negotiation, such a unity? Should the Protestant denominations mark time, as Knox recommends, until the option of a "return" to the Catholic and Apostolic Church becomes real and imminent? Or will this larger unity be better served by the churches of COCU taking the great step toward union among themselves?

Relationships with churches of Eastern Orthodoxy are quite different for the COCU participants than those with the Roman Catholic Church. Yet Orthodoxy must be kept within the field of vision of Protestants who seek greater unity, whatever the attitude of the Orthodox may be to them.

Still more pressing are the claims of various other Protestant denominations upon COCU, claims made simply by their existence, not by their protestations of desire for unity. Neither Baptists nor Lutherans nor Pentecostals nor other evangelical bodies are among the COCU members. It is their choice, not COCU's, which keeps them out, however friendly their relationships may be. Therefore, as elements of so-called "mainstream Protestantism," the denominations of COCU are caught in tensions existing between the Catholic and the Evangelical extremes. They could be kept in a static, neutral position indefinitely, while rapprochement and unity were being sought in both directions. But it is highly questionable whether such a position could be long maintained before the still too fragile structure of COCU would collapse for lack of movement toward union.

It is unnecessary for critics to keep reminding the COCU advocates of the danger of remaining narrowly Protestant. The Plan speaks very clearly to this issue (*A Plan of Union*, II, 19, p. 12; V, 13, pp. 27–28; IX, 1–10, pp. 73–74), as does the name which has been tentatively proposed for the united church, the Church of Christ *Uniting*.

(5) *Nationalism*. A comment sometimes made by opponents of COCU is that such a united church in America will undoubtedly foster the spirit of nationalism. They indicate the present increase of the isolationist mentality in this country. It is a reaction of undeniable strength and scope against the quarter-century of American aid, involvement, and military adventure throughout the world. And they point to developments in certain countries of Asia and Africa especially, where in recent years there seems to be a coincidence in Christian thinking of both nationalistic spirit and desire for church union. Therefore, it is argued, unions such as

COCU represents should be defeated; and the international and supra-national relations, both denominational and broadly ecumenical, should be strengthened and animated.

Since this kind of accusation refers to what might be rather than what is, there is no way to demonstrate beyond further doubt whether it is valid or invalid as a point against COCU. Certain comments are in order, however. And the first is that the protagonists of the Plan would agree with the critics in deploring the rise of a nationalistic church. Used in contrast to patriotism, the mood of excessive nationalism is already too widely extended in many denominations. It threatens to transmute Christian faith into civil religion, equate discipleship with citizenship, and render the churches quite impotent for prophetic witness and action. The question is not whether sanctified nationalism is bad, but whether it is likely to be a concomitant of church union. And that is very doubtful, for these four reasons.

(a) We live in a time of such extensive political, economic, and cultural interdependence of all nations that narrow nationalism is an anachronism.

(b) The fact that Christians in the new nations of Africa and Asia have disengaged themselves from ecclesiastical colonialism, enabling their churches to become autonomous and their practices indigenous, does not necessarily mean they are seeking church union within their lands because of nationalism. They take pride in their new status of nationhood, to be sure; and as Christians they want to show that the churches are not beholden to foreign authorities.

(c) When established churches of past generations and centuries were erastian and otherwise unduly nationalistic, their attitudes were due in part to their insularity and to lack of communication and regular contact with churches of other lands. All that has changed completely today. The World Council of Churches, the organizations of denominational families, and the many international agencies for ecumenical cooperation on special causes have created a many-stranded network. Travel by jet plane has contributed to the proliferation of ecumenical conferences and consultations, as have other technological conveniences. For churches to return to former states of isolationism because of their nationalistic fervor is quite unthinkable.

(d) There is more than a suspicion, finally, that the efforts to discredit church union by evoking the specter of nationalism are motivated by the desire to promote international denominationalism at the expense of Christian unity in particular countries or regions. Such motivation may derive from sincere conviction and theological reasoning. But those who place denominational or confessional loyalty above the need for visible

Christian unity in the places where people live are kicking against the main trend of ecumenical theologizing on the nature of unity.

In summary at this halfway mark of the chapter, then, the following assertion can be made. Supporters of *A Plan of Union* do not under any circumstances want or expect a united church which is characterized by monolithicity, uniformity, centralism, narrow Protestantism, and nationalism. Such criticisms arouse anger and cause confusion; as such, they are effective for combating the trend of church union. But it is doubtful in the extreme whether they have any basis in fact or in sound theological reflection. Moreover, they have been anticipated by the COCU participants and fended off by paragraphs in the Plan itself.

III

There is strange irony in the fact that a singular virtue of COCU may prove to be its point of greatest vulnerability.

It is to COCU's credit that three of the nine denominations participating in it are predominantly of Negro, or black, membership. In none of the several dozen union schemes presently under consideration in the world can there be found so large a proportion of black Christians in relation to whites and others. Given the political and social circumstances of the United States in the decade during which COCU has developed, the involvement of the three denominations, as well as the many black Christians in other churches, is both remarkable and commendable.

With respect to polity and tradition, most of the black Christians represented are Methodists. Their questions put to COCU on matters of doctrine, ministry, and organization are not very different from others. Singular, pertinent, and provocative, however, is their clutch of questions about white racism.

With cognizance and due notice of certain recent changes in the attitudes and practices of the predominantly white denominations, it is asked of them by black people whether there can be any confidence that fully nondiscriminatory equality may be expected for all members of the united church. Certainly the present condition of the mainly white denominations is insufficiently reassuring.

The COCU Plan makes some efforts to take account of this deep-rooted problem. In many contexts, wherever safeguards against racism are pertinent, professions of equality and nondiscrimination are made (*A Plan of Union*, V, 16, p. 28). Promises are made that positions of church leadership will be open to black members. And in one paragraph (*A Plan of Union*, II, 17, pp. 11–12), as though employing a euphemism for "reparations" to oppressed people and their descendants, it is declared that provision will be made "for the compensatory treatment of those who have been excluded in the past."

By themselves, written promises in the Plan are not of sufficient power to persuade skeptical black Christians that the union will prove to be in their best interests, which means also in the church's best interests. More significant will be the actions and policies which reflect the attitudes and ideas of the white Christians, insofar as these come to reveal the diminution and disappearance of prejudice.

I V

Chapter V of A Plan of Union designates and describes the bases, formulations, and some of the content of the doctrines of faith which will be constitutive of the united church. It is the work of theologians of the several denominations, who spent long hours and days in discussing and drafting this most debatable material. In the past years, churches have divided and new schisms have occurred because of theological disputations. Now the COCU delegates have endeavored to specify the theological grounds on which these ancient divisions can be overcome.

The more concern people show about something, the more vehement their reactions to those with whom they disagree. Christian faith is a matter of ultimate concern. Therefore, the criticisms of this chapter have been as vigorous as they are mutually contradictory.

Exponents of modern critical and radical theology find the chapter archaic, traditionalist, and thus irrelevant.

The two Presbyterian bodies in COCU are the only confessional churches of the nine, in the sense that they formally adhere to the great Westminster Confession and are accustomed to a doctrinal system informed by Calvinism. Some of them have joined the friendly observers belonging to the Lutheran and Roman Catholic churches, expressing dismay over the Plan's imprecision, eclecticism, and inconsistency of doctrine.

Contrariwise, some Episcopalians say of A Plan of Union that it is too much inclined toward a united church which assumes a confessional stance; this would be a disagreeable to Anglicans, who profess the "faith once delivered to the saints" but do not like to have it too precisely formulated.

The Christian Church (Disciples of Christ) is not readily accommodated by the chapter because it embraces so many creeds and confessions of faith—against all of which the Disciples have long contended, calling them human inventions, not scriptural truth. And the Disciples have supporters among people of liberal theology in all the nine denominations.

It has never been easy for divided churches, even with the most positive and charitable intentions, to arrive at doctrinal definitions which are satisfying to all. In America today, during the time of the break-up of old formulations and the consequent confusion and obscurity of theology, this difficulty is aggravated. But when all things—really *all*—are considered, it is hard to see how any such diversified group of denominational representatives could have produced a statement on faith superior to this one. It proclaims a trinitarian witness to God, acknowledges the unique and normative authority of Holy Scripture, gives due recognition to the authority and influence of Tradition and traditions, accepts the Apostles' and Nicene creeds as the classic expressions of faith, respects and intends to use a variety of other creeds and confessions, encourages the articulation of the Gospel in contemporary language, and promises to express this faith through liturgy and witness in the world. And it says all this in less than five pages! These elements of the chapter are clearly recognized as including explicitly or implicitly the essentials of Christian faith. And yet they are presented in such a way as to allow at least as much latitude of belief and interpretation as presently obtains in each of the denominations by itself. Can more be expected at this stage of the move toward union?

V

The nearer the time comes when a definite position respecting the Plan must be taken by the denominations, the more vigorously will the proposed structure and polity be challenged. These matters affect immediately the daily life of the constituent churches; they are the issues about which most members become aroused.

COCU has presupposed the truth of an insight often expressed in the ecumenical movement—namely, that a united church must include elements of three types of polity: congregational, presbyteral, and episcopal. The Plan reflects this admixture. And because it does, the persons who adhere most tightly to each of the three are most critical of the effort to comprehend and blend them.

The strongest advocates of congregational autonomy are members of the Christian Church (Disciples of Christ) and the United Church of Christ. The latter includes most of the churches once known as Congregational-Christian, which joined the Evangelical and Reformed Church in 1957 to form the present denomination. Many Congregationalists have still not reconciled their minds to accepting the presbyteral type of polity in this body; and they feel all the more resentment toward the draft COCU plan, which introduces the further element of episcopacy. In spite of the care taken by COCU to provide for the decentralizing of governance, as already indicated above, the Plan is hardly to be considered consistent with historic Congregationalism.

The local unit of the united church, for example, is not the congregation as such, but the parish. And the parish is a cluster of smaller congregations and task-oriented communities. Whatever benefits may be foreseen in this parish model, it clearly represents a break away from the practice of local autonomy. Parishes would in turn be subject to the direction of district councils, presided over by bishops; and districts would be subject to regional councils; and the regions to the national assembly. On paper, this is seen to be a plain structure of top-to-bottom hierarchical control, or if not literally hierarchical, at least a descending order of church councils and courts.

A decisive indication of the break from congregational autonomy is the provision made for the ownership of church property. Following a transitional period, during which existing policies regarding title would be maintained, the parish would become the owner of local property; but all property would be held for the benefit of the whole church, meaning that ultimately, in the event of the dissolution of a parish, the district would become the legal owner (See A Plan of Union, VIII, 34, p. 61; X, 48, p. 80).

In spite of this proposal regarding structure and ownership, it seems to many Methodists to be "a sell-out to Congregationalism." Such, indeed, has been the expressed criticism! There are two main reasons for this remarkable objection: property ownership and the appointing of parish ministers.

In the United Methodist Church, for example, all property is owned ultimately by the whole denomination, and held in trust for it by boards of trustees at various structural levels. This is believed to be an essential condition of the so-called connectional system of the church.

Connectionalism also is believed to require what has been known for two centuries as the itinerant ministry. While this summons up romantic memories of preachers on horseback, moving about their circuits, it means literally today the appointment system. The Methodist bishop, acting in consultation with district superintendents and committees of local churches, has the final authority to place ministers in local churches or special appointments as well as to remove them. In contrast to this exercise of episcopal authority, the calling or "settling" of parish ministers in the Episcopal Church is a purely congregational matter.

Logic permits no hope for a reconciling of the strictly congregational and connectional systems of church governance in a manner satisfactory to all parties. Adamant adherents of either system might seem to have only two choices: either to contend vigorously within COCU for the writing of a polity which is essentially like their own; or else to reject and oppose the Plan altogether. A third alternative, however, would mean forfeiting their intransigency in favor of flexibility.

With respect to the settlement of ministers, the Plan does propose a method which presumes to conserve both congregational and episcopal authority. It makes *time* the variable. Unless a parish committee could agree on, and secure, a minister within six months of the time the place fell vacant, the bishop would appoint a minister. But this appointment would still be subject to conditions affecting his permanency. It is not yet known, however, whether this proposal can win the support of the four Methodist denominations. And there is evidence that it is being severely criticized. As Bishop John Wesley Lord declared, the appointment system "is believed by many to represent the genius of the United Methodist system which must be protected at all costs." [6] Do "all costs" include final rejection of church union?

In the presence of this seeming impasse between the congregational and connectional polities, it would be premature and foolhardy to suggest a facile solution. Also, it would scarcely be convincing to the antagonists to claim that the proposed Plan is right and they are wrong. Obviously, a good deal more study, discussion, and negotiation are needed: and also, more significantly, some experimentation with practices consonant with those suggested in the draft plan. Since neither side really believes its position to be *de fide*, or known through divine revelation, the pragmatic tests of authentic communal life, effective mission at local and national levels, and faithful stewardship of personal and material resources must be applied.

The relative reticence of Presbyterian critics with respect to these issues of polity would seem to indicate their general satisfaction with *A Plan of Union*—despite the lingering hostility toward bishops which is derived mainly from memories of ancestral strife in Scotland and England.

There are Episcopalians, however, who are decidedly dissatisfied with the Plan's stated concept of episcopacy and with certain aspects of the discussion of ordination. Without opening up the whole box of disputes and polemics affecting the doctrine of ministry and episcopacy, we can fix upon two contested features of the Plan: the place of the laity in ordinations, and the recognition of Methodist bishops.

"In all ordination rites, including particularly the laying-on of hands, representatives of all offices and orders of ordained ministry in the church and *representatives of the laity* shall participate. This participation signifies that ordination is an act of the whole church" (*A Plan of Union*, VII, 33, pp. 44–45, italics added). A colloquium of theologians representing varieties of Anglican perspective agreed in 1971 that the problem of lay laying on of hands is likely to be insuperable in the consideration of the Plan by the Episcopal Church. This is not because Episcopalians demean the laity. They cite with approval the practice of Eastern Orthodox churches in having the laity participate in the selecting and affirming of priests and bishops. But laying hands on the heads of ordinands is, in their view, a matter of order. In theory, at least, all members of the church accept the ordained ministry, and particular candidates, as gifts of God; but in both theory and practice, only bishops ordain. (Whether Episcopalians would likewise object to the laying on of hands by presbyters and deacons is less clear.) To be sure, the Plan does not state that laymen ordain, but their participation is intended to signify the corporate role of the whole church.

The difficulty for many Episcopalians with respect to the nature—as distinct from function—of the episcopacy is just as formidable. The acceptance of the threefold ministry of "presbyters, bishops, and deacons" by COCU was due to the positive estimate of this historic pattern on the part of delegates from all denominations; they recognized, too, that it was a *sine qua non* for the Episcopal Church's participation. Then quite rightly they wrote into the draft plan the provision that "accepting and maintaining the historic episcopate . . . neither implies, excludes, nor requires any theory or doctrine of the episcopate which goes beyond what is stated in this plan" (*A Plan of Union*, VII, 57, p. 49). Up to this point they were following precedents well tested in other union schemes of the past fifty years in which Anglicans have been involved.

In only two plans of union other than COCU's has it been necessary to make a choice about the unification of Anglican and Methodist episcopates. In only one has it been achieved. This was the union which brought the Church of Pakistan into being in 1970. It might have happened in the same way in North India, had not the Methodists withdrawn awkwardly at the last minute. In all other unions involving Anglicans and Methodists, as in South India or Ceylon or even the proposal in England, the Methodist churches have been without bishops. Methodist bishops were invented in 1784 in the United States.

Episcopalians understandably raise a major question about the nature of the Methodist episcopate. (The function is another matter.) Do the Methodist bishops claim to stand in the historic succession? No. Do they claim to belong to a third order of ministry, apart from presbyters and deacons? No. Then are they bishops? Yes. But what kind of bishops?

The proposed service of inauguration of the united church involves the unification of the ministries by mutual recognition and by prayer. In the prayer they acknowledge before God the limitations set upon the ministries because of past divisions, and they petition God to unite the ministries according to his will. In this most critical action, no distinctions are drawn among the three orders. There is a symbolic act of the laying

on of hands *in silence* by all participating ministers. Then all the people
together declare their acceptance of these presbyters, bishops, and deacons as their ministers (*A Plan of Union*, Appendix I, 37–41, pp. 88–89).
Thus, in accordance with VII, (60) of the draft plan, "All who are bishops
in the uniting churches will be bishops in the united church after the
service of inauguration."

Some would say that Episcopalians are here being asked to do what
they might in turn ask Roman Catholics and Orthodox to do: namely, to
leap past certain circumstances of past history which call episcopal continuity into question and to achieve unity through recognizing that God
wills the divided churches and their ministries to be one. The same, in
effect, is what many Episcopalians are prepared to do in the COCU
Plan with respect to the ordained presbyters. If these can be recognized
without "re-ordinations"—a much used word which is logically and theologically impossible—cannot Methodist bishops be recognized without
"re-consecration"? This question relates directly to the earlier criticism of
COCU as constituting an impediment to closer unity with the Roman
Catholic and Orthodox churches. But no resolution of the difficulty can
be suggested that is without its anomalies. None can be theologically
defended except in terms of the doctrine of "economy" or special dispen-
sation.

VI

The criticisms so far discussed are not the only ones which have been
launched against the Plan, of course. Some have pointed out that the
Plan reflects in too much detail the passing concerns of the period 1969–
1970, and that it will soon be dated. True enough—which is why amendments and modifications must be written in response to criticisms.

More damaging—indeed, shattering for some minds—is the charge that
the whole enterprise of church union is now obsolete. Prophets of the
day, whether clinical or gloomy or both, declare that the crisis of the
churches and of Christian faith itself is now so acute that the survival
of Christianity has displaced the survival of denominationalism as the
commanding concern. Who cares about denominations anyway? And
who cares about the church in modern society? In response, it must be
said that the persons responsible for COCU are not at all oblivious to
the present crisis. Nor are they blind to the urgency of using Christians'
resources for the struggle to attain justice, peace, and human values in
society. Nor are they driven to despair by the warnings of a suddenly
apocalyptic, or slowly pathological, demise of the churches.

A favorite way of detracting interest from COCU is to insist that church
renewal (spiritual or human renewal may sound better) is more urgently

needed than union. This implies inevitably that we are faced with a choice of renewal or union, but cannot have both. It is an illogical implication as well as a false choice. The same mode of detraction used to be employed by those who declared that Christians want spiritual unity rather than organic union, or again by those who pitted mission against unity.

It is the earnest and avowed intention of the advocates of COCU that union, rennewal, and mission are all indispensable, and that none of the three must be purchased at the expense of the other two. Moreover, there are many who argue that it is precisely the lack of sufficiently wide and authentic unity which now inhibits mission and keeps the churches closed to the renewing impulses of the Spirit.

The coming united church must not be a mere amalgam of the denominations as we now know them. It must be the communal expression of the perennial power of Jesus Christ, with the new concepts and forms appropriate to the time.

The ecumenical movement has shown, and recent experiences have verified, that we cannot return to the denominationalism of the previous decades and before. Nor does the present condition of the churches give us much assurance that the present form of denominationalism is satisfactory for the realizing of renewal and effectual mission. In effect, the participating denominations in COCU have committed themselves irretrievably to some new form of unity. They have reached the point of no return; they cannot go backward in time, nor stand still. Can there be a new, acceptable, and desirable form of unity which is entirely different from the Plan of COCU? Possibly. But it will have to be proved both by valid criticism and by imaginative planning that an alternate scheme will enable the churches to fulfill their calling to mission and service more faithfully than by the way of union.

NOTES

1. John McQuarrie, ed., *Realistic Reflections on Church Union* (Albany, N.Y.: Argus Greenwood, Inc. 1967), p. 37.
2. "United Methodism, COCU, and the Future Church," *Christian Advocate*, Vol. XV, No. 3 (February 4, 1971), p. 8.
3. *Realistic Reflections on Church Union, op. cit.*, pp. 27–29.
4. See "A Catholic Perspective," in *COCU: A Catholic Perspective* (Washington: USCC Publications Office, 1970), p. 35.
5. "The COCU Plan of Union and Catholicity," *The Christian Century*, Vol. LXXXVIII, No. 42 (October 20, 1971), p. 1229.
6. "COCU Plan Would Change Methodist Appointive System," *Christian Advocate*, Vol. XV, No. 3 (February 4, 1971), p. 12.

12

Councils, Consortia, and COCU

STEPHEN C. ROSE

This brief essay sees COCU, fundamentally, more as creative process than fixed plan, more as a notion of church union, mission, and renewal than as the superchurch model so dear to her detractors. Seen as process, COCU differs from councils and consortia, for these latter already exist institutionally as ecumenical programs. COCU exists as a "faith and order" process. This essay will argue that COCU can be seen as a significant breakthrough, mediating between what could be called "the new ecumenism" and the ecumenical impasses revealed by analysis of Protestant-Orthodox councils and consortia. Space limitations permit no more than an outline of an argument that would require considerably more fleshing-out to stand up against critical scruitiny.

I

There are two general meanings of council within the church. The first may be called *authoritative councils*. These councils—convened by the early church and sporadically through the years by the Roman Catholic Church—were decision-making bodies of limited duration endowed with a considerable degree of authority, seeking solutions to pressing theological-ecclesiological problems. In general terms, the *authoritative council* is one which defines "faith and order" issues in order to enable the church to exist faithfully during her time in history.

The second sort of council rose up more recently and now exists as one—perhaps the main—Protestant-Orthodox approach to ecumenism. These are the *non-authoritative councils* which exist at one removal from the autonomous denominations which compose their membership. They have no direct congregational constituency. They developed primarily under the influence of mission-oriented Protestanism as cooperative vehicles for programming. There is a sense in which non-authoritative councils become, potentially, barriers to church union. Since they are federations of autonomous churches, they give the implicit impression that ecumensim has more to do with the cooperation of existing bodies than with a process by which these bodies might more fully manifest their unity, particularly on the local level. Example: researched by Booz, Allen, and Hamilton found that constituent churches of the National Council of Churches wished the council would play a greater role in "faith and order" discussions; by and large the NCC has shied away from any such function.

It can be argued that all churches need, from time to time, an authoritative conciliar process as a means of *aggiornamento*. Within separated churches different polities provide varying possibilities that such processes can emerge internally. Thus the United Presbyterian Church produced a new Confession during the 1960s. The central contention of this essay is that *the principal barrier to ecumenical advance has been the absence of an authoritative conciliar process interdenominationally.* Protestant-Orthodox councils have been unable to provide a bridge from denominational autonomy to church union. There has, by and large, been no "faith and order" process rising from Protestant-Orthodox councils that can move beyond the contradiction rising from the non-authoritative nature of such councils. Hence one gets at conciliar meetings the aura of an ecumenical charade, and looks more to the legislative assemblies of autonomous churches (or to Vatican II) for examples of authoritative conciliar action.

II

The failure of the churches to come to grips with their own need for *aggiornamento* is partly responsible for what might be called "the new ecumenism." During the 1960s, acknowledging both the intransigence of autonomous churches and the beginnings of stultification within the conciliar movement, the World Council of Churches defined ecumenism anew with the phrase "all in each place." Here emerged (non-authoritatively, to be sure!) a suggestion that ecumenism could no longer be seen exclusively in terms of existing church institutions, it had to extend to the whole inhabited earth. A corollary implication: present denominational and ecumenical structures should not inhibit a spontaneous, pluralist ecumenism from arising among "all . . . in each place." To some extent this was merely an acknowledgment of a new reality which was expressing itself in myriad ways:

> Intercommunion in Southern prison cells;
> Random clusters of churches locally;

Jesus communes;
Confrontations between secular prophets and church establishments;
Evangelical interest in social justice;
Liberal Christian longing for personal, evangelical depth;
A general longing for "renewal" and "revival"; etc.

Confronted with this "new ecumenism", there has been a twofold response in the churches. Some have interpreted it as the "shaking up" which is the prelude to the healing of the church's divisions and to the renewal of Christian life and mission. Others have reacted negatively, believing that most of the "new ecumenism" is merely the capitulation of the church to the world. Thus we witness, on one hand, denominational resurgence and loss of interest in past forms of ecumenism. And, on the other hand, we see the alienation of "new ecumenists" from the churches. It is precisely this situation that underlines the need for an authoritative conciliar process to enable the churches to move creatively during the present time. What has just been described—this twofold response to current developments—may well be no more than a playing-out-to-the-end of the tragic liberal-evangelical split which, with racism, is really the principal dividing factor within the American church. An authoritative conciliar process would be charged with determining how the churches, in all their dividedness, can come together, how they can participate jointly in their common self-discovery, how they can heal the wounds of racism, faithlessness, and parochialism that show like stigmata on their separated bodies.

One interpretation would argue that we should not hesitate to let yet another liberal-conservative, modernist-fundamentalist, social-activist—evangelical split rend existing denominations and ultimately create a new conservative-radical realignment similar to that which rose in the wake of the abolitionist movement. Such an argument could be sustained by Marxist logic, not to mention the self-preservation instinct.

The hope of this essay is that such a split would *not* be perpetuated, that an authoritative conciliar process might have the effect of moving beyond the false dialectics of liberalism and conservatism to create a church both evangelical and service-oriented. Despite the reality of denominational resurgence today, who can miss the possibility that the Spirit is leading each denomination through the crucible of its own past dividedness, to be sure, but also toward the vision of how a more valid church might be developed in the future, a church combining compassion and contemplation, biblical preaching and social out-reaching, Christ-centered theology with a universal concern for the whole human being? Who honestly wishes a perpetuation of vapid liberalism or tired, uncreative evangelicalism? Who wishes to cede all religious initiative to expressions of the new ecumenism that are rising in profusion beyond the institutional churches? A valid conciliar process cannot usurp the Spirit in the work of moving the churches in the way that God intends, but if, as Christians, we are obliged to seek the marks of the Spirit's work, we may tentatively locate them in the effort to create a new church that seeks to overcome old contradictions and divisions. Clearly, though not without reservations, the author sees COCU as one expression of an authoritative conciliar process operating interdenominationally with openness to the Spirit and genuine concern to heal the wounded body of Christ in this prideful and problematic nation. It is authoritative because it is no more than what the churches freely embody of it in their own lives. It is a vehicle for the promulgation of developing principles of church union, renewal, and mission and is potentially a bridge between denominational autonomy and church union, between a truncated Establishment ecumenism manifested in the non-authoritative conciliar movement and the new ecumenism of "all in each place." For COCU is not one institution pitted against others. It is a process to which separate churches have committed themselves. It cannot coerce—that is the province of power. It *can* pool wisdom and enhance vision—that is one province of authority.

It can be argued—and has been—that the involvement of but nine denominations in COCU is evidence of its limitation as a manifestation of ecumenism. This viewpoint neglects the fact that three central traditions within Protestantism—free church. episcopal, and reformed—*are* represented in COCU. It has also been observed that COCU is not international, that it suggests the formation of a national church. This is surely not an objection that councils of churches in the U.S. could make without first examining themselves. It is indeed true that a Church of Christ *Uniting* (the very name implies the unfinished character of the potential institution) would have little international significance if it were marketed abroad as a U.S. product. But, as a process, COCU deserves study internationally because it offers an alternative to the stalled "faith and order" processes of the World Council of Churches and of other national and regional councils. If the imperialism of the Christian church is to be rooted out, there needs to be a growth of autonomy among colonized churches, but also there must be a struggle to convert the consciousness of the oppressive church. COCU as a process is neutral and could be adapted to many situations. But it is worth noting that COCU in the United States represents one of the few arenas in which questions of faith and order must be considered specifically in relation to the problem of the past racism of white Christians and the current ambivalence of the black community toward white-inspired notions of integration. It can be argued that racism and the mutually debilitating split between evangelicalism and liberalism are the principal thorns in the flesh of American Protestantism. Whether or not COCU is able to provide a process by which these issues can be partly resolved is immaterial to the thesis that COCU is a valid, authoritative conciliar endeavor. But if COCU were the matrix within which these problems were creatively dealt with, who could doubt that the Spirit himself was working through this particular form of ecumenism? These lines are written in painful awareness that articulate black churchmen have scored COCU as "white folks' business." The injunction, however, that the church be one is not black, white, or red—it is biblical. If black churches should withdraw from COCU, it would seem less a signal to disband than a warning that the process of attaining oneness has far to go, and a specific rejoinder against the formation of a racist church.

To summarize to this point: COCU represents an authoritative conciliar process on the Protestant ecumenical scene, dealing with "faith and order" issues and forwarding a process of participatory ecumenism that integrates the institutional churches involved with the new ecumenism of "all in each place." By refining principles of union, renewal, and mission, and by inaugurating a plan of union that will involve the church in each place in common conversation, COCU—institutionally a weakling —exhibits authority evidenced by the free response of divided churches to its prayer and vision.

III

Both non-authoritative councils of churches and, to a lesser extent, consortia reveal the ecumenical impasses afflicting Protestantism. The impasse created by councils has already been described. Very simply, the councils can exist only by the implicit assumption that church disunity is normative, and they encourage denominations to feel they are being more ecumenical than they are. But, before suggesting how such councils might relate to ecumenism in the future, let us deal with the question of consortia. For purposes of this essay, consortia may be defined as ad hoc, nonconciliar, non-ecclesiological forms of cooperation between church bureaucracies. This distinguishes consortia from the new ecumenism because consortia relate to already existing church bodies. It could be argued that consortia are one of a number of structural phenomena that have emerged from the failure of churches and councils to produce adequate forms of ecumenism. From the church side, councils have been inadequate. From the councils' side, churches have not entrusted them with sufficient ecumenical responsibility. In the author's view, the culpability is mutual.

To speak of consortia as an ecumenical way forward raises the question of whether, and on what basis, the church should be a program agency, a distributor of funds, a philanthropist, a world-shaped bureaucracy, a fighter of battles in the secular realm. Some consortia are nothing more than marriages of convenience between existing bureaucracies, producing cooperatively various educational and service resources. Others exist more particularly as conduits for church funds, most aimed at extending the churches' social mission. A good example would be the Interreligious Foundation for Community Organization (IFCO), which seeks to serve as a broker between the churches and oppressed Americans. If one concedes that the ecclesial positions of both councils (as presently constituted) and consortia are tenuous at best, then the only question is whether, as program agencies, they function well by some agreed standard. But if one is concerned about ecumenism within the whole spectrum of organizations that call themselves churches, one must not drop the ecclesial question prematurely. The ecumenical movement has had few hesitations about committing the churches to social positions and defining the church as a program agency. But the churches—particularly the local churches—have been less and less willing to be "represented" in such a fashion. Perhaps the most practical legacy of the uncreative split between evangelicalism and liberalism is the question: should the church be involved in politics, or should politics not be left to the individual church member, the layman? This question masks the issue, however, for logically it stands to reason that the political wisdom of a council or consortium or church does not depend upon the size of the decision-making organization. Thus the individual lay person who is involved in politics stands as much chance of being wrong—if judgments are to be made—as a consortium or council does. The real question has to do with *process*. It is not *who* speaks for the church but, rather, *how* the church speaks! If councils and consortia do not in fact represent the bulk of the church members, this is just as important, ecumenically, as the possibility that the World Council of Churches may know more about Africa than a congregation in Iowa does. And it is just as important to ecumenism to resolve this issue of process as to reach firmer clarity on the nature of ethical decision-making among Christians. There is no simple answer. That the church should minister to the blind, the lame, the captive is hardly in doubt. What is needed is a process by which these concerns, and others, will not become so politicized as to make immanents of transcendents, to confuse allegiance to a secular cause with heresy, on one hand, or faithfulness, on the other. Both liberal and evangelical churches are at fault here. Both would profit from involvement in an authoritative conciliar process.

Without attempting to resolve this seemingly insoluble dilemma—this problem of Christian identity and worldly identification—let me suggest

that the terms *ministry of the laity* and *decentralization-participation*
suggest fruitful directions for the ecumenical-minded. *Ministry of the
laity* suggests that, no matter how collective the church's program decisions are, or whether we speak of individual or group witness, it is the
laity who should be at the forefront in dealing with secular issues. Not
only this—their involvement should be in non-ecclesial "task forces" such
as envisioned in the COCU Plan: a practical resolution to Troeltch's
debilitating distinction between the sect and church. Conversely, in
breaking the patently clear domination of the church by ordained clergy,
bishops, and church bureaucrats, we must restore the ordained to their
proper function. *Decentralization-participation* suggests a process by
which church establishments can begin to take seriously the idea of
ecumenism as "all in each place." Such a process would insure in the
future greater communication between the levels of the church and
emphasis on the possibility that leadership is not confined to any particular
level—it may emerge from central Iowa just as it might emerge from
Geneva, Switzerland. One need not berate the witness of the upper
bureaucracies of the churches, for it is often in accord with solid biblical
theology. What is being criticized here is the process of evasion that takes
place when a liberal bureaucracy refuses to engage in solid theological
and personal reasoning with its local constituency.

Consortia at the national level tend to take issues like lay ministry and
decentralization-participation with some seriousness. Insofar as both
councils and consortia can assist in developing processes of participation,
decentralization, the enhancement of lay ministry, and ties between
churches and the new ecumenism, it may be that they will move us toward the goal of church renewal which is the vision of authentic ecumenism. It is precisely because the COCU *Plan of Union* embodies such
concerns that it warrants support.

How then should councils, consortia, and COCU relate? A provisional
answer: COCU is an interchurch "faith and order" process which offers
American Protestants a participatory forum for moving from one stage
of ecumenism to another—from the non-authoritative conciliar stage to
the "all in each place" stage. (In my view, it is this "all in each place"
stage which offers the most promising prospect of healing the great divisions within the church—those between Orthodoxy, Rome, and Protestantism. Thus the current talk of bringing Rome into the councils seems
to me far more related to conciliar self-preservation and sociological factors than to viable ecclesiology. It would, indeed, be more logical and
less confusing to invite the Roman Catholic Church to enter, in some
form or fashion, the COCU discussions and other discussions where
existing churches are exploring mutual possibilities under the rubric of
"all in each place.") From this it would appear that councils ought either

to aspire to a COCU-like role, moving from tentative to authoritative work in the realm of faith and order and supporting COCU, or to join with consortia in becoming experimental task forces, new voluntaristic forms of church mission—of the ministry of the laity. One or the other. Possibly both. But not the current amalgam of purposeless self-survival, punctuated with imaginative programming and courageous action, to be sure, but in this sense more sectarian than the churches, because unwilling or unable to see that ecumenism must somehow mean the healing of animosities within each church as well as among churches.

Finally, having sought to put forth COCU as the institutional mode of a move toward new ecumenism—as an authoritative conciliar process— it would only be honest to share some existential problems that I feel about the whole enterprise of dealing with current church structures in terms like relating COCU, councils, and consortia. So deeply in myself do I feel my own lack of faith, my own sense of directionlessness, and my own sense that somehow prayer, meditation, and individual action may be the only way I can even claim with integrity to be nominally Christian—that I would willingly bury this and all other past efforts to nudge structures, renew the church, stimulate action, if there could be but one common experience of grace for me, and for others, that would remind us all of the life and freedom and love and justice that is the precious pearl offered, I believe, by the Holy Spirit. Thus existentially my allegiance to COCU has hardly a thing to do with fine structural thoughts. It is simply a forum that I have felt a part of and where I thought processes of revival were operative. I have felt the same in congregations that harbor their old people and "straight laymen and women" and harried clergy, where nonetheless there is the glimmer of life and some of the very social concern that is thought to exist only in movements outside the church or in the upper bureaucracies. But I have also felt this possibility of the Spirit within the denominations, even in their solemn assemblies. And so I feel almost like thrusting aside the argument and simply affirming all that is happening as the possible prelude to the revival—a late awakening—that may well shatter our familiar structures and create, not a peaceful new world, not an easy future, but at least the possibility of an ecumenism that is broader and deeper and more prayerful than what I have known ecumenism to be in the past.

13

Church Organizational Behavior and Ecumenical Possibilities

ROBERT C. WORLEY

If one could stand in a position to view Protestant church organizations, the scene might look as follows: profound distrust and alienation between all levels of church organizations—national boards and program agencies, theological seminaries, middle-level judicatories (districts, conferences, synods, or presbyteries), and congregations. Within church organizations at each level the same conditions exist. The degree of distrust and alienation varies from organization to organization, but these same basic conditions provide the dominant climate for most church organizations. Delightful exceptions are difficult to find. The political, historical, and theological bases of such alienation and distrust are rarely dealt with in overt, constructive ways, thus creating the conditions for further alienation and distrust.

Churchmen and churchwomen have not paid sufficient attention to these conditions in church organizations. In fact, we have tended to run from conflict, differences, turbulence in church organizations. We look to extraterrestrial forces for the significant intervention to clean up the mess we have made, or we pretend, through theological rationalization, that what we currently experience is really God's creation rather than our own. The argument has the following components: Church people are Christians. They use Christian language. Because they are Christians and they use religious language, the Church will be Christian.

Through such reasoning church people are never encouraged to look at

The studies from which the conclusions presented in this paper are made were funded by the Department of Educational Development, the National Council of Churches. Gratitude is expressed particularly to Eli Wismer, the executive of that department.

their creation, a human church organization. The purpose of this essay is to sketch a way of viewing church organizations as human organizations subject to the judgment and direction of Christian faith. The future of the church, either as independent denominations or as something new, more effective, and more Christian, depends upon a better, more appropriate understanding of ourselves. The forces working against ecumenical Christendom are at work within denominations, promoting distrust and alienation. It is necessary to look at the key factors in church organizational life in order to understand the behavior of church organization today.

Goals and Church Organizational Behavior

Human beings are characteristically purposive in their behavior. The most important feature of man is the purpose or goal to which he will commit himself. To deny man the means to express commitment to the purposes or goals important to him is to deny that which is most important and which most significantly characterizes him, his goals. Man is his purposes or goals. These goals are expressive of his values, ideological and/or theological commitments. They reflect that which has "captured" him. It is superficial to note that there are different qualities and depths to these values and commitments. This is taken for granted. The important fact is that he acts as a person in church organizations to express these values and commitments. It is not even important to acknowledge whether we agree or disagree, even though we may, with these values and commitments which are expressed in his goals.

When we look at church organizations, we see men acting out their values and/or theological commitments in the goals they seek to achieve. The goals of men have multiple expressions. They can be seen in the personal goals of men as they act in church organizations. They are also readily seen in the personal goals of men for a particular church organization. Many laymen have a personal goal of experiencing Christian faith through particular hymns and a particular style of sermon. This personal goal is expressed in a goal for the organization as they work on worship committees to influence the selection of hymns and styles of sermon. It may be expressed also in their effort to have the congregation employ a minister who preaches as they desire, and selects hymns which match their personal faith and commitments. Ministers, laity, and young people have goals for themselves and for the organization as they participate.

The goals of persons must be seen in relation to the goals of the organization in which they participate. Organizational goals can be divided into three categories—order, economic, and ministry and mission goals. Order goals are those directed toward the maintenance of practices of faith and life in the organization. Economic goals are directed toward adequate financial support for the organization. Ministry and mission goals are directed toward the expression of Christian faith in witness and service both toward members of the organization and toward the world. The goals of persons and their personal goals for the organization are expressed in relation to the organization's goals. If personal goals and personal goals for the organization cannot be expressed through the organization's goals, apathy, frustration, alienative activity, and eventually removing oneself are the result. If there are differences in priority between personal goals and organizational goals, the same aberrative behavior can be seen. When a member is committed personally to mission and ministry goals and the organization's priority goal is order, controlling the life of the Church in traditional practices, conflict is inevitable.

Most church organzations are goal-oriented in that they have numerous goals related to worship, the budget, attendance at church services, youth, women, scouts, etc. These goals are usually implicit and unexamined. Priority among goals can be seen only by looking at the budget (how money is allotted), and at the use of time by clergy and laity. Few church organizations are goal-directed with goals and priority among goals clearly established and visible to all members.

The argument of this essay is that the most significant variables of any church organization are the goals and primary tasks toward those goals. The goals may be explicit or implicit, examined or unexamined, and competing and conflicting. In order to see the goals of any organization, budget allocations, use of time by staff and volunteers, agendas and minutes of committees, processes for incorporating persons into the church, processes for directing persons and other resources into different goal-task groups, and the messages and products made visible as output of a congregation should be examined. There are numerous goal-task areas of congregational life—i.e., Christian education, stewardship, community service, etc. These goal-task areas are in direct competition for resources with all other goal-task areas, and they exist always within some implicity or explicitly determined priority ranking. The perceived importance of each goal-task area determines the amount and kind of resources available.

A major factor influencing the ranking in any goal-task area is how well the activities of a particular area enable the congregation to cope with the internal and external challenges. Motivation and intensity and degree of involvement are increased in a congregation when goals are perceived as appropriate and necessary to persons in the organization. Appropriateness and necessity relate to environmental conditions. The more a goal helps the church organization gain control over uncertain features in its environment, the more appropriate and necessary it is.

The goal of effective youth ministry in a community where there is a drug problem in the high school or where groups of young people engage in vandalism of church property becomes appropriate and necessary in that environment. If goal attainment (effective youth ministry) is successful, then the congregation has gained a measure of control over its turbulent environment.

But the goal of effective youth ministry may be given a quite low ranking among goals. If this occurs, apathy and/or alienative involvement may occur by members who think this should be a priority goal. Non-achievement of the goal occurs. Effectiveness in achieving the various goals of church organization depends upon how these goals are perceived by the total organization and the implicit and/or explicit ranking of these goals among other goals.

The need for understanding the relation between personal goals, organizational goals, and the environment should be apparent (see Figure 1 for a schematic way of viewing these relationships).

In church organizations there are different constituent groups, each of which is more or less committed to achieving the goals of that part, and which may manifest antipathy to antagonism toward goals and leaders of other parts. It is easy to imagine the different goals and tasks embedded in different parts of an organization, and the differing populations which they serve—youth groups, Christian education, stewardship promotion, worship services, adult study groups. Parts are subjected to different degrees of stress from the populations they serve. Stewardship committees experience different stress than do youth-work committees from different groups of persons in the organization. Church organizations are biased toward responding selectively to different kinds of stress by different members and their professional leaders. Organizationally, stewardship committees and new-member committees may be facilitated in optimum ways while youth-work committees may be thwarted and prevented from adequate response.

Church professionals also suffer from the organizational dynamics related to achieving goals. The stress which the organization places upon church professionals and their relations to one another too frequently creates conditions which work counter to collegiality and successful goal attainment. Most parish organizations do not have the flexible structure and processes to facilitate multiple goals and tasks with different professional specialists related to these goals and tasks. Rather than organizational goals, most parishes have goals of different parts with their own budgets, constituent groups and professional specialists in competition (overtly and covertly) with other parts and the professional specialists of these parts.

The organizational requisites for effectiveness in goal attainment and

FIGURE 1

SUMMARY OF RELATIONS BETWEEN VARIABLES IN CHURCH ORGANIZATIONS

Organizational Assumptions	Goals or Purposes	Environment	Structure	Polity
God at work primarily in the church; organization not influenced by environment; sufficient resources internally for needs. Resist undersired influences from environment by sealing off.	Known, clear, simple	Stable	Rigid	Historical confessions of faith; traditional norms; historical precedent; written rules (constitutions, by-laws, manuals of policies and procedures); controlling climate to maintain stable internal life.
God at work in both church and world. Environment influences organization. Resources in environment needed to achieve organization's goals. Both negative and positive influences in the environment.	Unknown, multiple, complex, ambiguous, competing and conflicting, uncertainty about best means to achieve goals.	Turbulent. Diverse constituencies; insufficient knowledge of constituencies; changing coalitions which support different goals.	Flexible	New confessions of faith for present moment. Create conditions for coping more effectively through increased human communication; feedback mechanisms; planning; consensus-forming processes; political processes which mobilize persons and increase the size of the dominant coalition; leadership development; organizational development; team-building; sensitivity training.

collegial relations between professionals and groups of laity are common organizational goals, a flexible structure which facilitates appropriate and effective responses to stress in different parts of the organization, and communication and decision-making processes which maintain commitment toward multiple and diverse common organizational goals. These are almost self-evident characteristics of collegial organizations, but there are few church organizations which have developed collaborative strategies not only among pastors but also among different goal-oriented groups.

The confusion and tension in church organizations is due primarily to the multiple and diverse goals of an organization and the inability organizationally to respond to persons and the environment which built this dynamic relation into the organization. Personal goals and goals for the organization and the needs which environment builds into an organization are never dealt with adequately. Consequently, there is always tension building around the most significant aspects of man, his goals, and the multiple demands of a changing environment. The ways in which persons, their goals, and the environment are dealt with in most church organizations increase the distrust, and the insatiable appetite for more explicit actions of clergy and lay leaders to demonstrate they can be trusted. In a society in which the environments for each church organization and for parts of that organization are different, and the goals of each organization and parts consequently are different, trust is not easily achieved. Environment plays a crucial role in the formation of goals of church organizations—a role we do not understand well, but which we must seek to understand better if increased health and effectiveness are to develop in church organizations.

The primary objectives in Chapter II of *A Plan of Union* provide for the conditions in the united church in which goals and multiple changing environments can be dealt with so that Christ's church can become increasingly effective in mission and ministry. If the primary objectives are achieved in united churches, then the goals, resources, and capacity for significant witness and service will develop in the various environments of the church. *A Plan of Union* envisions a church engaged in expressions of ministry and mission in multiple and changing environments. Embedded within *A Plan of Union* is a more appropriate understanding of the church's relation to its environment than denominations have had in the past. We turn now to look more closely at the relation between church organizations and their environments.

Environment and Church Behavior

The church when viewed from a panoramic perspective is a huge, bureaucratic system composed of congregations, middle judicatories, and denominational organizations. Each level of this system has operated as though it were a closed system and need only respond to internal environmental variables. For example, Boards of Christian Education have concluded that the important variables are (from their persepective and as they understand them) teachers, students, church education committees, middle-judicatory church education committees, and particular age-group or teacher curriculum needs in the case of church education strategy. They have assumed that the environment of every other church organization involved in denominational church education strategy can be ignored. Boards of Christian Education have attempted to achieve their denominational educational goals through a closed-system strategy by creating a monolithic central network which controlled resources and professional staff. Across Protestantism, Boards of Christian Education are being dismantled as they seek a new, noncontrolling relationship with those who are their constituents. This phenomenon can be seen at every level of church life. Decentralization, the word denoting increased responsiveness to the challenges of particular environments by church organizations, is seen in congregations and middle judicatories. Committees of congregations desire more resources and autonomy to achieve goals in relation to particular environments. Districts, presbyteries, synods, and conferences are brought to virtual paralysis by groups of clergy and laity who demand an increasing amount of the organization's money, staff, and power to achieve goals in relation to different environments.

The assumption of a closed system is a colossal error. All human organizations in Western culture are open systems varying in the degree of openness and the environmental variables which influence them. In viewing church organizations as an organizational phenomenon through an open-system perspective, the impact of environment upon different levels and types of church organizations can be seen. The uncertainty which a turbulent environment, such as ours, introduces into church organizations can be dealt with only when an organization assumes that a turbulent environment will introduce uncertainty and indeterminacy into its life, and then begins to search for and discover means for achieving more certainty in its life and program. It will not do this as long as it assumes that it is a closed system at all levels and hence can ignore environmental variables.

Developing mechanisms for dealing with uncertainty as an organization while still focusing on the achievement of goals is a first-order activity for church organizations. All church programming takes place in an organization which is affected dramatically by its environment. Environmental effects alter the nature of church goal achievement through programming at each level, so that the old closed-system assumptions are outmoded with their strategies of controlling resources, program, and personnel. Instead, open-system assumptions which lead to the development of strategies of coping to achieve organizational goals must be adopted. This means a new noncontrolling relationship between levels of church organizations and within church organizations if the necessary degree of positive interdependence and the mobilization of human and other resources necessary to cope in at least minimal ways with the environment is to occur.

Church life is such that in our environment there are diverse groups which make up the constituency of each organization. No organization has sufficient knowledge about its constitutents. Their personal goals and personal goals for the organization are relatively unknown. Our hunches and guesses about constituents are poor substitutes for processes in which they can make this information available in their language and in relation to current organizational goals. We also have an inadequate understanding of how these constituencies change in terms both of their goals and of the potential political coalitions which are necessary to support the goals of any organization. The environment produces new conditions for church organizations, which necessitate new structures, communication, decision-making (political) processes, and new polity. Thus far, church organizations have been overwhelmed by these environmental factors, and have yet to turn their attention to coping with the challenges of this environment. The assumption that the environment can be ignored will lead only to increased tension, frustration, apathy, and ineffectiveness.

A *Plan of Union* has in Chapter VIII, "Organizing for Mission," prescriptions for an organization which focuses on priority mission and ministry goals and on flexible open structures which will facilitate initiative and participation in congregations and parishes.

> The structures of the church shall be determined by what the church is in its given nature and by what it undertakes to do in obedience to Christ; in this sense, structures shall be functionally determined. Hence, such structures shall, from time to time, be established, changed or eliminated as needs arise or conditions of life arise or conditions of life require. These structures shall be open for experiment, exploration, testing and evaluation, with maximum emphasis upon local initiative and widespread participation [A *Plan of Union*, VIII, 3, p. 56].

The kind of organization advocated in A *Plan of Union* is essential for faithfulness in witness and service with the variety of goals which persons have for themselves and for church organizations, and in the context of multiple, challenging environments. Stable, inflexible, closed organizations are inappropriate and mitigate against expression of Christian faith in the world of men.

Components of Church Organizational Effectiveness

Clarity and explicitness of goals in relation to particular environments are primary in understanding church organizational behavior. The basis for movement toward a significant future, either as a congregation or a parish in the COCU Plan or as a denominational organization or new ecumenical creation, is the goals in a particular environment, not a structure. The structure of an organization is required to serve the goals in a particular environment. The goals of an organization are the basis for judging whether persons or organizations should join together in any structure. Common purposes are the precondition for a future together in any form. When these purposes are known, then a structure can be created to serve them.

The role of structure in achieving goals has not been studied in church organizations, but some observations can be made which point to needed research. In a stable environment in which tasks are simple and known, a stable structure supported by a few standardized rules and procedures is adequate for goal attainment. Most church programming until the end of World War II took place in a relatively stable environment, and the tasks related to programming in education, mission stewardship, etc., were comparatively simple and known. But today the environment is turbulent, the tasks of church programming are increasingly complex, heterogeneous, multiple, and frequently unknown. For example, standardized curricula, teaching methods, and classroom procedures have become obsolete. Each congregation is invited to construct its own curriculum. But the congregational structures still tend to be rigid, rather than flexible and able to reflect and facilitate goal achievement in a turbulent environment. Many congregations despair because the standardized rules and procedures are no longer viable, but the alternatives of more effective human communication, congregational goal setting and planning, and a variety of feedback mechanisms have eluded them. In most church organizations leaders and followers have been unwilling to find alternatives to traditional practices, rules, and methods. Alternatives in a turbulent environment with tasks that are complex, unknown, and multiple are bound to be costly in terms of human energy. The human communication necessary for effective consensus formation requires different patterns of communication. If the goals related to mission or church education or any other goal area are to be known, understood, and supported with the necessary resources, then congregational communication about these goals is required. No elite group can announce the goals or tasks related to these goals and expect automatic support. Patterns of congregation-wide communication through clustering or area grouping, telephone networks, and effective congregational meetings are needed to develop a consensus around the goals of congregations. In many congregations leaders and goal-task areas are mismatched so that the leaders reflect not goal priorities of a congregation, but a political process which produces nonrepresentative leaders who do not or cannot communicate with a constituency which must support the programs they devise. Or even worse, the leaders may approve programs, curricular resources, and teaching methods which are inadequate, inappropriate, and unresponsive to the needs and interests of a congregation. Or they may approve inconsequential goals which use a disproportionate share of resources. The goals they approve may create division, tension, and apathy which reduce the resources and the power of the total organization to achieve any goals adequately.

Goals, structure, communication patterns, and political processes are variables which function in every congregation. These variables influence each other in such a way that goals and tasks to accomplish goals suffer if structure, communication patterns, and political processes are not designed to facilitate goal attainment. This is obvious, but the focus in church organizations has not been on the nature of the organization which must accomplish the goal. We have been preoccupied with programs, and not sufficiently alerted to the church organization which must accomplish goals. Sick congregations may not be able to accomplish any goal effectively. This is true even when adequate resources, good program ideas, and all the rest of the church organizational apparatus are available.

Most church organizations do not have the decision-making (political processes to mobilize persons and their resources, and to maintain commitment to a diverse group of organizational goals. In church organizations there are differentiated groups of leaders who are related to different goals. This is the basis of the diffused power which is characteristic of church organizations. No group of leaders has all the resources necessary to achieve goals effectively. Few church organizations accept the leadership of any single group. Conflict occurs between the elites of different goal-task areas of church organizational life who have access to different resources and constituencies, and have different amounts of power to achieve goals.

Competition and conflict result when the structure of decision-makers does not correspond to the priority of goals. A minority of leaders rather than leaders from minorities rule in most church organizations. Every such minority has its own priority goals. It is extremely difficult for any minority to represent adequately the goals, leaders, and needs of other minorities. Such minority rule in which the goals of one group receive preferential treatment over the goals and leaders of others mitigates against collegiality between clergy and lay groups of an organization. A political system in which minorities rule is an organizational prerequisite for coordination of the goals of the various minorities within church organizations.

Many leaders of church organizations are concerned about the new attitudes toward polity, the standardized, written rules of conduct. They do not appear to be either helpful or functional in enabling an organization to achieve its goals more effectively. There is need to explore the issue of polity in church organizational behavior, particularly at moments when distrust and alienation renders all polity almost completely ineffective in assisting an organization to maintain that order necessary to accomplish goals.

Church organizations are unique among the kinds of organizations in that polity has had an important effect upon church organizational behavior. The polity currently applied in congregations was developed in an atmosphere of stability both internal and external to the organization. This polity, manifested in by-laws, constitutions, manuals, directories of worship, procedures, and confessions, was developed primarily as a protective mechanism to insulate or seal off from environmental influences in a more or less stable society. Polity which seals off and standardizes is no longer possible. Different parts of an organization with their goals, tasks, and specialized professionals stand in different relations to the external environment. The internal turbulence which results, and the stress which this turbulence from multiple, diverse groups places upon professional staff, works against collegiality. Polity no longer functions to enhance collegial relations. Rather than rely upon polity to insure order and viability as an organization, costly human communication is a prerequisite for collegiality. The human communication which is necessary to maintain effectiveness is costly in time, energy, and organizational mechanisms which maintain the multidirectional feedback flow of information from all parts of a congregation. In church organizations with multiple diverse goals, constituent groups which stand in different positive and negative relations to these goals, a turbulent or changing external and internal environment, human communication is the most effective alternative to order through polity, and a major means of maintaining the necessary flow of information which will facilitate collegiality between individuals and parts of an organization.

The alternatives to traditional norms, historical precedent, and written rules are increased human communication, new resources for theological reflection about the challenges to faith and life, feedback mechanism from constituent groups, planning, consensus-forming processes, political processes which mobilize persons and increase the size of the dominant coalition, leadership development, organizational development, and various human-relations skills. When written rules and historical resources no longer suffice, a new understanding of polity must emerge which enables persons through communication and decision-making processes to deal more substantively with those issues and goals which are most divisive. The old polity cannot hold the diverse groups and their goals together. New polity which enables persons to deal with issues and goals must be substituted. Written rules must be supplemented and, perhaps, supplanted by processes which facilitate inquiry, debate, and discussion so that a new consensus is built out of the commitment of persons to goals and issues, rather than to an organization and its historical way of maintaining order which developed in a more stable, simple society.

Structure, communication, decision-making, and polity all deal with power in church organizational life. Power is a substantive issue in church organizational life at this moment. Those who hold to closed-system assumptions believe that control can be maintained through some system of rewards and punishments. This day is almost over. The minorities have discovered that they too have power, perhaps more power than any single minority of leaders. The ability to bring about the dismantling of denominational program agencies through withholding of funds is but one illustration of such power.

But negative power which diminishes the total organization's ability to achieve its goals is no solution for the church of Jesus Christ. What is needed is an organization which employs those mechanisms to work through issues and diversity of goals to the point where once again such trust exists at least among a dominant coalition that the organization has power to achieve its goals. Because of the negative power now being exercised by individuals and organizations (congregations and middle judicatories) no church organization has the resources sufficient to accomplish its goals.

The use of negative power by clergy and laity, and the decline in power of congregations, middle judicatories, and national program agencies have pushed these organizations toward ecumenical collaboration as a way to increase the power to achieve their goals, particularly financial and ministry and mission goals.

A primary purpose of A Plan of Union is to increase the power of laity and church organizations at each level through an emphasis on local initiative, equitable participation and representation (A Plan of Union, VIII, 14–19, pp. 58–59), and, most important, through the very concept of the parish itself. The parish, with its diversity, multiple congregations, and increased resources, is able to be much more powerful in relation to its environment and other levels of church organizations. The concept of the parish is probably the most significant new creation in A Plan of Union. If the parish is developed in local communities, the power of Christians to implement their goals of ministry and mission will be greatly increased.

A note of caution is needed. The vision of a parish organization which A Plan of Union contains will never be implemented, or, if implemented, will fail, unless appropriate polity, communication, and decision-making processes be developed. There is nothing in the parish design which will provide the capacity to deal with the differences and conflicts arising from these differences. New polity mechanisms are needed!

Ecumenical Possibilities for Church Organizations

While some may point cynically to collaboration necessitated by an economic disaster as the primary reason, others, among whom I include myself, can point to forty years of church theology, a turbulent environment, and new mission and ministry goals as more cogent reasons for new ecumenical forms of church life. The disappearance of a stable environment has exposed the inadequacy of our mission and ministry goals, structure, polity, and closed-system controlling assumptions.

New ecumenical organizations must be based on common mission and ministry goals pertinent to the challenges of their environment. The first order of business in the creation of a new organization must be a goal-setting process which identifies the goals and provides the only relevant foundation for working together. The new creation will be as obsolete as any of the old ones it replaces if this is not done. This is true for ecumenical local parishes, middle-level and national church organization. There is nothing inherently good about a goalless new structure. The goals or purposes of the new creation are the significant element.

In our society, as the challenges become more complex and the resource needs greater, there is an inevitability to the process of trying to create church organizations which have the resources necessary to cope, to respond actively and even aggressively. No organization has the needed resources of ideas, money, or people. Ecumenical creations provide the greatest potential for achieving goals effectively. The claims of God in Christ upon his people for a faithful, effective witness propel us toward defining our common goals and creating organizational forms which facilitate persons and organizations in their faithfulness.

The last generation of Christians was captured by a vision which caused them to create new mission forms in hospitals, homes, settlement houses, colleges, trade schools, boarding schools. Mission through institution-building was an appropriate form for meeting the needs of the poor immigrants at the turn of the century. The needs have grown greater, the challenges more intense and complex. Economic development, housing, health care and welfare for the poor, quality integrated education, and peace are societal problems that are not met with the same kind of institution-building with which we have been familiar, and which seems from our perspective to be safer and less stressful on the church.

The means for witness and service to God's work in this complex society are loaded with controversy and conflict. The need for resources seems overwhelming. It is in fact overwhelming if we proceed alone. Effective witness and service to God in this society depend upon the mobilization of faith commitments of persons around common goals at every level of church organizational life, and then the creation of new organizations which will encourage persons to use their resources for the achievement of goals which are responsive to the needs of our society.

A *Plan of Union* points us toward the creation of new organizations at every level of church life—not just new structures, but new organizations. We are directed toward a continually changing church, a church which changes itself for the sake of more effective mission and ministry. The process of uniting is a process, an active, dynamic, creating process which always seeks to overcome the static, closed, inappropriate forms of church life. A *Plan of Union* contains in its prescriptions for new church organizations at each level, directions, styles, and forms which are far more appropriate for the expression of Christian faith in our time.

14

The New Generation and COCU

MARTIN E. MARTY

The Consultation on Church Union represents an idea whose time had come in the 1960s. It then suffered the fate of suddenly changing times, and to many its own time seems now to have passed. Since something of what it pointed to is valid and offers promise and hope, responsible leaders serve as custodians of its traditions and intentions. One day its time may come again.

The early 1960s: how hard it is now mentally to recreate the world in which the hopeful announcements about the birth of the Consultation and the possibility of a "Church of Christ Uniting" were first made. A historian might find it easier to recreate for a coming generation the ethos and spirit of the Council of Nicaea or, more easily, the "violent tenor of life" when the late medieval Catholic councils were held than to try to make believable the climate of the early 1960s.

The world of the white Anglo-Saxon Protestant mattered, then, in ways that it does not at the moment. Of course, throughout the decade the COCU leadership has been in the hands of men and women of uncommon breadth of racial spirit; during the years of discussion black religious leaders have also taken a responsible part. On the spectrum of openness or closedness toward racially inclusive models, COCU heads have symbolized the open end. But the proposal naturally did not grow out of the experience of Third World churches. It is not expressive of generalized Christianity, Eastern Orthodoxy, Roman Catholicism, or the religion of the recently oppressed in North America. It is quite understandably in continuity with several centuries of church patterns that had been developed largely by North Americans of provenances connected with the British Isles. There need be no criticism of or judgment upon COCU for this element of its genesis. Everyone has to be born somewhere; everything reflects particular origins. Had it been born elsewhere, it would reflect elsewhere's *Gestalt*.

The fact of its lineage, however, served it ill during the ensuing decade. The break-up of the older (ca. 1954) "integrationist" models in American Protestant church life caused internal strains which show up whenever black and white COCU leaders exchange views. They would show up even more if the kind of black spokesmen who are somehow religious but also somehow out of COCU's symbolic orbits were to be drawn into them. Meanwhile, America has been discovering, largely in Catholicism but also in Protestantism, the enduring power of lower-middle-class, often non-WASP peoples: "ethnics," backlashers, middle Americans, silent-majoritarians—people regarded sometimes with condescension and sometimes with fear. They are in any case people whose religious experience was not encapsulated in the traditions embodied by COCU denominations. Public curiosity has shifted toward these, leaving COCU groups at the margins, so far as expectations are concerned.

This is not to say that WASP power has disappeared. Tens of millions of Americans belong to the churches of these families; their hold on various establishments remains impressive. There is great potential for good or ill within them. The point here is simply that at the moment these belong to the "givenness," the background against which newer dynamisms in American history show up. Few are curious about the details of their existence because they are simply assumed, even if in the forms of caricatures and stereotypes.

Secondly, COCU was born of an age when a kind of liberal optimism was prevailing. The religious revival of the 1950s had just showed signs of tapering off, but churches were still full and often paid for, membership was growing or holding its own, young people were being brought for religious instruction in the denominations. Most of the COCU leadership was critical of many dimensions of the revival: its ethical default, its esthetic faults, its evocation of success syndromes. But COCU profited from the institutional strengths that were the legacy of the previous decade. There was reason for wise men to hope.

They were finding new company. Not only was there reason to believe that they could make a dent on the great social injustices of the day, through movements of racial integration and the promises at first of a New Frontier and then of a Great Society—two semisecular incarnations of "Kingdom of God" imagery—but they were finding compatriots in the religious field. If only the Protestants would set their house in order, they could begin to express an openness toward Roman Catholicism. The spirit of Pope John was regnant; Vatican II had been announced. The world of religion mattered: the secure Catholic Church with its hundreds of millions of members was soon to unleash new spiritual power. COCU showed that Protestants knew how to relate to that power.

That world seems irretrievable today. Renewed Catholicism is largely in shambles, at least for the moment; intransigent Catholicism hangs on, but offers the world almost no hope. Institutionalized religion does not matter in the world as it did a decade ago. Social change (long weekends, high-rise buildings, mass higher education, economic affluence-and-nervousness) has made it difficult for institutions to rely almost automatically on the support of church members gained in the Eisenhower Era, and impossible for them to be automatically dependent upon the children of those members. Theological creativity and uncertainty ("death of God," *et al.*) suggest to members and nonmembers alike that the churches are not able to present unifying and salvific symbols or promises. Epochal changes in religion are going on.

The COCU dream was tied, more than anyone then knew, to the spiritual tinge of the secular ethos of that day. The major promises and prophecies relied on pictures of a kind of technopolitan utopia, the kind of kingdom prefigured in Gibson Winter's *The New Creation as Metropolis* or Harvey Cox's *The Secular City*. It is hard to believe now that once men believed that something of these post-Christian utopias could be foretasted. It is hard to remember that wise men could hope that cities would be governable, or that Harvard technocrats in the Kennedy administration would share responsibility for miring the nation in a militarily and morally plotless war. Few now like to be reminded of a day when they shared hope that "man in control" would rule, that computers could be idolized or even believed in.

COCU was, of course, not a simple product of, advertisement for, or public-relations agent of that world. But it was built on the idea of rational programming: negotiating committees would smooth out differences between traditions; complex bureaucracies would help assure the forthcoming church a place of some influence near the ears of the mighty.

That world fell apart in the mid-1960s, when Vietnam heated up, Watts-Detroit-Newark burned, student radicals rejected the proffered models. In its place came competitive promises, of a world of "permanent revolution" which would destroy the continuities off which COCU-type churches lived (for they were putatively part of established structure), or of a mystical millennium which was simply non- rather than anti-institutional. Mystical: people turned to the Eastern religions instead of Western continuities; they rejected consensus and committee life; they sought alternative styles of community and new symbolization. Millennium: because "the Age of Aquarius" or its cognates served to project futures in which the transcendent could be expressed extra-ecclesiastically.

One could go through almost all the revolutions of the 1960s and see how they militated against the potential success of COCU. In the early 1970s some savants saw signs that there were returns to the ethos of the 1950s. Worship in the White House East Room suggested governmental support of *status quo* religion; COCU could represent the left or cutting edge of that civil religious sphere. The young were allegedly neoromantics, filled with nostalgia, weeping their way through the revolution at *Love Story* and paging through old family albums in which papa's church played a part. Jesus revolutions and catholic pentecostalism were often described as merely the most colorful of a large number of backward-looking phenomena in religion. But to this time none of these mood changes have made life easier for people in COCU denominations.

Those who look for what Halvdan Koht called "driving forces in history," then, look elsewhere for what COCU had set out to deliver. "Black power," "women's liberation," "communes," "sensitivity," "behaviorism," and other condensations of complex movements drew more attention. This is nowhere more visible than in the religious press of the COCU churches, where editors may occasionally and almost dutifully report on what COCU is doing; but when they want to attract and hold readers they turn elsewhere for copy.

One reads of COCU documents as best-sellers, no doubt because there are channels for their dissemination in the churches and programs in which they are being discussed. No one has checked to see if they are best-read documents; my impression is that they are not, that most church members do not know of their existence or do not feel threatened by their ignorance of them. Perhaps people have taken some polls about acceptability of COCU; I have not seen them. One could guess that there would be amiable public acceptance of the ideas, since most Americans in most years welcome the attempts of most people to find consensus and to come together.

Resistance would probably come the closer one approaches the pillars of churches most threatened by attempts to put new foundations under them. My journalistic instincts tell me that COCU does not "catch on"; the world I know best, that of theological education, provides me with devastating personal documentation of the problem of COCU's idea and promise. Years pass on the lecture circuit or in class, seminar, and forum without a single question having to do with anything implied by COCU ever coming up. Everything else is mentioned; I never let ignorance inhibit discussion, and make it possible for audiences and students to extrapolate toward infinity in the range of admissible subjects. COCU does not draw attention. Yet COCU represents a world that ought to hold attraction for seminarians and theological leaders of tomorrow, and as a historian and ecclesiologue I should be held responsible for comment on relationships to entities like COCU. Were I asked to lead a conference on COCU at any theological school of my acquaintance, I would be tempted to rent a phone booth which could hold a prospective audience.

All this sounds as if it is implicit criticism of the men and women who dreamed of COCU's success, or as if it treated them as poor custodians of its developing life. I leave such criticism to others, having no reason to fault poeple who were making the best of what their day had to offer, only to see that day disappear. These were, as I have said above, "wise men" who were hoping, and one does not see any more courageous, audacious, or adventurous ecumenical pioneering among the contemporaries of the people of the early 1960s. If one looked closely or had responsibilities for directly furthering COCU's fortunes, he would find motivation for criticism. There are no doubt self-seekers, people of low imagination, non-adaptable insisters on their own ways, intransigents, and petty people, but I do not care whether or not there are. They are not really holding back the Church of Christ Uniting.

So the decade has to be seen as a time of ironies for Protestant ecumenism. COCU came to its highest point of achievemeut at a time when few cared. It picked up ecumenical dreams at least as old as the Evangelical Alliance of 1846 and carried them further than anyone else had carried them, but not many backers shared the dream. It set out to overcome "separation" at a time when symbol-makers now set a new premium on at least strategic "separation" in various racial, sexual, generational, or other movements. COCU leaders inevitably, despite their efforts at simplification, seemed to play into the picture of bureaucracy at a time when bureaucracy was being rejected. They arranged ecumenical furniture inside the burning houses of the inherited institutional churches, in a time when more watched and fewer helped put out the blaze. They faced the problem of denominationalism at a time when denominationalism was being discerned as no longer the central offense—if it ever had been—in Christendom.

The result has been that COCU is ordinarily damned with faint praise as few organizations have been. In a diffuse, noncommittal way, people who are told about it tend to agree that it is a good idea. But as they draw closer they find little to which to extend enthusiasms. It is praised with faint damns by people who worry about what it is of which they will be deprived by participation. It is damned with vigorous damns by young anti-institutionalists or by alternative-institutionalists who blame certain metropolitan-cosmopolitan "conspiracies" for whatever goes wrong in the world. And its leaders have to issue press releases announcing that COCU is not "dead" and implicitly scolding the necrophiles who like to find dead things around and, when they are not around, like to declare live things to be dead. Argument over that issue never was of much importance or worth. In simplest terms, the issue is not whether COCU is alive but whether it is "interesting," or can become so.

History may pass COCU by because most people are more secular than are its spokesmen. "Most people" includes most church people, men and women who may be members of a local parish where they are integrated into some social group and some pattern of meaning. But they do not buy theological books, they are not curious about Christians beyond the local region. They are bored by long discussions about levels and types of offices of ministry; biblical arguments for one style or the other are not compelling to them. They find that COCU meets neither of two tests that are vital to them inside their "secular envelope." On one hand, it does not seem to inconvenience them, to stand in their way, to assault their sensibilities—as do many political and social movements in the secular *oikoumene*. On the other hand, it does not suggest to them great boons or bounties which they would not otherwise possess.

If the public has grown to be more secular than COCU, that same public paradoxically is also in many ways more "religious." The 1960s were a decade of revolutionary change in the prospects offered to humans in their social organization and even in their sensibility or consciousness or world-view. As part of their new strivings, they often gave evidence of perpetuating quests for meaning, and employing explicit religious symbols to do so. They looked once again to the occult-metaphysical sectors of life for some clues to the transcendent. Many of them reexplored Eastern religion or the "primitive" styles of Amerindian or African perspectives. The drugs-and-communes world attracted others. Within Christianity the young who had been scorned by elders as being too nonreligious turned around and embarrassed them by being too religious, "freaking" for Jesus or someone else.

The problem with the new religious spirit (aside from the questions of ephemerality, faddism, and the like) was that it was too anarchic, too resistant to channeling and domestication, to be of much direct benefit to people in the leadership of COCU churches. COCU did not embody the actual hopes or minister to the manifest fears of such people, and they turned elsewhere. In a formula that I have found attractive, they sought "the immediate experience." In psychologist R. D. Laing's terms, they were looking not for a theory of experience but for an experience.

Now, the main-line churches certainly would advertise themselves as value-creating societies, as locales where profound experience of the transcendent is offered. But they suffer from sometimes apt and sometimes inept public criticism and dismissal. Their traditions are prematurely overlooked because they seem to have been exhausted. The new seekers do not often inquire about Jakob Boehme or Meister Eckhart or

Teresa of Avila or Blaise Pascal for traslatable visions, turning instead to shamans and gurus of other lineages. As a Christian and as a historian I do not always rejoice in these rejections, but I must understand them; I may feel that some of them are superficial and temporary, but they lead me to empathize with those who have to live off revision of those traditions.

COCU suffers, third, from the fact that its reforms stand somewhere midway between the two realities people most regularly seem to be related to. These are times of great mistrust of remote bureaucracy and great love for the most immediate circle. We have spoken of the times as characterized by a "new localism." Nationalism resists the United Nations or One World integrative spirit. Ethnicity serves as a counterforce to American homogenizing pluralism. Collegians move out of "impersonal" dormitories to find each other in communes or small private enclaves. Catholics now find less sustenance in the large impersonal gatherings of the mass and, if they work through the church at all, hope to find it in small cells.

Nowhere does this localism show up more than in Protestant churches. While the decline in Protestant institutional participation has not been drastic, the growth of nonconcern or suspicion in relation to "Geneva" "475 Riverside Drive" or "denominational headquarters" has been startling. Insofar as the church parallels what they already find fault with in the world, they have little use for it.

There may be uncreative and ugly sides to the new localism. It may represent attempts to screen out conflicting signals and to help people build self-justifying forms around themselves. But there is also an attractive side: the religious experience, whether or not it has to do with mass movements, has to be ratified and certified in more intimate groups. The clan no longer serves in the day of the too small and claustrophobic isolated nuclear family. The town is going or gone; but the religious circle can serve.

COCU is perceived by the uninitiated as one more cluster of remote elitist committees, bureaucracies, or evidences of the managerial revolution. To the initiated it often appears to disrupt the new localism through its admittedly most drastic and creative innovation, the new parish which resembles the Catholic "diocese" of earlier history, the agency of interconnection between local cells. They see the larger "parish" without recognizing the promise of the smaller "congregations" and even possibly smaller intentional "cells" in these. So COCU is rejected as halfway between their greatest fears and their greatest hopes.

It makes little sense to criticize details of COCU unless one makes up his mind about the larger context in which it suffered its vicissitudes during the first decade of its life. It is not necessary for everyone to agree with my reading of these fates, but it seems impossible to move further unless one at least faces and makes up his mind about them. Only then can there be some sort of turning toward positive reconstructive work in forms appropriate for our decade.

The reader who has followed this essay thus far may not be emotionally ready to want to take that turn. Its thesis has been that the men and women who envisioned and stimulated COCU grasped perfectly the spirit and needs of their moment or even their epoch—but that the epoch was itself coming to an end at that very instant. It implied throughout that, ever since, a swift sequence of new threats and promises, styles and world-views has appeared—almost all of it representing surprise. If that is the case, why trust our reading of the situation in the early 1970s, especially since there is now much of fashion and faddism in the forces that give such trouble to COCU: anti-institutionalism, pervasive secularity accompanied by neoreligiousness, mistrust of bureaucracy and love of the local? Perhaps by publication date everything will have changed again. Perhaps. Therefore talk for the future will have to take in a wider range of contingencies.

Here are some outlines toward reconstruction, uttered as provocations and not as programs.

1. It is important for COCU leaders to do what they can to escape any palace-guard protection, any hall-of-mirror illusions. Because elites talk to each other, they can create the impression that they are discussing a "real" world; they profit most by talking to those who do not share their world of discourse.

2. While what they hear may ordinarily be devastating, one would hope that they would keep their morale. In spite of all that has been said, something of what they are about strikes many of us as being very precious. They represent a further advance in removal of the old offense that may have kept many people from taking seriously Christian promise. "Is Christ divided?" was a question that elicited more scandalous response at a time when Christians were perceived to be chiefly competitive, not acceptant of each other's mission. When they became basically acceptant, that scandal began to be removed. The point has been made to the world: Christians are essentially united and are seeking practical manifestations of the unity which is always seeking them, is seeking expression through them. COCU is a more audacious attempt to further such symbolism than were the cozy intradenominational "mergers" or the rather relaxed conciliar or federative patterns.

COCU can stand, then, as a weak but durable symbol over against "separationist" movements, whether these follow national, ethnic, racial, sexual, or generational and interest-group lines. The "driving forces of history" may move with these separatist voices, but COCU can consolidate some gains, can patiently work toward reconciliations. In the Christian vocabulary, reconciliation is the ultimate word. Separation, identity-seeking, partisanship may be functionally necessary for individuals and groups at various stages of development. One must understand drives toward these in our homogenizing "integrative" world. But the theological premium cannot be placed on mere separation; separation is a penultimate, not an ultimate in Christian intentions. COCU can possibly serve as a reminder of that.

3. COCU has begun to permit a sharing of resources among Christians; it is the first of the practicable ecumenical patterns which does not *simply* work to smooth out everything in the name of "consensus" and it does seem to turn to the separate traditions with some hope.

These are not times in which we look for homognized, packaged, stereotypical prescriptions in secular or religious life. People resurrect old coats of arms and family trees; the more sensitive and gifted people seek ethnic restaurants and buy recipe books which allow at least a sampling of other cultures; some at least travel outside the Hiltonesque or Howard Johnsonian range—where every place is like every other place—and they come into actual contact with cultures which keep their identity and enrich our own. This is an age in which liturgies and hymnals should probably be loose-leaf and not permanently bound, so hungry are people to hear some reinforcing word from other contexts, and to share the sense of immediacy and discovery that can come with these. We well know, should the Church of Christ Uniting come into being, that COCU will not be able to resist publication of hymnals (which few will use and none will enjoy), liturgical fabrication (which will probably be tolerated, but which will at best serve as base for improvisation), and the like. But COCU expresses the intention to let a catholic range of voices be heard, and someone should be worrying about skeining together the anomic and disparate voices of our anarchic and anti-institutional age.

4. The attempt to jostle the current self-seeking congregations by a new parochial pattern shows at least that COCU is trying. It may not succeed; it may find that the consequent ecclesiological entity may be born without its most audacious form finding acceptance. But the debate that can occur before people again lapse into the deadly forms they have come to enjoy or employ for finding security can be creative.

We have already alluded to the COCU institutional problem: its revision is not strong enough to counter imageries of the "superchurch" and "remoteness" or the "impersonal." But it is hard to come up with better models, at least to provoke thought about what we now call "congregations" and what men celebrate in their present dysfunctionality for Christian mission and service. In this sense COCU shares in the pathos of our moment, something which we all suffer. We are too far into a cultural revolution to be able to find much power or hope in the existing forms, but are not far enough into it to be able to envisage effective new forms. The "emerging viable structures of ministry" offered in the "meantime" of the past decade or two have largely come and gone as a result of the stage of revolution in which they were offered.

Can one go further, and suggest other elements that should be built into any reconstruction of the COCU ideal? From this point on, one can only speak in general terms and see whether programmers can pick them up. I believe there are ways to advance the discussion, but must ask pardon in advance from those who may regard the mode of their presentation as flippant. They are not intended to be so.

First, the ecumenical models of the future do not seem to relate to those which began bureaucratically, were nurtured by committees, or sought consensus. The actual way in which Christians have related to each other ever since the basic ecumenical point has been established differs vastly from this. It is characterized by what might be called *ad hoc* ecumenism: ecumenism which finds profound if temporary manifestations and leaves certain deposits behind it on which permanent "organization" and expression can be based.

If one wanted to translate this into Southern dialect, it would be an ecumenism based on a phrase something like the invitation "Y'all come!" The utterer of such an invitation may not mean literally that all men should come; I am not sure whether or not Christians always mean it either. But the inviter does mean that people in range of a voice recognize that they are free to come within the context of their predispositions and in ways compatible with their more profound commitments.

Ad hoc ecumenism is also "secular ecumenism"; it has been evidenced when Protestant-Catholic-Jew-agnostic band together for social justice or artistic expression without worrying about confessional consensus. They are drawn by the magnet, the object, the burden, the promise, and cannot wait until guidelines are all ready. Those of us who have experienced such "y'all come" secular ecumenism can testify that it often runs deeper and is more profound than are those "community Thanksgiving services" or metropolitan ecumenical stagings which seldom reach beyond superficiality.

The "y'all come" of COCU's future could be uttered even as committees continue their quiet backroom work. Let the organization become the staging area, the forum, the arena in which Christians as Christians find places of expression outside of and beyond rather than within consensus. Let the invitation and the rewards be so rich that no one will want to stand outside. At present, members of non-COCU denominations seldom experience or express a sense of deprivation. Yet some things go on there in the name of Jesus Christ which they cannot pass up except to their or the cause's detriment: COCU could become the enactor of such occasions if it did not wait for consensus.

The "y'all come" model can be expressed in a slightly diffrent way, also by reference to a rather flippant-sounding slogan: "Run up a flag and see who salutes." This picture suggests that Christians have already found each other in extremely casual ways as part of a "mass." If somehow the spirit of Christ is formed in another, I bear his burdens, share Christ's wounds with him, and offer reasons for the hope that is in me at his side. But his confession or tradition, his primal apprehension of reality, his habit or manner or community may ordinarily keep him at a distance.

Then someone "runs up a flag to see who salutes"—around some social program, theological motif, or esthetic evocation. Out of that mass, some respond while others remain disassociated or unaffected. We become part of a "public"—just as when one attends a theater he or she stands the risk of becoming part of a public. People are still far from intimacy; they may not even meet, but they profit from and contribute to something with energy and potential.

It seems to me that this symbolization is important in the day of "new localism," when the great danger is that people turn narcissistic and elitist within their small response groups. A network of symbols has to be developed, nurtured, and propagated.

So COCU would self-consciously cultivate the artists and writers, the poets and dancers and dramatists, the gifted and sensitive people who influence others; it would serve to be alert to the mass media of communication and to those in that world who convert masses to publics. It would devote itself intentionally to this symbolic network and its sustenance.

While both of these phrases suggest a high degree of informality and adaptability, life in the future of COCU would be characterized by intentionality. It might be said that in 1960 for the last time people could put together a Christian organizational dream in America and expect it to draw "automatic" Christians. Tomorrow no one will be a practicing Christian out of habit; those who will be left or who will be there afresh will have come to the faith around some specific project or projection: what can I do for Christ through the Church (or what can it do for me) to further this or that understanding or cause?

COCU cannot express the "intentionality" of the current components, the denominations. It must seek its own. A narrow focus and a limited range of projects and projections tomorrow would mean death, in every cultural change. If COCU sees itself chiefly as a staging area for ad hoc ecumenism and as the main coordinator of a symbolic network, it can allow for the fulfillment of many others' intentions, those connected with small groups where signals are clearer and more decisive.

From some points of view, the picture I have described is so broad that no intentionality can be expressed. One could say, "But then, only those Christians who would want to be 'out' of the Church of Christ Uniting would be out of it; what does this do to definition in the Church?" Answer: definition comes elsewhere. We have plenty of definition and do not need more; what we need now is a locale for interaction. Consolidation of gains there may be; growth in grace could be expected; hungers for new stages of institutionalization appropriate for a new culture and a new Christian witness there will be. But for now, COCU has to be more expansive, less concerned with consensus and committee.

Scenario for the future: one day the remains of once powerful Catholicism have to be regrouped. The Orthodox presence in America will be "at home." Blacks will be far enough along in assertion of identity and freedom that they can risk "integration" because it no longer is on someone else's terms. Young people will have holy-rolled and freaked, and their movements will either have faded away or have been transformed into some new institutional self-reforming patterns. Liberated women will be "together." The current denominational lineages will be too weak and blurry to offer distinctiveness to anyone. Yet the spirit of Christ will seek embodiment. A Church of Christ Uniting that has remained almost protean in form, catholic in outlook, particularist where particularity comes naturally, will be better poised to host and house these emphases than would the consensus-plus-committee organization that speaks so little to the needs of a new generation.

15

The Taste and Smell of
Our Salvation and COCU

JOHN PAIRMAN BROWN

[These are the things I wanted to say about the unity of the Church, and the unity of men and women in the face of monstrous critical tasks, just as they came out of my typewriter. They are critical of the COCU Plan of Union. They are also not in any strict order of logic, but as they were actually layered inside my head. As an editor of other people's writings, I could have relayered them in a more rational order. I was afraid, if I did, that the criticism would come out rational and external, and not (as it really is) the criticism of one who has been faced with the same problems as the makers of the Plan and has been compelled by history to take a different road. After some reflection, I decided that justice to truth would best be done by letting the words stand as they came.]

Unity of what? Let us not be too confident about answering quickly, "Unity of the church." Church union, the phrase on which the COCU process rests, in various ways is inadequate or ambiguous.[1]

The New Testament envisages less the unity of the Church than the unity of humankind. COCU literature rests its Biblical case almost exclusively on John 17:21 "that they may all be one." The *Plan of Union* comes close to implying that this is an historical word of Jesus (*A Plan of Union*, II, 1, p. 10). Also it downplays the strong separatism of the context in John, "they are not of the world" (John 17:15). Who are intended by "they" of verse 21? The preceding verse gives the Evangelist's answer: "I do not pray for these only [the apostles], but also for those who believe in me through their word." I suppose the author had in mind Christian congregations of Asia Minor in the late first century with their clear boundaries. But by the generality of his language he positively invites our reinterpretation. Through the word of the first apostles and many others, the word has gone out to the ends of the earth. In our days it reached out (among others) to Boris Pasternak, Gandhi, Thich Nhat Hanh. Do they believe in Christ? In the biblical sense of the verb, they do: they trust and commit themselves to the principle or "word" that he represents far more than most of us.

Similarly, when Paul says in Galations 3:28 "you are all one in Christ Jesus" I suppose he primarily has in mind a restricted group of people, "as many of you as were baptized into Christ" (Galatians 3:26). But the words that come between suggest that Paul is reaching out to a larger vision of unity: "There is neither Jew nor Greek, there is neither slave nor free, there is neither male nor female." A larger vision is stated very explicitly in I Corinthians 15:22, "For as in Adam all die, so also in Christ shall *all* be made alive." The context suggests that some classes of people will have priority in the new life, but hardly gives us any ground to limit the generality of that "all." Even more sweeping is Romans 11:32 "For God has consigned all men to disobedience, that he may have mercy upon all." Here formally it is Israel and the church that are under discussion; but Paul had ways in Greek to say "both" if he had really wanted to.

There is a strong theme of what I may call the "church incognito" running through the first three Gospels. The important thing is not to say "Lord, Lord" to the historic Jesus but to do what he tells us (Luke 6:46)—or, alternatively, to do the will of his Father in heaven (Matthew 7:21). The important thing is not whether a man is "following" the legitimate apostles but whether he is truly casting out demons (Mark 10:38–40). "As you did it to one of the least of these my brethren, you did it to me" (Matthew 25:40).

In general, the New Testament sees the coming of Jesus as an event whose consequences are not soon exhausted. He represents the first, and the adequate, appearance in history of a principle which gives the human race a new center, our body a new head. The church (or whatever body the Sermon on the Mount addresses) is a nucleus of the new unity for mankind: it is the salt of the earth, the light of the world, a city set on a hill (Matthew 5:13–15). But that light is not put under a basket; it is set in a stand, and gives light to *all* in the house.

Our newspapers call for a unity of mankind regrouped around new tasks. And our newspapers, after the Bible, are our principal source of revelation. "Because the church lives in the midst of history those faithful in mission find themselves continually in a new context and therefore continually faced with a new agenda" (*A Plan of Union*, III, 6, p. 16). I open the paper and what do I read? "The sea is dying"; "Prisoners are not disposed to wait for reform"; "The war is destroying this country far more surely than it destroys Vietnam." All these things, even the decay of the biological environment, were foreseen and stated again and again in our Scriptures. The promise we were given is that a power beyond the newspapers will reverse the damage; he makes a new sky and earth, he sets the prisoners free, he smashes the weapons of war. Why should we believe the promise? Do we have any evidence that God is really doing those things? Yes, we do. And our evidence is the appearance in history of a community of people on whom there is laid a commitment to do those things. They have taken seriously the commands: "Let the land rest and lie fallow" (Exodus 23:10); "Undo the thongs of the yoke" (Isaiah 58:6); "Put your sword back in its place" (Matthew 26:52).

How do we recognize that community? It does not necessarily call itself by the name of God. As it was said to Cyrus the Persian, the anointed of God:

> I surname you, though you do not know me.
> I am the LORD, and there is no other,
> besides me there is no God;
> I gird you, though you do not know me. [Isaiah 45:4–5]

Since there is only one power beyond history, there is only one history; and whoever does the true work of history is the servant of that power, whether he recognizes it or not. From the beginning to the end of biblical history, from the beginning of history until now, the story is the same: the eldest son, the legitimate heir, proves unfaithful or unworthy, and it is the younger son, the illegitimate, the outsider, who enters into the inheritance.

We live at a time in history when names and things have gotten very far separated. Institutions which call themselves by the name of God and of Christ are among the chief of those that are doing the works of pollution, oppression, war. Conversely: the majority of those who are doing the works of restoration, justice, peace, do *not* call themselves by the name of God. That remnant of us who *both* call ourselves by the name of God *and* try to do the works of the Spirit have a double task laid on us. On the one hand, we should bring names and things back together again. That means trying to help people in the churches read the revelation in the Bible and in the newspapers, and discover those commandments on which their salvation stands or falls. That also means helping people in the secular movement for peace and justice discover their true roots in the movement of God in history, for without those roots they will in the end wither.

But we cannot count on bringing names and things wholly back together again. Because normally a new thing doesn't find its true name until it has emerged full-blown into history. And so we are faced with our second task: a clear choice of loyalties. Is our place with the institution which has the name of God's will but not the reality; or with the reality, even without the name? Put that way, the choice imposes itself. Which means that our concern is *more for the unity of those who are doing God's work than for the unity of what is formally called the church.* And this is not merely a tactical decision. For the New Testament texts we looked at say very plainly that the new way which Jesus illustrates and brings in is the only possible basis of unity. If a large part of what calls itself the church has seriously diverged from that way, church union is impossible or undesirable or both. The church in Europe was united in 1500, fragmented in 1600. And its fragmentation was related very precisely to the rediscovery of important truths about the nature and work of the church.

Thus my initial difficulty with the COCU process is that it has been almost exclusively concerned with the unity of the church, rather than with the unity of the movement for peace, justice, and the environment. I can imagine the response: "We are not concerned to reform the church, but to reunite it." Is it conceived that reform will spring automatically from a united church, or more easily than from a fragmented one? But neither the old tight unity of the Roman Church nor the new loose unity of, say, the United Church of Canada is speaking the prophetic voice we need to hear. I had always assumed that unity followed reform rather than the opposite way around: "Seek ye first God's kingdom and his righteousness [or justice] and all these things will be added to you" (Matthew 6:33). In a preliminary way this happened in the civil-rights movement and in the peace movement; Christians of all sorts committed to those struggles found quite unexpectedly that the barriers between them had fallen—as well as the barriers between Christian and Marxist, black and white, male and female, person and person generally.

In fact, there are all kinds of reform movements inside the church or at its fringes. If COCU had made a determined effort to work for the reunion of the *whole* church, it would have had to deal with issues of peace and justice. But in fact it represents no more an effort to reunite the whole church than the whole of humanity. If it achieves its utmost success, it will have reunited the *church of the American ruling class.* (The only important ruling-class churches left out are parts of the Catholics and Lutherans; but they have never as a whole been part of the ruling structure like the six white denominations represented.) I am sorry for the bluntness of this Marxist analysis, but I don't know any other way to put it. The principal reform element which the proposed *church* includes is the *middle-class liberal intelligentsia:* seminary professors, social-action coordinators on the regional and national levels, suburban lay people oriented toward peace or ecology. But it includes hardly a single reform-minded congregation; those which accidentally formed have tended to drift out of the denominations into the new *ad hoc* or underground ecumenism. And each wing of that liberal intelligentsia is frustrated by the class interests of a much larger group. The lectures of the reform-minded professors are excerpted and ignored by their students (except for the minority who end up professors or outside the structure themselves); the programs of the coordinators are cut down by the budget committees; the suburban peace agitators are stifled and contained by their neighbors.

The fundamental original decisions behind *A Plan of Union* meant, in fact, the exclusion of all the mass-based Christian groups in America which might have asked actual reform as a condition of their participation. It will be instructive to list some churches which are absent from the scheme.

1. *Black Baptists.* The three respectable and upwardly mobile black Methodist churches have been included. But the black spirituality which produced King, Abernathy, and the whole civil-rights movement is lacking.

2. *Catholics.* The absence of the Church of Rome, besides elminating from the COCU process Irish policemen, Polish steelworkers, and the like, has also elminated the Catholic worker movement, the catholic resistence of the Berrigans and their companions, the radical nonviolence of the Chicano farm workers under Cesar Chavez.

3. *The peace churches:* Brethren, Mennonites, Quakers.

4. *Pentecostals* and other groups which might introduce an unpredictable element into the timid COCU liturgy.

5. *Action-based task forces.* The reform energy of the white COCU denominations themselves has all flowed into para-ecclesiastical organizations struggling on specific issues: antiwar, for social justice, conservation, farm-worker support, etc. An optional place is allowed for these in the scheme of union, but there is no specific recognition of any existing group or requirement that certain Commissions must be formed.

6. *The Third World.* Because this is an *American* scheme, relating strongly to the old National Council of Churches but hardly at all to the World Council of Churches, Third World issues are excluded. The new Catholic-pentecostal alliance of Latin America appears no more than do Chicanos here; the black revolutionary movements of Africa no more than black revolutionaries here; and so on.

What change in the present bad ways of doing things does the Plan promise (or threaten, depending on your point of view)? Locally, not much. The key provision is in *A Plan of Union* VIII, 25 (p. 59): "The district shall take the practical actions necessary to assure that all of the parishes within its area shall include the different races and socio-economic groups of the whole area." The force of this is diluted by a couple of considerations. First, the parish can break itself down into congregations and task groups. In one local discussion on COCU I attended, a conservative supporter of the scheme took it for granted that existing congregations going into the new parish could maintain themselves as "clubs of like-minded people doing things in their own way." I am not sure the times are propitious for the emergence of a tough-minded discipline in any kind of organization. Nowhere in the Plan is there the kind of authority which could actually push through any kind of *Sunday busing*. People drive out of their neighborhoods now to seek a congregation of like-minded people; are they likely to drive out of their neighborhoods to be exposed to a congregation of different-minded people? But further, there is little use in the gerrymandered parish boundaries if the different races and socio-economic groups of the whole area are not represented in it. For example: In a typical town of California's Central Valley, COCU union would pull together in a solid bloc the white grower and merchant churches which now compete at least on an ecclesiastical level. The Catholic Anglo parish would find it easy to relate to the new structure. Even more isolated and threatened than now would remain the white pentecostal congregations, the black stroefront churches, and the Catholic Chicano parish.

I understand that, in spite of these facts which pull the teeth from the new parish concept, it remains distasteful enough to conservative lay chancellors that they are likely to try and block the Plan. Is that opposition consistent enough so that the COCU scheme can be seen as a clear blow against racism? I don't think so. In the enormous mass of minute concrete details which the Plan envisages, I see no guarantee at all that racial unity would emerge as an unambiguous issue. The covenant statement (Chapter I) of the Plan says that the churches agree to "struggle against racism, poverty, environmental blight, war, and other problems of the family of man" (*A Plan of Union*, I, p. 9). And the Plan makes explicit provisions, such as they are, only for racial balance. It is silent (so far as I can discover) on: peace education; income sharing between rich people and poor people; the problem of divided loyalty in military and prison chaplaincy; ecology action; social change as a criterion for church investments. The only hard hammering-out of conflicting interests which the Plan shows is in the area of church government. Even here it remains ambiguous on the one point of church government where fresh winds are today blowing: the ordination of women.

How far at this point is *A Plan of Union* open to modification? Not very far, I should say. The denominational enabling actions can be read in Vic Jameson's pamphlet "What Does God Require of Us Now?" All but a couple refer to the specific 1970 *Plan of Union* document. I assume that people are anxious *not* to have to go back to the denominations with a different document for approval. That means: efforts to build specific commitments into the united church would have to be done through its own structures as they are formed, rather than through amendments to *A Plan of Union.*

Should I—should people who see things more or less as I do—work actively to support *A Plan of Union?* That would seem to be the immediate practical question. But to answer it, we have to answer a prior question: What is likely to take place if the union at some point acquires good chances of actually happening? We could invent one of those fun retrospective scenarios of how it happened, but the danger of projecting our hopes and fears is too strong. Let's try to think about it fairly.

In 1972 I see the energy of the denominations at low ebb; it strikes me as improbable that they will push through to the union out of their own resources. But at any time in the next five years I can imagine a number of external events that might well pull America's ruling class together. Such events could be: accidental explosion of a nuclear bomb in some inhabited place; sudden appearance of a new and dangerous level of pollution; the collapse of marine life in the Baltic or some other inland sea; massive deaths from hunger and/or disease in Bengal; a black armed uprising in America; new communist governments in Southeast Asia; a series of socialist victories in Latin America; serious inflation or some other fiscal breakdown; heavy repression of white and black radicals in the U.S.; counterinsurgency and air war by the U.S. in the Middle East. Any one of these events or a combination would generate serious social disturbances in America. Moderate liberals and moderate conservatives in the churches might have enough incentive to sink their differences and present a united front. Nothing but *A Plan of Union* would be available for them to crystallize around. Emergency conferences of denominational executives would be held. Noncenter groups of all sorts would splinter off. Radicals in the three black Methodist churches would go out and join their brothers. Anglo-Catholic parishes and dioceses in the Episcopal Church would split off on the issue of apostolic succession. A large bloc of the Southern Presbyterians would go into a lily-white synod. Theologically liberal congregations in the U.C.C. would switch to the Unitarians or continuing Congregationalists, depending on their political orientation. Perhaps the Methodists would hold together best, for the Plan does have a kind of Methodist ring, with its bishops but lacking a developed theory of the episcopate.

So there the united church is! What does it look like? It has 18,000,000 members and 60,000 pastors. (I added together the figures from *Yearbook*

of American Churches 1971 and assumed twenty-five per cent losses.)
Nearly half of it is the former United Methodist Church. It is not much
smaller than the American Catholic Church, which in 1969 also claimed
60,000 pastors and 48,000,000 members (the latter figure, unlike the
Protestant ones, includes children under thirteen—and probably even
more nominal or apostate members). It far overshadows the Southern
Baptist Convention, with its 29,000 pastors and 11,500,000 members,
which remains America's one regional established church. As governing
bodies on every level are shuffled, new coalitions and groupings emerge
weekly. There is a gigantic power struggle among the former denominational executives to retain their former level; many more jobs than were
originally contemplated are invented to satisfy them. (See the ideal description of the "Transitional Period" in *A Plan of Union* X, pp. 76–82.)

At the same time the United States generally is in deepened social
crisis—we had to assume a crisis to motivate union in the first place. Advocates of law-and-order and of social justice are locked in combat at
many levels of government—unless the issue has already been decided.
Both parties in the state appeal to the new church, as well as to the
Catholic Church here, to act in fact like the church of America. The
same conflict is going on in the united church—complicated by the struggle between black and white executives, which has no parallel of the
same intensity in the state. The biennial or annual meetings of the National Assembly in its 1,500-member plenaries (*A Plan of Union,* VIII,
116, p. 69) pass elaborately compromised resolutions on social affairs,
which the General Council of forty-five or more people supplements and
tries or fails to carry out.

In the continuing posture of the Third World, overseas missions do
not loom very much larger than today. Consolidation of the nine churches
has brought about some actual administrative economies. On four levels
—parish, district, region, nation—there is a gigantic budget for home
missions and social change, up for grabs to whoever presents the best
case or wins the closest access. A large minority of conservatives complains that the decisions are too liberal, and sets up its own scheme for
mission giving. A smaller minority of radicals also complains that the
decisions are too "liberal." On the one hand, an independently funded
conservative evangelical mission society emerges. On the other hand, the
radicals jell into an opposition.

The steady rise of the gross national product is not affected by these
changes. (I didn't list a major depression among possible crises; it might
very well be a good thing, but I don't see it in the cards.) If anything,
the social position of the American ruling class is stabilized a little by
its consolidation into one church. The annual military budget remains
not far under ten per cent of the GNP. Destruction of the planetary

ecology continues to accelerate. If racial war has been avoided here, the gap between American affluence and Third World poverty continues to widen. Family life in the united church remains torn by divorce, alcoholism, emotional breakdown, and the youth rebellion. Beatniks, hippies, dropouts, street people all have contributed features to a new style of youth culture, which is kept alive by a new form of universal national service, extended now to women also.

All right now. Those of us who all along have been struggling to work and witness for peace, simplicity of life-style, justice to poor peoples, piety to the creation—how do we relate to the new church thing that has happened? Secretly—or, better, openly—we get a few of our people into high slots in the social-justice task forces. There they siphon off some funds for our projects—but can never be fully counted on when most needed. The permanent headquarters staff in Lincoln, Nebraska, evolves an impenetrable style of public statement, which avoids total subservience to the U.S. government—at the cost of never committing itself to actual definite risky action. The old denominational peace fellowships, Clergy and Laymen Concerned, and the Fellowship of Reconciliation have put together a working radical peace coalition. But they have lost a lot of their strength to the new National Church Task Force on Justice Between Nations, which publishes commission reports and makes it clear that it, and not the radical coalition, is the peace spokesman for the united church. The same pattern comes about with racial justice, ecology groups, population planning.

And there my crystal ball clouded over and cracked! I'm afraid it was a kind of futuralogical scenario, after all. Before it fades away like other dreams, let me ask: How do I relate to it? In some respects it would be easier than the struggle now—more like the situation of Catholic radicals who know that for the rest of their lives they can count on the same monolithic enemy. The united church of America would be a sitting duck, a barn-door target for the Word of God. It would be fun to not have to take responsibility for its actions, for its inactivity. . . .

All the same, for the decreasing number of us who remembered how things were before, the united church would be there as witness to our failure—our failure, above all, to persuade the American ruling class that it should *not* consolidate its class interests. I feel that a criticism must be made of the well-educated and well-intentioned men, some of them my friends, who put the Plan together: they took up the wrong concerns and set the wrong priorities. The appearance of one big ruling-class church in America would mean that no poor people's church could enter into it without simply being swallowed up. Was it their plan to start negotiations with the Roman Church from a position of strength? That is too much like Mr. Nixon's plan to build more missiles to enter into disarmament talks on a basis of parity. . . .

And so in the end I have to conclude, No, I do not want to take the COCU road nor to point others onto it, because it would mean rejecting other roads which offer more hope. Probably it was good that we should reconnoiter the COCU road this far, to be sure what it looked like. Perhaps it is not very likely that the nine churches will take it, after all. Did our scenario, like other visions of the future, seem improbable? I think it did. And the biggest improbability, to my mind, was this: that the church executives who can say no to the Plan would at the moment of truth (in spite of crisis) lay themselves open to all that hassle and say yes. They had to pay lip-service to the idea of unity, at least as far as putting the Plan together. Now let us all agree that there are many roads—roads which lead directly to real elements of union and renewal, roads which, above all, do not exclude each other. Let me just state very briefly what some of those roads have been.

Selma. In the churches of that small town a fellowship of black and white, Catholic and Protestant, was born; the friendships made there still hold our movement together.

The peace movement. As the meal of Christ has again and again been repeated in the streets and jails of America, outside and inside the barbed wire, nobody was excluded; a working community grew up around the actual tasks of the Gospel.

The farm-worker ministry. The initial burdens of nonviolence, labor, risk were taken up by plain, poor Spanish Catholic people. They then simply declared that "anybody who refused to eat a grape" was part of the farm workers' union—mostly middle-class Protestants.

And so on. These actual deeds of unity were precious to us, both for themselves and because they pointed ahead to the broadest imaginable type of church union in the future. In these actions, Quakers and people from the peace churches were just about reconciled to the established churches that they had come out of—for the best possible reasons, Gospel reasons. The COCU plan shuts once again the doors that had seemed to be opened.

But that is not the primary consideration; the primary consideration, as I said at the beginning, is to build an inclusive unity of all people, wherever we can find them, for the critical life-and-death tasks that we are faced with. When that unity has begun to exist, it is also necessary to perform the symbolic act of calling it by its true name. But until the new reality has come to birth, there is nothing to give a name to! A *Plan of Union* does not give any adequate reason why conscientious people should adhere to the church, united or disunited, in the first place. I believe that omission was deliberate; I can only see it as irremediable.

In times past, church renewal—whether through union or separation—has happened only when men and women saw their life and salvation at stake. Any lesser motive is insufficient to motivate the struggle. Today we know that our life and salvation stand or fall with peace, justice for poor people, the restoration of the earth. Knowing the faults of our own heart, and our neighbor's heart, as we do, we are persuaded that only through the Gospel have we even a fighting chance for those things. And unless a page tastes and smells of our salvation, even though it has printed on it every other church word twenty times over, we cannot recognize it as the Gospel.

16

A Way Ahead:
The Church of Christ Uniting

WILLIAM JERRY BONEY

What's wrong, if anything, with COCU? "It's fine except a hundred years too late" (an editor). "It's interesting, but a hundred years too soon" (a moderator).

Remarks heard in a group studying *A Plan of Union for the Church of Christ Uniting:* "Well, I can see why you Presbyterians would like the plan—after all, it's *your* government." "Do *we* have bishops?!" "No, it's Methodist, really." "On the contrary, isn't it low-church Episcopalians who have the least to shift?" Etc., etc.

Remarks from the same occasion, but now between those over thirty-five and a group of students: "The parish is unrealistic. People are wedded to the congregations." The parish is the *only* thing right with *A Plan of Union.*" "No, he's right, the parish is unrealistic—a lot of furniture-moving but finally a difference without a difference. It's still the institutional game."

From here and there: "COCU is a chip off the old One World thing." "Blatant nationalism!" "It would rob black people of their heritage." "But the whole point is more forced integration (Sunday busing!)." "The Anglo-Saxon middle class and black friends, together at prayer."

A Way Between and Ahead

Almost every contested discussion of the Consultation on Church Union, in fact, *though largely unwittingly,* puts COCU and the proposed Church of Christ Uniting in the middle. The *de facto* placement is correct, but unseen for what it is. COCU *is* an effort of the pioneering, risk-taking middle. However, the early seventies are little equipped even to notice such a venture. The way of the times in and out of the churches is to expect in everything polarization, and in much to achieve it: left, right; winners, losers; too late, too soon; etc. The middle is the space overlooked as you peer at "them" or "that" over there. The pioneering or far-out middle is simply out of view excepting for rare glimpses, being left and right, up and down, from that which is overlooked.

To use terms borrowed from Colin Williams, Donald Mackinnon, and others, COCU is trying to steer a creative course between institutional fundamentalism—the hallowing of yesterday's structures (regularly confused with those of the New Testament or early church)—and institutional docetism—the failure to take seriously the embodiment of the body of Christ, the church. This is also the course of Hans Küng, that very model of a stubborn man of the far-out middle. Küng has written: ". . . the Spirit of God, if domiciled in the Church, is not domesticated in it. He is and remains the free Spirit of the free Lord not only of the 'holy city,' not only of Church offices, not only of the Catholic Church, not only of Christians, but of the whole world." [1] "Domiciled" but not "domesticated": a balance that has very little to do with the Golden Mean (a placid near-in middle); a view of the Spirit that permits neither fundamentalism nor docetism.

The tenth plenary of the Consultation, meeting in Denver in 1971, found some participants wishing to say that the Consultation was a process and *not* a plan. This suggestion meant different things to different persons. Insofar as it meant the Consultation must now be a process of growth involving more and more of its members with each other and together with others, and not be narrowly content with forming a plan— the plenary heartily concurred in its final documents. Insofar as the expression re-underlined that the Consultation seriously expects extensive revision in the present draft plan—all could agree. Insofar as it meant for a few let's enjoy the courtship for whatever it's worth—and may it be great!—but not really desire or expect a union: *this* the tenth plenary in no wise agreed to.

The Denver plenary, 1971, persisted in "a way between." "We have seen more vividly than ever before the importance of mutual involvement among Christians . . . in the quest for the church which God wills," wrote the Denver participants in "A Word to the Churches"; but they had this to say as well: "We declare with a new conviction the gospel imperative to orangic union. . . . As his ministers of reconciliation we must find together those structures for mission which will enable us to serve the oppressed, the hurt, and the poor in ways not open to us in our separateness." [2] There is no doubt COCU is a process, and that it needs to become more fully a process—particularly by involving and hearing many more persons; but the needs are too serious, the faith too incarnational, to be guided by the maxim "getting there is all the fun." (This is said realizing there is no "arrival," not even union, with which a "uniting" church would stop.)

What is proposed is a way of considerable risk. It is a matter of consistently pressing for change well beyond the inclination of conservatives, but not enough to sate the appetite of the radical who feels no responsibility for indicating what better structures might come next. It is, in one sense of a widely loathed word, "liberal." No prudent man expecting to be heard nowadays would choose to be known as a liberal. We can be thankful that some perisist nonetheless in seeking a way between that might also be an advance.[3]

This "balance with risk" can be illustrated with regard to *A Plan of Union*. As all agree, the parish plan in *A Plan of Union* is a departure. It is a departure, however, within a total context of many continuities (most of them still creative). Without the parish plan, or if not this plan then *another*, the Consultation will have "flinched" at a vital point in the quest for a way between that is a way ahead. The Consultation cannot indulge in romanticism about structures (a form of cryptodocetism). Yet it *must* take risks that will be too much for many conservatives. This side of the double risk needs stress at the moment because there seems particular pressure to make the parish decidedly less of a departure in the revised plan than it is in the draft plan. The draft plan is traditional in so many other ways that it requires, if not this parish, then another "parish" to keep creative balance in the whole. If something with the serious, and admittedly threatening, potential for difference of the parish is not in the revised plan, then there is serious question as to whether the whole is worth the effort. Is not the key difference between union and merger (and the Consultation has rightly stressed that it does not intend a mere merger) that union, unlike merger, brings all into a new situation that is in *important* ways other than any have known before? (How many United Church of Christ congregations that come out of the old Evangelical and Reformed Church still think of themselves as not really UCC? *And* have been little challenged in this self-estimate? Not to mention Congregational Christians unaffected by the admixture of "Christian" in their congregational life, much less the grouping with the E&R's.) Plainly, it is possible to go to a great deal of ecumenical trouble and fuss—capped with stirring doxologies—for very little live difference as far as the average churchgoer is concerned. The plan for this *union* must have an excellent chance of making a creative difference *at the grass roots*, costly as that may well be.

The provisions of the parish plan in the draft plan can be *improved* only by persons committed to seeing that the element of serious "departure" for the local level of the church is not removed. Improvements are needed, to be sure. For example: it may well be that the black contributions need to be safeguarded and encouraged with explicit provisions that wherever possible there will be *majority* black parishes, and many parishes in which blacks will constitute a substantial minority. *No* black congregation should be pushed to enter a parish in which the total number of blacks from all uniting congregations is under a certain percentage. In another, though related, matter: it is necessary to ask whether there will be enough leadership slots in a new church guided by the draft plan. It may be that parishes will need to give away something in efficiency and economy in order to permit decision-making contributions from as many persons as possible. This consideration brings us to a topic where a breakthrough is most needed and particularly difficult: authority.

A Way Ahead in "Authority"?

The heart of the problem of authority in the church is reached with Hans Küng's realization that "the person who can advise and collaborate, but not participate in decision-making in a manner befitting his status, *is* not really the church, but only *belongs* to the church." [4] It is well known that Hans Küng has threatened traditional elements in the Roman Catholic Church, and embarrassed many with official responsibilities great and small who might consider that they in large part agree with him. No son of his church feels more acutely the responsibility to participate personally in the development of his church so that *all* of its members may *be* the church. Because this is so, authority has become the "neuralgic point" [5] for Küng as well as for Pope Paul VI. The Vatican II promises regarding collegiality, subsidiarity, respect for persons and personality, have not only remained largely unfulfilled, as Küng sees it, but, after *Humani Vitae*, almost mocked. (The Synod of 1971 hardly disproved his analysis.)

It is gratifying that a number of Catholic theologians, none of whom entirely agrees with Küng, have resolved that the present crisis precipitated by Paul VI (and Küng) is, after all, one of opportunity. So it is a time not for "holding the line," much less for repression, but for a new look at the meaning of authority and the exercise of authority: the meaning of confidence in the Spirit, and the ways of acting upon that confidence. [6] All Christians claiming to rely on the guidance of the Spirit in their church *should* be able to recognize that these are *their* theologians at work on their problems.

Unfortunately, it is all too easy for Protestants hearing of "The Infallibility Debate" to conclude that this is a Roman Catholic matter, and remark that if Catholics want to progress in humanity in their decision-making they should become "democratic" *as we* are. How easily, though, the few manage the many in Protestant "democracies." How frequently the many, when they *are* heard, show little evidence of having sought the mind of Christ. The decision of the Southern Baptist Sunday School Board in the fall of 1971 to recall the complete press run of materials dealing with blacks seeking church membership (which included a photo of black and white children together)—because "it could have been construed as improper promotion on the part of the Sunday School Board of integration in the Churches, which is an individual church matter under Baptist polity" [7]—speaks for itself. To be sure, many Baptists —white, black, Southern and otherwise—would insist that their polity requires an assumption of more responsibility and courage by the associational church than this decision reflects. Presbyterians have had their misdirected heresy trials, conducted according to all the rules of a good representative democracy. Methodists have occasionally avoided the "issue" and Spirit by ducking behind (really burrowing within) their ample polity. *Have* we a polity—*any* of us, in or out of COCU? Or do we seek one to come? Surely, the latter.

Granted there is no conceivable polity (set of arrangements for making authoritative decisions and carrying them out) that cannot be used as a defense against the Spirit; but *is* the COCU polity a step ahead?

Chapter VIII of *A Plan of Union* provides for a carefully ordered system of legislative bodies with executives and courts at four levels, a pattern of representative democracy much like that most of the COCU denominations have already known. The plan includes safeguards against the concentration of power at the national level. It contains checks and balances between the levels, and between responsible parties at the same level. Hans Küng might passingly envy aspects of the arrangement. Nonetheless, on balance, the present draft plan for a Church of Christ Uniting does not contain a creative advance in decision-making provisions beyond that which the participating churches have known.

As suggested briefly above, a weakness of the parish plan at present is that it will allow far fewer persons to participate in official decision-making than have a recognized niche in the nine churches. The answer does not seem to be to provide for a parish council of vast size (that is not ruled out by *A Plan of Union*, VIII, 33, p. 61), although, to repeat, the number of council members could well afford to be larger than considerations of efficiency and economy alone might dictate.

The problem is that representative democracy as we have experienced it has a record of including minorities only slowly and grudgingly, if at all. Can the CCU be yet more fully human in its authoritative ways and styles than the city halls, the statehouses? Than the Presbyterian Church, U.S., and the United Methodist Church? This is a particularly important question for the minorities whose humanity requires that they not again be silenced, and for the majorities whose humanity requires that they not fall further into callousness. New styles and ways of decision-making are desperately needed in our society and in our churches without a doubt —at the very least, meaningful modifications of the inherited forms and procedures.

The way between and ahead for the COCU in the matter of authoritative decision-making might well include further incorporation of elements of "participatory democracy" within the basic frame of a system of representative democracy. Many things, admittedly, have been called "participatory democracy": Woodstock, a picket line, a riot, a Town Meeting, a Friends' Meeting, the governing ways and means of certain religious orders. Strictly considered, the phenomenon has to do with proceeding by a consensus of all involved. Less strictly, it refers to shared feelings of belonging and agreeing that can be brought about in any of many ways.

The draft document *A Plan of Union* is not without participatory features. At the parish level, the annual parish meeting can be such an occasion, although present meetings of the type are only rarely such. The provision for task groups connected to the church at all levels could turn out to be far more significant. The internal directing of these groups could typically be by consensus. Furthermore, representatives from the task groups of the parish could *regularly* be invited and expected to sit with the parish council without a vote but with full privilege of the floor. Task groups related to the district could include experimental communities with much the same autonomy and responsibilities as parishes, but not necessarily with a council, and perhaps without clergy.

So much can be suggested as possible. But are there indications of a tangible sort within the life of the Consultation today of "humanizing" in decision-making?

The Denver plenary of the Consultation showed sensitivity and ingenuity in providing for wider participation in its proceedings. At Denver 48 per cent of those present had not previously attended an assembly. Over 50 per cent of those participating were in nonvoting categories such as "accredited visitor," "invited guest," etc.—but the important point is that at this plenary the distinction between voting and nonvoting participants was not as it had been before. All persons accredited to the assembly, whether or not they were voting delegates, had the privilege of the floor in plenary sessions, and a full voice in the work groups. The result was simply a different meeting, a more fully "listening" assembly. Whether or not this same arrangement will pertain at the succeeding plenary, where more votes must be taken than at Denver, remains to be seen. There is good reason to believe, however, that the eleventh plenary will keep continuity with the new start of the tenth.

Those who demand of the Consultation—rightly!—that it begin now to show *something* of the difference the CCU might make, should consider seriously Denver as an expression of sensitivity for new ways and styles of decision-making. At the same time, the Consultation must not leave the Denver experimentation as a *cul de sac,* unreflected in arrangements for coming plenaries *and* in the revision of *A Plan of Union.*

In an address delivered to the Denver plenary, Peter L. Berger made an appeal for a "stance of authority" among Christians, a new sense of Christian conviction and willingness to speak with conviction.[8] The appeal is in order—in fact, much needed—so long as the misunderstandings Peter Berger hoped to avoid are in fact avoided: authoritarianism, and theological and ecclesiastical conservatism. (How difficult it is to speak as he spoke and not be misinterpreted by some is indicated by the report of the Berger speech in *Time,* October 11, 1971, headlined, "The Death of Relevance.") The student of Hans Küng will take as the core of "ecclesiastical conservatism" unwillingness to see one's church develop more truly human—inclusive, representative, responsible—ways of making and carrying out decisions. There is a way of appealing for authority (as confidence) that appears to minimize serious listening to the world and therewith shows scant concern for finding new modes of exercising authority. It is not enough—indeed, it can be harmful—to appeal to authority, speak with authority, if one fails to see Christian authority properly itself as developing—in dialogue with the world, in response to the Spirit (John 16: 12–13).

Confident and Listening (United and Uniting)

A way between and ahead is one of confidence, and of listening.

Confidence in some fundamentals is indispensable, as Peter Berger has pointed out. New listening extending to fundamentals is also indispensable.

There are a variety of interpretations of John 17 and other "unity" passages in the New Testament. Some of these run heavily to stress on "spiritual" unity, or otherwise variously explain and condone the present church dismemberment. For their part, those committed to the Consultation on Church Union take as a fundamental:

> The Church is one.
> Yet the disunity of the visible companies of Christian people obscures this reality. In a world of repression and anarchy, a renewed church is called to a new unity. This oneness in the church is required for the credibility and effectiveness of Christ's mission. [*A Plan of Union,* II, 2–3, p. 10].

Many of those so committed and engaged in the Consultation are, as alleged, Anglo-Saxon, middle-class, and over thirty-five. They could not be unaware that these givens make it difficult for some others to hear them, and with reason. Of late they have sometimes hesitated to voice their views, even—or particularly—in those matters where they have firmest convictions. This is false modesty, an improper expression of guilt and/or fear that does no credit to themselves or to those who are rightly wary of them. As H. Richard Niebuhr observed: "It is not evident that the man who is forced to confess that his view of things is conditioned by the standpoint he occupies must doubt the reality of what he sees." [9] This much can be said to men with prior conditioning of every sort, not excluding that by privilege.

It should be encouraging to these sometimes intimidated ecumenists that they are joined—indeed, well *preceded*—in their convictions regarding "unity" in the New Testament by a goodly company of those in America and abroad whose "givens" are not their own. And, of course, they are opposed by a legion of Anglo-Saxon, etc., Christians—and others —here and elsewhere.

Two questions above all confront those engaged today in the process which is the Consultation on Church Union: do they have confidence still in their originating goal? And, if confident, are they also open—can they listen and learn?

With regard to the first, as just noted, intimidation is real, self-doubt is not unknown, but resolve is an even more apparent fact. This "off season" for wide popular interest in COCU (and ecumenism generally) has revealed those engaged in the Consultation process to be there with tenacity, and after Denver one must add with increasing boldness as well. Is it possible, however, for a resolved, tenacious fellowship also to be open? *This is the crucial question.* There are those, of course, who say the Consultation is now incapable of further serious listening and growth. It is reported as a well-known fact that COCU cannot be translated beyond its native sixties.

Do the process and the draft plan bear indelible marks of having been born and raised in the sixties? Of course. Is COCU therefore dead or moribund? No more than anything else stemming from earlier years *must* crumble with the coming of a new age (or agelet). If the Consultation had no seriousness and honesty in expecting extensive changes in the draft document, A Plan of Union—all would be finished. If the Consultation were not a process "peopled" very largely by those alive and participating in the seventies—it would be dead. If the Consultation were a club whose leadership had been permanently set ten years ago (which the tenth plenary belied)—it would be beyond recall. None of these fears, or "ghoulish" hopes, fits the Consultation.

On the other hand, COCU has some special answering to do about its listening, participating, and growth now that the seventies are here.

Does this process begun earlier *show* itself open to new voices speaking of separation, liberation, consensus, *ad-hoc*-ism, localism, individualism, etc.? Can it listen and participate fully and wisely, knowing there are tensions *among* the emphases of this day, and knowing that most of those persons it must listen to and work with are paying scant (at most) attention to the Consultation?

"A Word to the Churches from the Consultation on Church Union, Denver, Colorado, 1971," opens wth these paragraphs:

> Ten years ago our churches set out in quest of a united church faithful to our Lord's intention for a reconciled and reconciling community ministering to a divided humanity. In the first years of the· Consultation we felt the Spirit speaking to us primarily through one another as we shared the faith we have received through our separate traditions. At Denver his voice has come to us particularly in the anguish of the oppressed as we listened to the cry of Chicanos, American blacks, and a black South African, with the hurt of Attica, Vietnam, and East Pakistan heavy on our hearts. We have tried to face our work with determination to find a form of church ready to serve and suffer in faithfulness to Christ our Lord.
>
> In this mood we reaffirm our commitment to continue together in this venture of obedience.[10]

Is this shift largely verbal? It could be. But the Denver recommendations to the Consultation churches for concrete actions give additional indication of "shift" and effectual listening: "take steps as are necessary to promote racial justice and to provide compensatory treatment," "encourage and grant freedom to . . . congregations to participate in the forming of model parishes," "change delegations . . . to provide a more equitable representation of minority groups and women, and do so according to a formula to be recommended," "include . . . at least one youth twenty-five years of age or under" and much else.[11] The important conversations over a period of time between the National Committee of Black Churchmen (NCBC) and the Consultation staff should be mentioned; and the reader might refer again to what has been said above about the makeup and participatory features of the tenth plenary. Still the evidence that could be marshaled of new listening by this unconsummated-process-almost-without-a-budget is hardly more than begun.

Is there *really warrant* for the opinion that COCU will not survive in the seventies, much less serve? That view seems far more precarious than the situation of the Consultation. But what then is the meaning of the obvious lack of wide interest in COCU? Why does it seem to be way down on the priority lists of even active COCU-related Protestant churchmen? A large part of the answer has to do, as noted earlier, with the difficulty of a polarized, crisis-riveted time in noticing a venture in the middle, no matter how creative. But a neglected fact and a neglected interpretation, do in significant *part* account for the greatly underestimated further fact that year after year the COCU denominations pass up the chance to get out of the Consultation and usually, albeit routinely, express some satisfaction at being in.

The neglected fact is that it is the denominations as we have known them that are less and less viable. For them, sooner or later, something like a Church of Christ Uniting is a necessity if transition without enormous loss to better vehicles is to be accomplished at all. The denominations show unmanageable strain in many ways, including that from escalating local cooperation and *unions* flowing freely and often "unconstitutionally" across and around them. When all is probed, the denominations do *not* stay in the Consultation, as some critics imply, because it is not worth the trouble to get out. They continue because many leaders at least suspect (and have reason to hope) that a Church of Christ Uniting is "untimely" today *because it belongs to our future,* and not because it belongs to our past (which it does also).

The neglected interpretation is already in what has just been said, but perhaps a semiparable will also help convey it. The cook at certain hours is harried. If one watches what the cook most frets over when busiest in the kitchen, one might conclude that the cook's priorities are keeping rolls from burning, answering the phone, making a salad, washing dishes, removing a child from danger and the cat from the garbage. At the moment these are priorities, they have to be. But at the back of the stove simmers the main dish—not forgotten, hardly watched. Before long we will eat. (Of course, during dinner the phone may ring, etc.)

In all this some things of importance are said about expectations of the future. Again Peter Berger has been most instructive: we must, he said, avoid the error of "projecting the indefinite continuation of present trends in the future." [12]

The decades go by in ever fewer years. The sixties were at least two if not three "decades." Every indication is that the later seventies will contain at least one further "decade." The Consultation cannot "close on" the early seventies any more than with the early sixties. We can be assured that whatever is to come before the 1970s are past will not be a simple "Amen" to the years *circa* 1972. We can also be sure there will be no return to the Kennedy years, or any others. Nonetheless, is it not quite possible that American society and its church institutions will once again, and sooner than many suspect, be able to give an *honest* "yes" or "no" to a proposal regarding institutions that is neither a call to "stand pat" nor an attempt to pump-prime the eschaton?

Will not Christians sooner than later, precisely for the sake of their new ecumenical, grass-roots, ad-hoc achievements, seek forms—and largely new forms—for overview and connection? In short, if the churches are not to vanish—and the reliable promise of the Spirit is that this will not happen—can they not be expected to return again and again to the full agenda of renewal and reunion, overcoming all forms of fundamentalism, docetism, and fatigue?

It may just be a humbled, strengthened, many times purged and heartened Consultation on Church Union that finally provides the vehicle for the achievement of new flexible institutions for much of American Protestantism. If this turns out to be so, it will be because the fathers of the Consultation, and those who joined them on the way, resolved to be confident in a direction toward which the Spirit compelled them, and open to the fresh leadings of the same. They proposed and persisted toward a church "United and Uniting." "The specific purpose of this union is not the merger of denominations, but the formation through union of a dynamic united and uniting church. This pilgrimage has at its ultimate goal the unity of the whole church" (*A Plan of Union*, II, 24, p. 13).

A church seriously committed to manifest unity with *all* Christians is a church seeking solidarity with all men and all creation. *It is a church whose founding impulse should bring it ever again to renewal through serious openness to another, and another, and all others.*

It is necessary to stress, however, that the Consultation is quite aware that it is not the only or necessarily the primary place where the Spirit is at work for unity and renewal. Not even enthusiasts who have occasionally spoken of COCU with a touch of triumphalism believe this. It is enough to be *one* fellowship-in-becoming with openness to the unitive, reforming Spirit. The work of the Spirit in the Church of South India is an invaluable gift to a CCU in America. So are the achievements of united churches in Canada, Japan, Zaire (Congo), and elsewhere. The Consultation must never overlook or undervalue the historic and ongoing responses to the Spirit of unity and renewal among Lutherans, Baptists, Pentecostals, Roman Catholics, and so many others in the United States alone. The enormous ecumenical, worldwide advance that was Vatican II by itself puts the COCU efforts into perspective, and at the same time, together with these other expressions (and still others—the Berrigans, Willy Brandt, Helder Camara, Camilo Torres, Malcolm X), underlines its true importance.

An Orienting Possibility

In the place of a conclusion, here is the "story" of a possibility. The story is not predictive. That is, it is not about anything which "must" or even "likely" will happen "anyway." It is a sketch of what could be an orienting possibility. The possibility exists, depending upon whether or not it engages men and women who will both work and wait for it. Through interest shown in various versions—e.g., those of Douglas Horton and Hans Küng [13]—this engagement has already well begun.

During the 1970's and eighties the spirit of John XXIII and the influence of Vatican II proved increasingly subversive within the Roman Catholic Church. Vatican II was officially reinterpreted at many points, but never "domesticated." John XXIII was canonized, but his holiness could not be contained. Synods were still held occasionally to help link the bishops more closely to the Vatican. Greater and greater care was taken to see that new bishops were "loyal" and "sound." But, for all the pains and anguish, the center held less and less, to the detriment of that visible worldwide frame for unity that was a gift for all Christians in the stewardship care largely of Roman Catholics. The turning point came when it became apparent even to curial moderates that "Ultramontanist" ways and styles in the late twentieth century were not only not preserving the unity of the Roman Catholic Church, but were the greatest impediment to *that* unity as well as to fuller unity. Hans Küng's suggestions (and by this time those of many others) for development beyond "papacy" to "petrine ministry" could now be heard even by a sizable number of bishops and *monsignori*. Significantly, fewer of these prelates felt they had to hold that defense of the irreducible *skandalon* of the Gospel required rejection of further development of the Teaching Office.

So it was that in 1990 a pope was elected who took the name and ways of John XXIII. He proved—in the words of Hans Küng—to have

> a genuinely evangelical and not a juridical-formalistic and static-bureaucratic view of the Church. He [saw] the mystery of the Church in the light of the gospel, of the New Testament: not as a centrailzed administrative unity . . . but as one Church realized authentically in the local Churches . . . everywhere forming one community as the one Church of God and thus linked with the Church of Rome as with the center of their unity.[14]

By the year 2000 a number of communions of Christians were in discussions that included the Roman Catholics. Anglicans and Roman Catholics had begun these talks around 1980, but only after 1990 were others persuaded to join. What they were discussing was a church that might or might not be known as "Roman" (though of course including a very large "Latin Rite"), but extending to many more Christians—among many things—a petrine focal point, or ministry for unity. No one spoke any longer of "uniate" relations.

The world at large took much less notice of what the churches were trying to accomplish than had been paid to Vatican II, reflecting the decreased percentage of Christians in relation to the world population, and a drastic decrease among all Christian groups on the northern half of the earth. It was not difficult for the churches discussing to acknowledge they needed each other in many ways.

In 2000 it was taken for granted that Connecticut bordered Tibet. The world really had no alternative but to explore ways of centralized coordination. The question was not whether the world would be "united" but on what basis, and at what cost to humanity before and after. It was almost laughable for some Christians in 2000 to regard the quest for a worldwide union of most Christians as "Constantinian." Buddhists, Moslems, Communists, Christians, Jews, and others, gathering each among themselves, found that these unities greatly aided their "wider" dialogues. Communists, notwithstanding their continuing deep divisions, were the best-organized and largest of the world-level "confessional" groups.

It would have been evidence of a gross loss of faith in their Lord and his mission if Christians had not sought each other worldwide as never before as it became *inescapably* clear that the problems and needs of men in 2000 were bound together earthwide (and beginning to be still wider).

The groups reaching out to each other included Roman Catholics, Lutherans (European and some American), the Anglican Communion, a vigorous group of South American Pentecostals (that had grown much closer to elements of the Roman Catholic Church during the revolutions of the later twentieth century), the World Alliance of United Churches, and individual denominations in various places, including black and white Baptist conventions. Other churches considering joining the union discussions included the Greek Orthodox, other Orthodox, and other ancient Eastern churches. The most helpful forums for the anticipation of these meetings were those provided through the World Council of Churches and other councils of churches.

The largest Protestant group in the United States engaged in the union discussions was the Church of Christ Uniting, a member of the World Alliance of United Churches, the Anglican Communion, and of other communions. (The Church of England itself was by this time a "United" and an "Anglican" church, as were churches in North and South India, Canada, Australia, New Zealand, and elsewhere.) Knowledgeable persons agreed that the major reason such a large and abidingly variegated segment of American Protestantism was open to world-level union in 2000 A.D. was that in the early 1980s the nearly atrophied "unitive muscle" within nine churches had at long last been fully exercised and it could now be called upon again. It was of great importance that twenty years earlier a "united and uniting" church had come to be in the United States.

In 2017—or did it all take place sooner?—a magnificent and quietly celebrated advance was made in the manifest unity of Christ's church on earth with the convening of a council in Jerusalem.

NOTES

1. *The Church*, translated by Ockenden, Ray and Rosaleen (New York: Sheed and Ward, 1967), p. 176.
2. "A Word to the Churches," *Digest of the Proceedings of the Consultation on Church Union*, Vol. X (1971).
3. Nelson, J. Robert, "Toward Ecumenical Convergence," *The Christian Century*, Vol. LXXXVIII, No. 33 (August 18, 1971), p. 972.
4. Küng, Hans, "Participation of the Laity in Church Leadership and in Church Elections," *Bishops and People*, edited and translated by Swidler, Leonard and Arlene (Philadelphia: Westminster Press, 1970), pp. 87–88.
5. Küng, Hans, *Infallible? An Inquiry*, translated by Quinn, Edward (Garden City, New York: Doubleday & Co., 1971), p. 50.
6. See: Kirvan, John J. (ed.), *The Infallibility Debate* (New York: Paulist Press, 1971); *Journal of Ecumenical Studies*, Vol. VIII. No. 4 (Fall, 1971); *America*, Vol. CXXIV, No. 16 (1971), pp. 427–433. For an account of Küng's career up to 1968 see Mary Daly's article "Hans Küng," in Boney, W.J., and Molumby, L.E. (eds.), *The New Day: Catholic Theologians of the Renewal* (Richmond: John Knox Press, 1968), pp. 129–142.
7. *Presbyterian Outlook*, Vol. CLIII, No. 42 (November 22, 1971), p. 3.
8. Berger, Peter L., "A Call for Authority in the Christian Community: An Address Delivered to the Tenth Plenary of the Consultation on Church Union, Denver, Colorado," *The Christian Century*, Vol. LXXXVIII, No. 43 (October 27, 1971), p. 1262.
9. Niebuhr, H. Richard, *The Meaning of Revelation* (New York: The Macmillan Co., 1941), p. 18
10. "A Word to the Churches," *Digest*, Vol. X (1971).
11. "Recommendations to the Churches," *Digest*, Vol. X (1971).
12. Berger, *op. cit.*, p. 1261.
13. Horton, Douglas, *Toward an Undivided Church* (New York: Association Press, and Notre Dame: University of Notre Dame Press, 1967). Hans Küng has written "proleptically" in most of his books; examples: *Freedom Today* (New York: Sheed and Ward, 1966); *The Church*, pp. 444 ff.; *Infallible?*, pp. 241 ff. See also: Boney, W. J., "The 1969 Synod: Ecumenical Thoughts," *Worship*, Vol. XLIII, No. 6 (June-July, 1969), pp. 353–361; and, Boney, W. J., "Ecumenism: The Loss and the Hope," *The Priest*, Vol. XXV, No. 9 (September, 1969), pp. 452–459.
14. *Infallible?*, *op. cit.*, p. 244.

17

COCU and the Wider Reality
of Ecumenism

JOHN F. HOTCHKIN

With ten years of work done, it would be noticeably tardy to complain that the Consultation on Church Union has a somewhat misleading title. No doubt its name was an apt designation of what the participating churches began at the time they began. Also it would be well beyond the mark to describe the present stage of their endeavors by a term so formal as "negotiation." Nevertheless, ten years have made it clear that the meeting of church traditions within the COCU involves more than what we usually have in mind when we speak of a consultation.

The first extensively recorded result of this encounter of church traditions was the enunciation of *Principles for Church Union*. In a real sense these Principles formed the charter upon which more recent steps have been taken. To that extent it can be said that *Principles for Church Union* guide the Consultation process and take precedence over any particular plan developed during that process. It is readily conceivable that on the basis of these Principles several different plans could have been sketched all of which would have reflected the same basis. At the same time it is clear that the Consultation, notwithstanding its name, is considerably more than a think-tank devoted to the research and development of various ecumenical models. It is seeking a single plan for union. The Plan which it has offered for study by the churches is no doubt revisable and, if need be, even replaceable. Yet, however many revisions of plans come before the Consultation in the time ahead, it seems unlikely that there will ever be more than one plan before the churches at a time. Multiple options have their use in imaginative research as well as in internal organizational restructuring. But to go beyond these ventures in an effort to open new paths for history it seems we must go beyond options and come to *a* plan. I mention this because it seems to me that even while principles and processes are of more fundamental importance than particular plans, still whatever plan the churches find successful in bringing together their people, their traditions, and their resources is a plan that will carry great weight in the ecumenical scene.

So even at midpoint one can begin to anticipate the impact of COCU on wider ecumenism. To be sure, the Consultation does not directly engage the entire spectrum of American Christianity. But it does cover a sufficiently broad band of that spectrum to be truly remarkable as much as it is truly catholic, evangelical, and reformed. The emergence in this country of the Church of Christ Uniting would be a reality to which others could scarcely remain indifferent. If this church succeeds in uniting values and perspectives which were previously thought to have limited compatibility and which different churches cherished and upheld in separation, the fact of the Church of Christ Uniting in itself will command serious theological attention for what it can reveal ecclesiologically. But more than this, the distinctive heritages coming together to form this church would endow it with a positive and principled openness to broader and deeper relationships with many other churches. Thus the Church of Christ Uniting will not only change the religious topography of the United States, it will undoubtedly occupy a position of central importance in the new situation that is created by its emergence.

Some, of course, are less than sanguine about the eventual outcome of the Consultation process. No one closely involved with that process would wish to see its difficulties minimized or its critics left unheeded, and certainly no one who has watched its development over a decade would feel inclined to offer definite predictions as to the shape or timing of its eventual results. If indeed the Consultation is somewhere near midpoint, its decisive outcome may be as far in the future as its beginnings are in the past. While that makes definite predictions risky if not impossible, it also suggests that COCU is not about to disappear. It represents more than a momentary inspiration. Having lived through the ever changing ecumenical moods of the last decade, it now seems to have generated its own momentum which will carry it much further.

Perhaps one reason the Consultation has come so far and can go much further is that it has found the practical wisdom not to attempt paper solutions to questions that only life can answer. Examples can be offered. The future of the parish is a question that faces all churches in America today. The Consultation has taken this question very seriously in its efforts to strengthen the resources available to the parishes of the united church. Still the fact remains that a significant number of Christians today do not regard the parish as the primary locale in which they live out their Christian vocation. It's quite possible that even the more resourceful parishes envisioned by the Consultation will not always attract their energies. Also the question must be raised whether in today's multidimensional society the church can effectively carry out its mission basing itself almost exclusively on parish units. The Consultation stresses the importance of the parish as a major component in church life, going so far as to propose that all members of the united church shall hold membership in a parish. At the same time it opens the door to alternative patterns of church life which it describes as "task forces." What the eventual importance of these alternative Christian groups will be as components of church life along with the parishes is a question which only experience can eventually answer. Similarly, the offices of bishops, presbyters, and deacons are positioned in the general scheme of things, but the existential roles to be filled by these men is not foretold in any great detail. Who can say what roles such ministers will play in the life of the church at the turn of the century? The answer to that question will probably best be found in the lives of the men whom the church calls to serve in these capacities. In this respect, it might be helpful to note that the Consultation is in a position not altogether different from that of the Roman Catholic Church. Neither can that church foretell the future exactly as it reconstitutes the distinctive ministry of the diaconate, as it ponders the demands placed upon the presbyterate, and as it tries to reorganize the episcopate for more collegial action. Again, the maintenance of both infant and adult baptism as practices which have strong Christian precedents may be a course dictated by wisdom. The unsettled issues surrounding these two practices may find resolution in a united church in a way that has been impossible so far in separated churches.

By refusing to foretell the unforeseeable or to respond to objections of the past that were meant to be unanswerable, the Consultation is far from papering over problems. Rather, it gives every sign of acting in faith at its time in history. The fact is that not all issues can be resolved by churches in separation. Many differences among Christians can be comprehended and coped with only in the context of a fuller unity.

Taking things in order, the Consultation has given a great deal of attention to insuring the "inclusiveness" whereby the full participation and rightful relationships of all members will be provided for in the united church, "embracing the unity of all persons, regardless of race, age, sex, wealth or culture." This inclusiveness is seen as "a visible aspect of catholicity" (A Plan of Union, II, 17, pp. 11–12).

Another side of catholicity is its extensiveness. The church which hopes to be united seeks also to be uniting. (A somewhat more detailed description of this side of catholicity is found in A Plan of Union, III, 23, p. 20). While the Consultation has properly given priority to building toward internal catholicity, the concern for catholicity in wider relations has never been absent from its considerations. In no sense, either internally or externally, does the Consultation accept exclusiveness as a characteristic of the church for which it is preparing.

As early as 1964 the records of the Princeton meeting stated: "We look forward to the fullness of unity in communion and communion in unity with all the people of God in accordance with Christ's will." [1] The same emphasis reappears later in A Plan of Union: "The united church shall seek communion and union with other churches in the U.S. and elsewhere in the world, including united churches" (A Plan of Union, IX, 6, p. 73). Correspondingly, "the united church will seek to maintain communion with those churches with which the uniting churches previously enjoyed communion. The unity of Christ's body is indivisible. To manifest it in the local community without expressing it in a broader area would be as defeating of ecumenical purpose as is preoccupation with world denominational or confessional unity without attention to other ecumenical options" (A Plan of Union, II, 19, p. 12).

In these references to the goal envisioned for its wider ecumenical relationships, it is particularly interesting to note that the Consultation introduces the term communion. This term is not commonly used in the COCU Principles and Plan. These normally rely on other words such as union and unity, also community, and sometimes terms such as solidarity, covenant, and company to describe the oneness of Christians. The fact that the term communion is used so rarely may heighten its significance when it does appear in COCU language. But we can also notice an apparent uneasiness about the word, for, when used, it is linked with either union or unity.

Perhaps one reason for this uneasiness is that the term communion has come to have various meanings. Sometimes it is used simply to describe altar and pulpit fellowship which separated churches agree to establish and share on the basis of a concordat. Such an agreement serves, for example, as the basis for sacramental exchange between the Episcopal Church and the Polish National Catholic Church, which are accordingly said to be "in communion." The world confessional bodies of the Lutheran and Reformed traditions are also exploring the possibility of establishing concords between their churches which would enable somewhat similar exchanges. While such arrangements allow for significant sharing between separate churches, they do not constitute nor of themselves necessarily lead to what the Consultation regards as the union of churches. In this usage communion appears more limited in scope than union. The discipline of a number of the COCU churches already allows for the occasional sharing of the eucharist as well as the pulpit with members and ministers of other churches, even short of a formal interchurch agreement. If these exchanges are to mark more than the extension of courtesy, they must be carried out in the context of a much broader commitment to unity. It may be for this reason that in describing wider possible ecumenical relationships the Consultation adds the word *unity* or *union* to its use of the term *communion*, in order to suggest that something more dynamic than a formal agreement to share pulpit and eucharistic fellowship is being suggested.

That impression grows stronger when one reads a statement such as the following:

> The uniting churches desire to form more than a new and more inclusive denomination. We seek full reconciliation with earlier and still separate Christian churches as well as we do with those of more recent divisions. The specific purpose of this union is formation through union of a dynamic united and uniting church. This pilgrimage has as its ultimate goal the unity of the whole church [*A Plan of Union*, II, 24, p. 13].

Seen in this light, *communion*, signifying full reconciliation, takes on a deeper and more consummate meaning. In this sense it is a stronger term than *union*, indicating that a goal beyond specific denominational mergers is being sought.

This is a long-standing use of the term *communion* as equivalent to *koinonia*, signifying oneness and wholeness in the Christian body. With this understanding, the ecumenist Jerome Hamer observed: "Every social group has its own particular form of unity" and "the Church's specific form of unity is communion." For this reason he regards *communion* as the structural name for catholic unity and the link binding the church.[2] One might go further and ask if in this sense the term *communion* does not convey a more penetrating insight into the unitive reality of the Christian body than is expressed even by the term *church* or *assembly*. It does seem that this communion is what the Consultation had in mind when it stated: "At the heart of the church lies its essential unity, a unity God-given and Spirit-nourished" (*A Plan of Union*, III, 8, p. 17).

If this indeed is what lies at the heart of the church, then it deserves much more searching reflection by Christians ecumenically. There is one highly illustrative point in *A Plan of Union* where the internal life of the Church of Christ Uniting is described as a communion. Not insignificantly, this appears in the section entitled "The Corporate, Personal, and Collegial Character of the Episcopacy." Here it is stated that as a member of the episcopal college the bishop is in "continued communion" with the other members of the same college and that "with openness to the Holy Spirit and with awareness of the conciliar principle as the consensus of the faithful people of God, the episcopal body works to strengthen the inner harmony of the church . . ." (*A Plan of Union*, VII, 65, p. 50). This is but the beginning of a more comprehensive view of the church as a communion. But it does indicate that the collegiality or communion of bishops is founded upon the communion of the Christian people whom they serve and represent.

Reflecting still more deeply, we may come to a common awareness that communion begins with the person of the individual Christian. It is here that the power enabling every manifestation of Christian communion has its source. The Christian through the grace of faith and baptism is brought into communion with the Holy Spirit. And it is through this grace and power that each one is able to achieve communion with all others. From such a perspective we can see that the communion of the Christian body does not reside on a plane somewhere above the lives of its individual members. Rather it derives its own reality from the power of their lives. At the same time we can see how sad and how distorting the effect of church separation can be on the lives of individual Christians, how it can hamper the full expression of that freedom to live openly as Christians which the Spirit has given them.

In an anguished world where so many have felt the sense of isolation that is instilled by the alienation of groups, by the immense complexity of organizations which structure society, and by competition, it may well be that nothing the church has to offer is of greater value than a recovered awareness of communion. The communion of persons at its highest level is an interpenetration of existences achieved beyond the range of language. This is the protean source of energy that makes human society both human and possible. Where it was not possible or only rarely and remotely attainable, men would find society a haunted shell in which they would be homeless. The *I* could never fully participate in the *We*.

A recovered sense of communion among Christians should lead to the increased awareness that the corporate life of Christians as one people is but a manifestation of the participation by individual Christians in the communion of *persons* who *themselves* are *one* and who have drawn us into their inexhaustible life.

If ecumenism is essentially the quest for communion, then we may ask why did not the Consultation on Church Union develop "A Plan for Communion"? Why, instead, is there such an explicit focus on "church union"? Does not this suggest that the Consultation's principal aim is the realignment of ecclesiastical structures? Disappointment is sometimes voiced over the impression that this is so and that this sort of enterprise does not really reach Christians where they live, that it is the "ecumenism of scribes and canonists." Others wonder if such a focus does not obscure the wider ecumenical impact of the Consultation. It is observed that the achievement of a coherent system of responsibilities—a polity that will be uniformly accepted and consistently applied—may be advantageous to the COCU churches; but it seems quite unlikely that all major churches, even in the U.S., will be able to achieve such a uniformly consistent pattern of church life.

At least two answers could be given briefly in response to such concerns. One is that against the background of a history of church separation, our awareness of the force and reality of communion has been considerably dulled. Unless the very concrete question of church union is faced, communion may appear to be little more than an abstraction conveniently invoked by ecumenists.

A second, more positive answer is that the Consultation is facing up to the demands and the power of Christian communion by emphasizing so clearly the inclusiveness that must hold the Church of Christ Uniting together. It is by reason of this inclusiveness which brings together men and women, blacks and whites, persons who have achieved wisdom through simplicity and persons of sophisticated intelligence, heeding all, that the grace of communion will suffuse with meaning the forms of union.

All Christians by reason of their faith and baptism, by reason of the grace that is within them, have a right to experience much more fully what it is to live in communion. All of us need to see how to go beyond self-contained denominationalism locked in its own embrace. All of us need to achieve the reach of faith that enables us to transcend cultural exclusivism and come to a positive appreciation of the fact that while our histories have made us a varied people, they do not force us to remain a divided people. We need to bring our differences of style and of judgment into the context of communion so that they can be comprehended and coped with, lest in separation we nurture them into fixations. We need to express our communion by finding serious ways to speak and act as a whole on matters that are of concern to all.

In a very direct way the Consultation is acting in response to these needs. In so doing, it is facing what all of us need to face. In the process it has become the most advanced and most concrete endeavor attempted in the ecumenical history of this country. At midpoint the Consultation is inevitably making it clear that communion is not something less real than union, and that in striving for union it is not seeking anything less real than communion. It is through the power of communion that the Spirit gives each of us that COCU will make its widest impact.

NOTES

1. Young, Franklin W., "One Table in Contemporary New Testament Studies," *Digest of the Proceedings of the Consultation on Church Union*, Vol. III (1964), pp. 119–142.
2. Hamer, Jerome, *The Church Is a Communion* (New York: Sheed and Ward, 1964), p. 209.

IV

THE WAY FORWARD:
NEXT STEPS

18

Dynamics and Possibilities

PAUL A. CROW, JR.

The tenth year in the life of a child is an amazing moment. The trends of his past begin to converge and find partial fulfillment. His history begins to take shape. In like manner the child of a decade is the carrier of a latent, formative future. All in all, a typical ten-year-old, according to the authorities in child development, is a person with good balance, amazingly adaptive, sensitive to his environment, conscious of his individuality. All these characteristics make him an adult in the making.

This is an apt portrayal of the Consultation on Church Union as it enters its second decade of official union conversations. These churches-in-covenant-toward-union find their pasts converging through a decade of listening, debating, and praying; they look more attentively toward a future shared by all Christians. At this point in its life the Consultation is reaching for balance and equilibrium, attempting to be open and flexible to the future God gives, alert to the life-and-death issues of the world, increasingly conscious of its uniqueness in the one ecumenical movement. Like any child or movement in process toward maturity, COCU sees evidence that a partial fulfillment of its past developments has been reached. Its participants are keenly aware of an unknown future still demanding to be charted and fulfilled.

The purpose of this chapter is to ask, "What next? What lies ahead—in potential and actual possibilities—for the Consultation on Church Union?" The intent is not to prophesy about the official discussions, but to explore some of the dynamics and practical possibilities in the immediate future, to focus on, according to Leo Cardinal Suenens of Belgium, "the concrete and practical progression of our painful path toward unity."

From Discussion to Decision:
Test Case for Commitment

Ecumenism is perennially in danger of conversations without commitment, discussions without decisions. Even within the Consultation on
Church Union, with its openness to dialogue, there is the temptation to
perpetuate the dialogue to the millennium without pressing to the
point where the churches give an account of the faith which they already
have in common. How deceptively easy this paralysis can be was observed by Cardinal Suenens:

> We are told and retold that God is patient; that is true and the world is
> ever full of people ready to use this patience of God to tread water and wait
> for better times. We must also understand that if God is patient—because
> we force him to be—he is also impatient, for he is love and love is always
> eager to communicate itself.[1]

The impatient critics, especially young people, are on legitimate ground
when they ask: are the churches serious about these ecumenical conversations or do they want merely a forum which will periodically ease their
guilt of disunion? Has not the first decade of conversations in COCU
produced a firm foundation for a united church committed to new dimensions of mission and community? This impatience is not without
warrant, though a society programmed by "future shock" could hardly be
expected to overcome four centuries of history in a decade. There is an
unwritten proverb that says the churches are willing to do anything for
the sake of unity except unite. Little wonder then that some of the
strident critics suspect that the snail's pace in negotiations is due not to
clear differences in theology and ecclesiology but rather to "complicated
rationalization of church laziness, fear of experimentation, unwillingness
to disturb vested interests of churches, congregations, or church agencies, or just passive commitment to the *total* mission of the Church of
Christ in his world." [2]

Decision is a realistic component of the church union process, if Christian reconciliation is related to obedience to the Gospel. Otherwise it
sails in an ethereal atmosphere, bound for a place in the never-never
land. The *kairos* for a united church depends on dual judgments of per-
severing patience and political propriety; yet a corporate decision, an
action in obedience, is called for if the process is to maintain its integrity. What cannot be done in such situations is to postpone decision
indefinitely, in the belief that theological study should not be rushed,
or that more time will necessarily quicken the ecumenical conscience
of congregations or other church bodies. "Real decisions have to be

made," states Bishop Lesslie Newbigin of the Church of South India, "at the time when real choices are presented. It is an illusion to imagine that we can take our own time about deciding. Decisions which we do not make at the proper time are taken out of our hands." [3]

Yet at this very point the Consultation faces a paradox. Christians and churches are called to make new and renewed commitments at a time when the mood among the churches and society is to be noncommittal. Among both youth and adults, all covenants and contracts are under evaluation and up for grabs. Those who see the walls of their traditional way of life crumbling, who are perplexed by rapid change on all fronts, find it difficult to think clearly of commitment and major decisions about anything except self-preservation. Marked by a "failure of nerve," the churches—institutions and policy-making councils—reveal a community uncertain of past commitments and wary of making any new ones. This paradox was analyzed in a penetrating way after COCU's Denver plenary:

> The malaise infecting the churches in the Consultation is due in large part to the fact that the decade saw the young alienated by the war [in Vietnam], the middle generations morally paralyzed by guilt over the Black Manifesto and its fallout, and the older generation simply exhausted and longing for retirement. In other words, a decade of alienation, demoralization, and fatigue is precisely the decade that should be calling the churches into accountability, but it is also the decade in which working toward organic church union seems to be a distraction from the enormous expenditure of attention on more immediate concerns. [4]

The crisis of church union—indeed, of the whole church—is a crisis of motivation, of fundamental commitment to the vision and the process of a reconciled and reconciling church.

The failure of nerve or demoralization in the church has severely affected, among other things, the quest for church unity. It has, in the first instance, caused some unity pilgrims to play the game of ecumenical *faddism*. Those who lose their sense of purpose often become entrapped in a frantic mentality of leaping from one position to another. They hope to find the golden formula that will bring instant change and fulfillment to an unsavory situation. In the offices of church bureaucrats and in the lounges of pastors, pronouncements have been heard which are reminiscent of the Corinthian situation. One says, "I belong to COCU," and another, "I belong to the National Council of Churches [or Key 73]," or still another, "I prefer JSAC [Joint Strategy and Action Committee]" or some other new ecumenical model. Others chime in, "I belong to none of them; I'm an unrepentant Presbyterian [or Methodist, or Congregationalist, or etc.].'' Such competitiveness rarely produces a worthy Christian fellowship or mission; nor does it usually reflect a genuine support and commitment to any form of renewal or reunion. More often than not it is a defensive tactic to avoid giving oneself and his jurisdictions of authority and influence to Christian reconciliation in any form. Like any dilettante approach, faddism in ecumenism is never fulfilling; nor is there the prospect of a real, enduring outcome.

A second obstacle caused by the church's current failure of nerve is *pessimism*. Ironically, it tempts those of different persuasions. It provides an excuse for the indifferent, a retreat for the tired, and a nagging irritant for the committed. This deadly condition roots, of course, in the contemporary crisis of faith and has counterparts in all aspects of theology and culture. Indeed, American Christians are on the verge of ghoulishness, a neurotic delight in finding no hope for any ideas, proposals, institutions, or persons. The ultimate form of the malaise hails "the death of an adversary in order to hasten his demise often before the adversary has really a chance to live." [5] While we must be realistic about this condition and work toward its healing, we need also to resist its neurotic tendencies. A story which came out of the Anglican-Methodist church union negotiations is instructive at this point. It had been agreed that a seventy-five per cent approval by both churches would be necessary to form a united church. When the votes were counted, the British Methodists exceeded the required vote with seventy-nine per cent, while the Church of England achieved only a 69 per cent affirmative count. The immediate result was to postpone church union while the negotiations resumed. As people around the world bemoaned (or celebrated) this vote as an omen of pessimism, one Anglican bishop was quoted with gleeful optimism. "Sixty-nine per cent, you say. How marvelous! It's the first time since the English Reformation that the Church of England has been sixty-nine per cent for anything!" No good purpose is served by a false sense of enthusiasm; nevertheless, we dare not delay or abandon our pilgrimage because of a fabricated pessimism. Those who know the biblical faith realize that pessimism is never the permanent condition of a Christian or of the Christian community. Neither is a situation ever without hope.

Any church union venture must necessarily live with a tension between patience and pessimism, between disenchantment and decision. Yet the eminent danger for the COCU churches—indeed, of all Christians—in the decade of the 1970s is not that they shall make bad decisions. The most crippling possibility is they shall make no decisions, and thereby jeopardize the integrity of who they are as the one people of God, their ability to tell in life as well as with lips the story of the Gospel, and their witness with the human community to its saving, liberating grace. Church union is a test case not only for Protestant sincerity toward ecumenism, to borrow Robert McAfee Brown's phrase, but for the future of the church in this place.

Church Union as Process

As the Consultation has engaged in honest reflection about its posture and tried to translate its intended dynamics into a changed situation, it has chosen to speak, especially since the Denver plenary, of church union as process. The idea is not completely novel. The Consultation's earlier history, for example, articulated in the "stages and steps" concept discussed at the Dallas and Cambridge plenaries, gives evidence of this concept. The current coinage, however, came from the second Conference on Church Union, sponsored by the Commission on Faith and Order of the World Council of Churches, at Limuru, Kenya, in April, 1970. One of the four major papers of the Limuru Conference, entitled "Education for Church Union—A Plea for Encounter," presented church union as "process" and/or "encounter" as its motif. Understanding and involvement go together. Work for a united church involves both theological homework and existential experience. "It means a person, a congregation, a tradition, or a board or agency are placed in encounter with the Gospel, with other Christian traditions, with one's sense of spiritual identity, and with the world." [6] This stance was discussed and commended the following year (1971) at the Louvain meeting of the Commission on Faith and Order. "The living adventure of negotiations," the Louvain report commented, "draws Christians into a new and unfolding experience of what fellowship may mean, of the implications of their own faith and of the part they must play in reshaping society more nearly according to the mind of Christ." [7]

Before this becomes a shibboleth, it is important to explore what we mean by church union as process. It has distinct and far-reaching implications for the Consultation's mood, posture, and methodology.

1. Church union as process means the primary focus is upon Christian community rather than upon organizational structures. Herein lies the most radical difference between church union and merger. A merger decrees new structures which seek to implement new ties between the divided parties. Union encourages new understandings, new relationships, new actions which lead to experiences in Christian community. Thereby church structures emerge from, and give visible expression to, the new sense of identity and community.

This focus should not be misunderstood as a disparagement of the structural dimensions of church union. Much of the ineffectiveness of past ecumenical encounters is due to a failure to translate reconciliation into the churches' polities and structures. If the experiences of unity and union are to be translated into the real religious life, structural changes are essential.

2. Church union as process implies a united church will not become a reality merely from one future decision on any plan of union by the legislative bodies of the participating churches. Rather, it will arise from these new experiences in community, these new relationships developed along the road toward union in worship, work, and witness among persons, congregations, and institutions of the different traditions. Consequently, church union is more than a matter of one decision; it becomes a series of major decisions related to the building of Christian community. It is conceivable that such community-building will threaten, even destroy, the previous alliances and community which have lost their meaning, as well as those existing structures which contribute toward isolation, not communication; oppression, not freedom in the Gospel.

3. The understanding of church union as process requires the involvement of all members of the churches. COCU cannot survive as the preserve of elite churchmen; it is least of all a project of similar traditions or those with kindred theologies, socio-economic status, or racial heritages. The fullness of its intent is to bring Christians of all sorts and conditions into the pilgrimage. Only so will the full impact of disunion and the difficulties of church union be perceived. Only so will the rich variety and plenitude of a uniting church be understood and experienced.

4. If church union is process, the commitments of a shared life will not be something realized only at some futuristic moment. It will lead the participating churches to changes in life-styles and priorities in such a way as to give evidence of the new fellowship. In other words, the Church of Christ Uniting will never produce instantaneous changes in the participating churches, effective on the day the service of inauguration is celebrated. If the spirit and style of the Church of Christ Uniting is delayed until then, the church will probably never sense the value of a fully committed fellowship with other Christians.

To illustrate this point, we can turn to Chapter II in *A Plan of Union* (1970), which identifies the primary objectives of the Church of Christ Uniting. These envisage a united church whose life is committed to:

—Faithfulness to God's revelation, judgment, and grace as known through the Scriptures and incarnated in Jesus Christ; yet openness and humility in mission to the world and toward structures for mission.

—Inclusiveness of the whole people of God in every aspect of the church's fellowship and ministry; yet appreciation for the contributions of particular persons, vocations, and communities.

—Norms of ordered life; yet the protection of genuine diversities and openness toward continual renewal.

—Continuity with the heritages of the uniting churches; yet openness toward a dynamic enrichment with other religious traditions and cultural influences.

These are not marks which must await actual union. They represent commitments which should find expression in the directions of the participating churches *now*. In such a spirit Denver's "A Word to the Churches" urged the member churches "to promote programs leading to the achievement of racial justice and compensatory treatment for minorities in the churches and in the nation, the sharing of resources among the constituent churches, and cooperative action in mission." Only in this way will the COCU process gain credibility among the skeptics and the disenchanted. In this way it will be a flesh-and-bones foretaste for those engaged in the process.

5. To speak of church union as process is to face the nature and role of *A Plan of Union* from a different perspective. Undoubtedly in some circles the route toward a united church is understood to depend solely on a document known as *A Plan of Union*. The assumption is that a revised and perfected Plan, properly interpreted to the grass roots, will bring about a united church. The only problem with this strategy is that documents do not produce united churches. Plans are the agents of dialogue and encounter. Eventually they are the basis upon which churches officially vote to unite, but a Plan is not the only basis for a new creation. More than consensus on paper is needed; that "more" is a process of growing together.

This in no way diminishes the importance of *A Plan of Union*, though some people have so misappropriated the process emphasis. The formulation, revision, and approval of the Plan is a crucial part of the process. We mean to convey, however, that a Plan is developed within a process, and the most mature Plan will come from the full involvement of a variety of persons and groups. In this light we need not be defensive about a particular text of a Plan. Finally, no Plan can completely resolve all the issues confronting divided churches. Early in the Consultation's plenary process this insight was stated by Kyle Haselden, the late editor of *The Christian Century*: "A proposed union which waits for a theological resolution of all differences never occurs. Many of the theological and ecclesiastical issues which divide the churches can be removed only in and by the uniting process." [8]

6. The acceptance of church union as process focuses attention and expectation on the *interim* relations and joint action. There are many joint programs and projects—educational and missional—which are permissible and urgently needed among the COCU churches. Such engagements in common mission and nurture could be not only signs of the pilgrimage

but enabling steps which bring the reality of church union closer to home.

7. Church union as process requires greater concentration on study and response, joint worship and joint mission at all levels of the participating churches, especially at the regional and local levels.

8. Church union as process involves careful attention to the timetable and its dynamics. Someone once quipped, "Timetables for united churches seem to be written by turtles and the lists of 'obstacles to re-union' by mountains-out-of-molehill men." Some would assume that to speak of COCU as a process as well as a Plan is to slow down the pace. Not so! Proponents and opponents will accept that the tempo of Christian reconciliation is calculated by God's time. But that assumption does not mean delays or a protracted timetable. (Why do mortal men usually translate references to God's purposes and will as requiring more time?) It could involve an "earlier" consummation of a united church, especially if interim sacramental and missional relations are established with seriousness and integrity.

The fact of a process does, however, bring to consideration several different timetables, each of which deeply influences the prospects of a united church. There are (1) the COCU timetable itself, (2) the processes and timetables of the individual denominations, and (3) the agenda and timetable of the world in which the churches and the Consultation live. Sensitivity to all three sets of dynamics is one of the pivotal phases of the process toward church union.

What has been said here about church union as process has not meant to be definitive but suggestive. In summary, the above commentary can be illustrated by the following diagram:

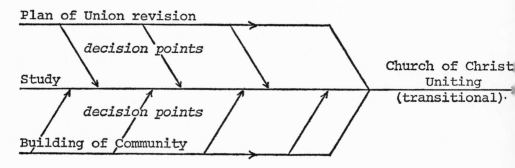

CONSULTATION ON CHURCH UNION PROCESS

Enabling Interim Steps

"Ten years ago our churches set out in quest of a united church faithful to our Lord's intention for a reconciled and reconciling community ministering to a divided humanity." [9] These pensive words began the message of the Denver delegates to their churches. They had come to test their goal and their commitment to the continuance of the process. On both counts the Denver experience recorded affirmative conclusions:

> We declare with new conviction the gospel imperative to organic union. As Christians who share that one gospel, we can no longer justify our institutional separation from one another. As his ministers of reconciliation, we must find together those structures for mission which will enable us to serve the oppressed, the hurt, and the poor in ways not open to us in our separateness. [10]

While full fellowship in Christ remains the goal of the Consultation, it now becomes apparent that certain interim steps could be beneficial to—indeed, are mandated by—this intention to pursue "a form of church ready to serve and suffer in faithfulness to Christ our Lord." These interim possibilities can be described as related to the eucharist, mission and structures, and local experimentation. They represent what Roger Schutz, Prior of Taizé, defines as "the power of the provisional"; they provide achievements for the moment, while awaiting, and making possible in the future, a fuller state of union.

Interim Eucharistic Fellowship. As we probe the possibilities of Christian community among the COCU churches, the natural inclination, pragmatic Americans that we are, is to think first of programmatic and cooperative projects. These are highly important and very much the controlling force upon most agendas these days. As I prepared an address for the Denver plenary on the immediate next steps in the Consultation process, I became convinced that both the signs of the times and the nature of the COCU venture require these nine churches, and any others who would join them, to move in the near future to interim eucharistic fellowship on a regular basis. The whole plenary took this proposal and made it its own, making it one of the two urgent calls put forth in "A Word to the Churches."

We should be clear about what this proposal is and is not. It is neither a sample of make-believe ecumenism nor a proposal for indifferentism. It is made—and should so be considered and implemented—as an exercise in Christian realism and an attempt to be responsible to the meaning of the Lord's Supper in these turbulent times. Such a shared eucharistic life would be a sign of the integrity of the church and a testimony to

Christian truth. What sharing "on a regular basis" means would be determined most effectively in each local situation. It could mean a joint service among the COCU congregations in a community at least four times a year.

Those who have opposed intercommunion in the past have been sincere in the belief that Holy Communion should be celebrated together by Christians of different communions only after union. This view, however, is rapidly being overtaken by events, and can no longer, I believe, be accepted as a sufficient rejoinder. Several factors make reconsideration worthy and decision urgent on this matter. First, the agony of a divided Table bears heavily upon the church's life and its witness to the world. As the Archbishop of York, F. D. Coggan, proclaimed to the recent Anglican general synod, "I think it is easier for God to forgive us any errors in the [Anglican-Methodist] plan of union than it is for him to forgive a church which persists in disunity at the table of the Lord and goes to the world weakened by that fact." Second, a significant pastoral problem is caused by the fact that joint celebrations of the Lord's Supper are taking place, even among churches whose theological definitions and canon laws preclude such events. Countless occasions are known where "underground" services of communion take place shared by those of episcopal and non-episcopal traditions, even among Roman Catholics and Protestants, who have witnessed together in some concrete human crisis.

Third, there are striking examples of consensus on the Lord's Supper, a consensus which includes churches of a broader spectrum than ever before. To mention only a few of the most significant: there are the Faith and Order statements at Lund in 1952, Montreal in 1963, and the special report received at Bristol in 1967;[11] the Lutheran–Roman Catholic consensus of 1967; [12] the historic agreement between Anglicans and Roman Catholics in 1971; and "The Eucharist in the Life of the Church: An Ecumenical Consensus," [13] a statement produced by Roman Catholic, Orthodox, and Protestant theologians. Not the least of these historic agreements on the Lord's Supper are those of the Consultation, which are recorded in *Principles of Church Union* and *A Plan of Union*.

A shared eucharistic life is reopened because of a reconsideration of relationships between those of episcopal and non-episcopal churches. For example, the Lambeth Conference of 1968 recommended "reciprocal acts of intercommunion" between an Anglican church and some other church or churches "where there is agreement on apostolic faith and order, and where that agreement to seek unity has found expression, whether in a covenant to unite or some other appropriate form." [14] The possibility of an interim eucharistic fellowship on a regular basis has deep implications for relations among the eight (all but the Episcopal) participating churches in the Consultation who have no barriers to intercommunion. In these churches the meaning of the Lord's Supper, the doctrine of ministry, and other practices present no obstacles to a fully committed fellowship at the Table. Yet this eucharistic openness has little or no bearing upon their relationships at the local, regional, or national level. United Methodists, Presbyterians, Disciples, AME's, and others only rarely break bread together, and then only under the stimulus of a special occasion. Even then, such services are often characterized by a feeling of strangeness, of being in someone else's church.

If these churches move into a sharing of the Lord's Supper on a regular basis, a much needed perspective and potential will be brought to bear on those disunities of racism, social alienation, and polarizations of all varieties which threaten to tear the body of Christ asunder again. This is not to suggest the eucharist as a magic cure-all; nor do I suggest that those separated in racial, ethnic, and political camps approach a common Table too easily. Nevertheless, no model of reconciliation has full validity unless it brings those of different backgrounds and persuasions face to face to break the one loaf and share the one cup. We need to confront each other at the Table in order that we may truly see Christ in each other. As a consequence, the attempts to overcome the hostilities and suspicions in our society—and in the Consultation—would be sustained by the joint celebration of the life, crucifixion, death, resurrection, exaltation of the living Lord, Jesus Christ.

Community and communion are inseparable realities; one without the other can only lead to distortion and denial of the true life together which God gives in Christ. On the one hand, when celebrations of the Supper are merely gatherings of those who look and think alike, the church loses the intent of the act to re-present the whole reconciling work of Christ. On the other hand, it is possible, especially in these times of frenzied polarization, to confront—either in study or direct action—the crisis issues of our society without facing the *real* issue: namely, God's overcoming of all alienations in Jesus Christ and his entrusting the ministry of reconciliation to all who confess his name. Where our coming together about the Table is mingled with our attempts to right the wrongs and heal the wounds of a broken humanity, a sign of spiritual health will nurture us.

Mission and Structures. Another next step, another dimension of commitment beyond mere talking, which deepens the process toward church union involves the COCU churches in enterprises of joint service and witness.

The normal inclination is to think of national boards and agencies when proposals of convergence in mission are made. This is understandable since these agencies have until recently been heavily involved in the

conciliar movement, where they have dealt with problems and program
from an ecumenical perspective. Certain of these divisions, such as the
overseas-mission executives of the COCU churches, have spent several
years in conversation about the possible coordination of the administra-
tions or the actual uniting of the various boards into one. A complexity of
problems has so far thwarted this prophetic attempt.

The area where the topic of structures for mission needs a desperate
airing and some ecumenically responsible decisions is the individual restructuring processes of the COCU churches. An interesting phenomenon
is seen in the fact that in the year 1971–1972 the six predominantly white
COCU churches are engaged, at varying stages, in major and comprehensive programs of restructure. Even among the three black churches
decisions of equal importance—e.g., the selection of episcopal leadership
—are on the horizon. The work of these restructure commissions could
bear an evil omen for an attempt at church union, or they could bring
good tidings of new ecumenical structural possibilities. It depends upon
the posture of the denominational restructuring. The inherent dangers
were identified in a communiqué in early 1968 from the Rt. Rev. Stephen
F. Bayne, Jr., Episcopal bishop and then chairman of the unofficial
COCU-FM group:

> Increasingly . . . we are troubled at the possibility that the issues and
> purposes represented by the fact of the Consultation itself may not be ad-
> equately taken into account by the constituent churches as they individ-
> ually consider and adopt the structural changes which seem appropriate in
> their particular situation.

Such attitudes and blind spots could effectively cause the restructure of
a particular church into a new confessional position or some other form
of isolation which fails to acknowledge the issues inherent in a church
truly catholic, truly evangelical, and truly reformed. "If the Consultation
is to be protected from the dangers of becoming merely a discussion
process," concluded the overseas-ministry executives, "we feel its member
churches must keep pressing the limits of joint action now possible to
them. This would suggest, we believe, that every structural change or
improvisation be tested, *inter alia*, by the degree to which it makes it
inescapable that the church in question is confronted, in its planning and
decision-making, by the implications of its membership in the Consulta-
ton."

Such reordering of priorities applies not only to national structures.
The Denver plenary gave particular attention and challenge to the middle
judicatories (dioceses, conferences, presbyteries and synods, etc.). In a
time when the roles of national staffs and agencies are declining, these
regional bodies now assume a larger involvement in mission, power of

decision-making, and the distribution of funds. Consequently, two of the ten recommendations from Denver to the participating churches urged the middle judicatories to become aware of the Consultation process in forming new ecumenical relationships, to seek relationships of counsel with the nearby middle judicatories of the other COCU churches, to strengthen their joint efforts in missional projects. It remains to be seen whether these regional manifestations of the churches will respond to such an ecumenical vocation; in some states they are clearly beyond such elementary endeavors and are moving toward some form of joint judicatory staff and ministry.

Local Experimentation. Another next step in the development of church union revolves around the life of people in local communities. Clearly, the top priority for, and the primary test of, the Consultation is to discover strategies, methods, resources in which the experience of unity and union can be fully expressed and internalized at the local level. Here we are dealing with a condition of dichotomy. Many Christians understand the fragmentation of the church and mankind through the daily life where they live, often in their work and families. People are divided into hostile camps, yet yearn for peace and wholeness. For them church union, properly understood, is a viable, though difficult, response.

Others are emotionally captive to disunions and parochialisms. Rather than a scandal, the divisions among Christians and within society are accepted as unavoidable and are judged to be situations to which persons and the church should accommodate themselves. For them the language of church union is a foreign tongue, talk of an alien experience. Ironically, church union is often thought to be a coterie of national church bureaucrats laboring to unite (and thereby save, goes the myth) their boards and agencies. The fact is those who lead these agencies often view the Consultation with as much mystery and fear as the uninformed layman or pastor. In reality the locus of church union is the local church and local community. Here, said the New Delhi Assembly, the frustrations and achievements are most deeply felt; here the possibilities are most often avoided. If it happens at all, it will happen there. Church union is a story about people who were promised a life together by the biblical message, but who, because of the divisions of history, or sociology, or sinfulness, are kept apart. Church union is a tale about local people—their response to the mandates of the Gospel of reconciliation and their common calling to minister to the needs of the brothers where they live.

One of the liberating possibilities would be for the churches not only to permit but to encourage, under appropriate guidelines, the setting up of experimental COCU parishes as outlined in *A Plan of Union.* Denver made such a request—namely, that the participating churches "take such steps as are necessary to encourage and grant freedom to their congregations to participate in the forming of model parishes." Already such experimentation, known as the cluster movement, is widespread in local communities. Some clusters arose in response to the Consultation; many found new relationships at the local level out of the need to face the pressing issues of mission in their locale. Such experimental developments need the full support of regional and national denominational bodies. They should be judged as neither acts of apostasy nor disloyal groups, but frontier expressions of the church's witness and ministry. This development presents the churches with a crucial decision which they cannot sidestep. If all such actions are judged as merely disobedient communities, then the churches may lose some of the most committed Christians to more radical forms of Christian relations which stand outside the existing forms of the church. The tragedy is double: the church will lose some of its most promising leaders, but by the same token its own processes of renewal and reunion will be deprived of the fruits of this experimentation. The churches in COCU must give high priority to engagement in these local ecumenical developments.

Conclusion. Predictions about the future of the consultation have been resisted in this chapter with "a soldierly discipline." The official conversations will continue toward the study and revision of *A Plan of Union,* and eventually be submitted for the moment of truth called decision. In the meantime other moments of truth will come and go in the local and regional study and response—to continue in other phases beyond June 1, 1972; in the ministries of denominational leaders who will be called upon to account for their ecumenical stewardship out in the open; in conversations where lay people will first have heard about COCU from reading venomous newsletters and then have to search for the truth guided by the innate desire to be faithful to the Good News; in seminary class rooms and coffee bars where anti-institutional convictions will be translated into options for a structured community which is more flexible, inclusive, and committed to a redemptive ministry in the human community.

What lies ahead for the Consultation on Church Union depends, of course, on the willingness and capacity of churches to pay the price of reconciliation and union. The price is not the loss of spiritual identity, or the minimizing of fervor for the Gospel. The price to each denomination, however, is its own death and resurrection. Denominations do not die gracefully, as their vindictive handling of earlier church union proposals reveals. Nevertheless, each church must be willing to entrust its treasures and its familiar patterns to the fires of death and to its living Lord, if a a new church is to be reborn.

The price of church union is high, terribly high. But so it was for God, who in coming to be among his people chose to endure the death and resurrection of his Son, our Lord Jesus Christ. There is no chance that anything less demanding will be asked of the church—his body—in its obedience.

NOTES

1. Leo Cardinal Suenens, "Unity of the Church—Unity of Mankind," mimeographed text of an address to the Commission on Faith and Order of the World Council of Churches, Louvain, Belgium, August 2–13, 1971.
2. Thomas Stransky, "Directions Within American Ecumenism," *Unitas*, Vol. XX, No. 4 (Winter, 1967), p. 297.
3. J. E. Lesslie Newbigin, "Which Way for 'Faith and Order'?", *What Unity Implies*, Reinhard Groscurth, ed. (Geneva: World Council of Churches, 1969), p. 124.
4. F. Thomas Trotter, "Toiling Up Pisgah," *The Christian Century*, Vol. LXXXVIII, No. 44 (November 3, 1971), p. 1284. This quotation records Dean Trotter's conversation at Denver with Dr. James I. McCord.
5. "On Ghoulishness and COCU" (editorial), *The Christian Century*, Vol. LXXXVIII, No. 19 (May 12, 1971), p. 579.
6. See Paul A. Crow, Jr., "Education for Church Union—A Plea for Encounter," *Midstream*, Vol. IX, Nos. 2–3 (Winter-Spring, 1970), pp. 82–100. Also published separately by the Consultation on Church Union.
7. See the report of Committee V: Church Union Negotiations and Bilateral Conversations, in *Faith and Order, Louvain 1971;* Faith and Order Paper No. 59 (Geneva: World Council of Churches, 1971), pp. 230–234.
8. Kyle Haselden, "Fusion at Oberlin," *The Christian Century*, Vol. LXXX (April 3, 1963), p. 422.
9. "A Word to the Churches," *Digest of the Proceedings of the Consultation on Church Union*, Vol. X (1971).
10. *Ibid.*
11. See Oliver S. Tomkins, ed., *The Third World Conference on Faith and Order* (London: SCM, 1953), pp. 49–59; Patrick C. Rodger and Lukas Vischer, eds., *The Fourth World Conference on Faith and Order, Montreal 1963* (New York: Association Press, 1964), pp. 73–80; *New Directions in Faith and Order, Bristol, 1967*, Faith and Order Paper No. 50 (Geneva: World Council of Churches, 1968), pp. 60–68, 141–143.
12. *Lutherans and Catholics in Dialogue*, Vol. III: *The Eucharist as Sacrifice* (New York: U.S.A. Committee of Lutheran World Federation and Bishops' Committee for Ecumenical and Inter-religious Affairs, 1967), pp. 187–198.
13. "The Eucharist in the Life of the Church: An Ecumenical Consensus," in *The Ecumenist*, Vol. 8, No. 6 (September-October, 1970), pp. 90–93. See Paul A. Crow, Jr., "Consensus, the Eucharist, and Union," and articles by four other commission members in *The American Ecclesiastical Review*, Vol. CLXIV, No. 6 (June, 1971).
14. *The Lambert Conference 1968; Resolutions and Reports* (London: SPCK, 1968), p. 42.

SELECT BIBLIOGRAPHY
OF RESOURCES

Select Bibliography of Resources

1. OFFICIAL REPORTS OF THE CONSULTATION

A Plan of Union for the Church of Christ Uniting. Princeton: Consultation on Church Union, 1970.

Digest of the Proceedings of the Consultation on Church Union for 1962 (Washington, D.C.), and 1963 (Oberlin, Ohio). Vol. I and II. (Out of print.)

Digest of the Proceedings of the Consultation on Church Union (Princeton, New Jersey), April, 1964. Vol. III.

Digest of the Proceedings of the Fourth Meeting of the Consultation on Church Union (Lexington, Kentucky), April 5–8, 1965, Vol. IV.

Digest of the Proceedings of the Fifth Meeting of the Consultation on Church Union (Dallas, Texas), May 2–5, 1966. Vol. V.

Digest of the Proceedings of the Sixth Meeting of the Consultation on Church Union (Cambridge, Massachusetts), May 1–4, 1967. Vol. VI.

Digest of the Proceedings of the Seventh Meeting of the Consultation on Church Union (Dayton, Ohio), March 25–28, 1968. Vol. VII.

Digest of the Proceedings of the Eighth Meeting of the Consultation on Church Union (Atlanta, Georgia), March 17–20, 1969. Vol. VIII.

Digest of the Proceedings of the Ninth Meeting of the Consultation on Church Union (St. Louis, Missouri), March 9–13, 1970. Vol. IX.

Digest of the Proceedings of the Tenth Meeting of the Consultation on Church Union (Denver, Colorado), Septmeber 26–30, 1971. Vol. X.

COCU: The Official Reports of the First Four Meetings of the Consultation. Cincinnati: Forward Movement Publications, 1966.

Principles of Church Union; adopted by the Consultation at its meeting in Dallas, 1966. Cincinnati: Forward Movement Publications, 1966. (Out of Print.)

Consultation on Church Union, 1967: Principles of Church Union, Guidelines for Sturcture, and a Study Guide. Cincinnati: Forward Movement Publications, 1967.

An Order of Worship for the Proclamation of the Word of God and the Cele-bration of the Lord's Supper with Commentary. Cincinnati: Forward Movement Publications, 1968.

Guidelines for Local Interchurch Action. Princeton: Consultation on Church Union, 1969.

Report of the National Conference on Program. Princeton: Consultation on Church Union, 1969.

2. STUDY DOCUMENTS

A Preliminary Outline of A Plan of Union; discussed at the Eighth Meeting of the Consultation on Church Union, Atlanta, Georgia, 1969. Princeton: Consultation on Church Union, 1969. (Out of print.)

Blake, Eugene Carson, *A Proposal Toward the Reunion of Christ's Church.* Philadelphia: General Assembly Office of the United Presbyterian Church in the U.S.A., 1961.

Brown, Robert McAfee, and David H. Scott, eds., *The Challenge to Reunion.* New York: McGraw-Hill, 1963.

COCU: A Catholic Perspective. Washington, D.C.: U.S. Catholic Conference Publications Office, 1970.

Day, Peter, *Tomorrow's Church: Catholic, Evangelical, Reformed.* New York: Seabury Press, 1969.

Enter Into This Dialogue. New York: Seabury Press, 1971.

"Issues for Discussion of *A Plan of Union.*" Mimeographed paper. Princeton N.J.: Consultation on Church Union, 1971.

Jameson, Victor L., *What Does God Require of Us Now?* A resource for studying *A Plan of Union for the Church of Christ Uniting.* Nashville: Abingdon Press, 1970.

Mathews, James K., *A Church Truly Catholic.* New York & Nashville: Abingdon Press, 1969.

Nelson, J. Robert, *Church Union in Focus.* Boston & Philadeplhia: United Church Press, 1967.

Osborn, Ronald E., *A Church for These Times.* New York: Abingdon Press, 1965.

Sense of Waiting. A Notebook of resources and background for a study of *A Plan of Union for the Church of Christ Uniting.* New York: Ecumenical Office of the Episcopal Church, 1971.

3. AUDIO-VISUAL RESOURCES

Something in Common. Visual presentation with recorded script conveying the people, process, and issues involved in the Consultation. Consultation on Church Union Distribution Center, P.O. Box 989, Philadephia, Pa. 19105. $5.00.

In Search of Union. LP Record of ten 4½-minute programs produced by Ecu-Media News Service. Consultation on Church Union Distribution Center, P.O. Box 989, Philadelphia, Pa. 19105. $2.00.

Sounds of Denver. Documentary cassette of excerpts from major addresses and discussions at 10th Plenary Session, September, 1971. Consultation on Church Union, 228 Alexander Street, Princeton, N.J. 08540. $3.00.

Conversations on COCU: The Denver Plenary Sessions (An Audio-Study Guide to the Current Process). Set of three sixty-minute cassettes with edited versions of major addresses. Thesis Theological Cassettes, P.O. Box 11724, Pittsburgh, Pa. 15228. $12.98 per set.

Comments on COCU. Interpretation and reflections on *A Plan of Union* on sixty-minute cassette. Consultation on Church Union, 228 Alexander Street, Princeton, N.J. 08540. $3.00.

"Frontiers of Faith" Series (1969), *Christian Unity: No. 1* and *No. 2.* Kinescope interviews between a news analyst and spokesmen for the Consultation on Church Union. Film and Broadcasting Commission, TV Library, National Council of Churches, 475 Riverside Drive, Room 852, New York, N.Y. 10027. Rental for one film: $8.00; for both films: $14.00. Scripts also available.

4. SELECTED ARTICLES RELATING TO THE CONSULTATION ON
CHURCH UNION 1970–1972

Andover Newton Quarterly, Newton Center, Mass., Volume 12, no. 1 (September, 1971).

Hazelton, Roger, "Consensus Theology: Reflections on the COCU Experience."

Peck, George, "Church Unity and the Future: Some Theological Tensions in the COCU Plan of Union."

McBrien, Richard P., "The COCU Plan of Union: A Catholic Critique."

Fackre, Gabriel, "COCU From the Ground Up."

Scalise, Victor F., Jr., "Diversity in Unity: The United Parish in Brookline, Massachusetts."

Canaday, Wilbur D., Jr., "The Vision and the Pain: A Clustering Experiment in Arlington, Massachusetts."

Austin Seminary Bulletin, Austin, Texas, Faculty Edition, Vol. LXXXVI, no. 4 (December, 1970).

Wharton, James A., "Traditions as Prologue."

Williams, J. Rodman, "The Plan of Union."

Jansen, John F., "The Plan of Union and the Worship of the Church."

Henderlite, Rachel, "Mission in the Church of Christ Uniting."

Stitt, David L., "Polity, COCU Style."

Bullock, Robert H., Jr., "Why COCU?"

Beazley, George C., "Church Union in Process." *The Christian,* Vol. 109, no. 17 (April 25, 1971), pp. 8–9.

———, "Write Your Plan of Union." *World Call,* Vol. 52, no. 11 (November, 1970), pp. 14–15.

Berger, Peter L., "A Call for Authority." *The Christian Century,* Vol. LXXXVIII, no. 43 (October 27, 1971), pp. 1257–1263.

Boney, William Jerry. "COCU at Denver, 1971." *Journal of Ecumenical Studies,*
    Vol. 9, No. 1 (Winter, 1972), pp. 218–221.
Brown, Robert McAfee, "The C.O.C.U.: A Contemporary Test Case," in his
    The Ecumenical Revolution. Revised and Expanded edition. Garden City,
    New York: Doubleday Anchor-Image Book, 1969, pp. 146–153.
Cate, William B., "Ecumenism on Main Street, U.S.A." Guest editorial, *The
    Christian Century,* Vol. LXXXVIII, no. 46 (November 17, 1971), pp. 1339–
    1340.
Christian Ministry, Vol. 1, no. 3 (March, 1970).
    Crow, Paul A., Jr., "Church Union at the Crossroads."
    Shepherd, Massey H., Jr., "The Liturgy of COCU."
    Penfield, Janet Harbison, "What's Been Happening."
COCU: A Catholic Perspective. Washington, D.C.: U.S. Catholic Conference
    Publications Office, 1970.
    Crow, Paul A., Jr., "COCU–The Potential of a Decade."
    Willebrands, Jan Cardinal, "An Address."
    Baum, Bishop William W., "A Catholic Perspective."
    Tavard, Fr. George H., "A Catholic Perspective."
"COCU 1970: A Symposium." *The Christian Century,* Vol. LXXXVII, no. 8
    (February 25, 1970).
    Crow, Paul A., Jr., "COCU at the Gateway in St. Louis."
    Nelson, J. Robert, "The Plague on Three 'Houses.'"
    Rose, Stephen C., "Process and Power."
    Stowe, David M., "COCU and NCC."
    Satterwhite, John H., "For Authentic Freedom: COCU and Black Churches."
    Blakemore, W. B., "Beyond Sectarianism: COCU and Roman Catholicism."
    Hallett, Stanley, "Church Union and Urban Missions."
    Doering, David, "Needed: A New Vision of the Kingdom."
    Bailey, J. Martin, "Ecumenism and Communication."
    Blake, Eugene Carson, "Seven Questions About COCU."
"COCU Alternatives." Editorial, *Christianity Today,* Vol. XV, no. 6 (Decem-
    ber 18, 1970), pp. 26–27.
"COCU's Coming Out Party." Editorial, *The Christian Century,* Vol. LXXXVII,
    no. 8 (February 25, 1970), p. 227.
Crow, Paul A., Jr., "Education for Church Union–A Plea for Encounter."
    Mid-Stream, Vol. IX, nos. 2 & 3 (Winter & Spring, 1970), pp. 82–100.
———, "Ecumenism and the Consultation on Church Union." *Journal of
    Ecumenical Studies,* Vol. 4, no. 4 (Fall, 1967).
———, "Update on the C.O.C.U." *World Call,* Vol. 52, no. 6 (June, 1970),
    pp. 6–7.
———, "A Plan of Union and the Church." Mimeographed address, 1971.
———, "Commitment for a Pilgrim People." *Lexington Theological Quarterly,*
    Vol. VII, no. 1 (January, 1972), pp. 21–30.
Ford, John T., "The COCU Plan of Union and Catholicity." *The Christian
    Century,* Vol. LXXXVIII, no. 42 (October 20, 1971), 1229–1232.
Gartman, Robert E., "Mother, God, and *A Plan of Union.*" *The Christian,* Vol.
    109, no. 17 (April 25, 1971), pp. 4–6.

Huston, Robert W., "A Plan of Union." *The Interpreter*, Vol. 15, no. 4 (April, 1971), pp. 11–14.

——, "In Search of a New Church." *The Interpreter*, Vol. 15, no. 15 (November-December, 1971), pp. 7–9.

——, "Progress Report on Church Union." *The Interpreter*, Vol. 14, no. 2 (February, 1970), pp. 7–10.

——, "What Has Happened to COCU?" *Engage*, June, 1971.

Jarman, William J., "A Closer Look at the Plan of Union." *The Christian*, Vol. 108 (July 19, 1970), pp. 4–5.

Kennedy, Gerald H., "Anti-COCU But Pro-Ecumenism." Reader's response, *The Christian Century*, Vol. LXXXVIII, no. 33 (August 18, 1971), pp. 985–986. Replies by William E. Bowles, Vol. LXXXVIII, no. 38 (September 22, 1971), p. 1111.

Lane, Martha A., "When Churches Take COCU Seriously." *Together*, Vol. XV, no. 9 (October, 1971), pp. 22–26.

Lexington Theological Quarterly. Lexington, Kentucky, Vol. VII, no. 2 (April, 1972).

Lindsell, Harold, "COCU: A Critique, Part I." *Christianity Today*, Vol. XX, no. 1 (October 9, 1970), pp. 3–5; "Part II," Vol. XX, no. 2 (October 23, 1970), pp. 8–12.

Lord, John Wesley, "COCU Plan Would Change Appointment System." *Christian Advocate*, Vol. XV, no. 3 (February 4, 1971), pp. 11–13.

Macquarrie, John, "The Consultation on Church Union, U.S.A., Plan of Union." *Faith and Unity*, Vol. 15, no. 1 (January, 1971), pp. 11–14.

Mathews, James K., "United Methodism, COCU, and the Future Church." *Christian Advocate*, Vol. XV, no. 3 (February 4, 1971), pp. 7–8.

Miller, Timothy, "Wither Unity? A Case Study." *The Christian Century*, Vol. LXXXVII, no. 29 (July 22, 1970), pp. 891–893.

Moore, Arthur J., "A Hard Look at COCU." *Christianity and Crisis*, Vol. XXX, no. 6 (April 13, 1970), pp. 67 ff.

Nelson, J. Robert, "Toward Ecumenical Convergence." *The Christian Century*, Vol. LXXXVIII, no. 33 (August 18, 1971), pp. 972–974.

"On Ghoulishness and COCU." Editorial, *The Christian Century*, Vol. LXXXVIII, no. 19 (May 12, 1971), p. 579.

Outler, Albert C., "COCU: Test Case for Ecumenism in America"; Lecture III, "Crisis Coming Up Dallas." Published privately, 1970. (The third of his McFadin lectures at Texas Christian University, 1970.)

"The Parish: An Interview with Lois Stair and William Thompson." *Presbyterian Life*, Special issue. Vol. 23, No. 18 (September 15, 1970), pp. 73–77.

Penfield, Janet Harbison, "Union From the Grass Roots?" *Presbyterian Life*, Vol. 24, no. 21 (November 1, 1971), pp. 18–21.

"Quiet Victory in St. Louis." Editorial, *The Christian Century*, Vol. LXXXVII, no. 12 (March 25, 1970), p. 349.

Rogers, Cornish, "Blacks and COCU: A New Honesty." *The Christian Century*, Vol. LXXXVII, no. 52 (December 30, 1970), p. 1554.

Rogness, Michael, "The Ups, the Downs, and the Plateaus of Ecumenism." *Dialog*, Vol. 10 (Autumn, 1971), pp. 281–287.

Rose, Stephen C., "A Hard Look at COCU." *Christianity and Crisis,* Vol. XXX, no. 6 (April 13, 1970), pp. 67 ff.

——, "COCU: Hope in Denver." *The Christian Century,* Vol. LXXXVIII, no. 41 (October 13, 1971), pp. 1189–1190.

——, "The Coming Confrontation on the Church's War Investments." *The Christian Century,* Vol. LXXXVII, no. 41 (October 14, 1970), pp. 1209–1211.

——, "Renewal Lives!" *Renewal,* Vol. 10, no. 3 (March, 1970), pp. 8–9.

Rossman, Parker, "COCU and the Cluster Concept." Reader's response, *The Christian Century,* Vol. LXXXVII, no. 48 (December 2, 1970), pp. 1457–1459.

Schaller, Lyle E., "COCU's Geographical Parish—How To Study It." *Christian Advocate,* Vol. XV, no. 3 (February 4, 1971), pp. 9–10.

Stookey, Laurence H. "The COCU Liturgy: Intent Versus Content." *The Princeton Seminary Bulletin,* Vol. 63, no. 1 (Winter, 1970), pp. 85–94.

Storey, William G., "An Order of Worship." *Worship,* Vol. 44, no. 2 (February 1970), pp. 109–111.

TeSelle, Eugene, "Ecumenical Reflections on the COCU Plan of Union." *The Jurist,* Vol. 31, no. 4 (Fall, 1971), pp. 629–637.

Trotter, F. Thomas, "Toiling Up Pisgah." *The Christian Century,* Vol. LXXXVIII, no. 44 (November 3, 1971), pp. 1284–1285.

Vischer, Lukas, "If Time Permits—Report on Church Union." *The Ecumenical Review,* Vol. XXIII, no. 2 (April, 1971), pp. 143–151.

Williams, Preston N., "The Ethics of Black Power," in *Quest for a Black Theology.* Eds. J. J. Gardner, S.A., and T. Deotis Roberts, Boston: Pilgrim Press (1971), pp. 82–96.

NOTES ON CONTRIBUTORS

Notes on Contributors

GEORGE G. BEAZLEY, JR., is the current chairman of the Consultation on Church Union. Dr. Beazley, after a 13-year pastorate in Bartlesville, Okla., became President of the Council on Christian Unity of the Christian Church (Disciples of Christ). He has held numerous official positions with the Consultation, the National and World Councils of Churches. He is editor of the ecumenical journal *Mid-Stream*.

WILLIAM JERRY BONEY is Professor of Theology in the School of Theology, Virginia Union University. Dr. Boney is a member of the Permanent Committee on Inter-Church Relations of the Presbyterian Church in the U.S., a Fellow (1968–69) of the Institute for Ecumenical and Cultural Research, and a co-editor of *The New Day: Catholic Theologians of the Renewal*.

JOHN PAIRMAN BROWN is Theologian in Residence at the Berkeley Free Church, Berkeley, Calif. An Episcopalian, he is author of *The Liberated Zone: A Guide to Christian Resistance*, historian of the Lebanese Forest, involved in the peace movement, and co-compiler of the *Free Church Prayer Book*.

PAUL A. CROW, JR., is the first General Secretary of the Consultation on Church Union. Formerly Professor of Church History at Lexington Theological Seminary, he is a minister of the Christian Church (Disciples of Christ). Dr. Crow is a member of the Faith and Order Commission of the World Council of Churches. He is author of *No Greater Love: The Gospel and Its Imperative* and *The Ecumenical Movement in Bibliographical Outline*, and co-editor of *Where We Are in Church Union*.

THEODORE H. ERICKSON, JR., is a Planning Associate with the United Church Board for Homeland Ministries. He has done extensive research as

251

252 Notes on Contributors

well as organizational work with ecumenical clusters of churches. His experience also includes work in housing and poverty programs for the City of Philadelphia. An editor of *The Journal of Current Social Issues*, Mr. Erickson is also a member of the Task Force on Local Church Clusters of the Consultation on Church Union.

GABRIEL FACKRE is professor of Theology, Andover Newton Theological School. Dr. Fackre is author of numerous books including *Humiliation and Celebration: Post-Radical Themes in Doctrine, Morals, and Mission; The Promise of Reinhold Niebuhr*, and *Liberation in Middle America*. He is a delegate of the United Church of Christ to the COCU Plenary.

JOHN T. FORD is Professor of Theology at the Catholic University of America. Father Ford has written numerous articles including two on the Consultation on Church Union appearing in *The Christian Century* and in *Unitas*. He is a member of the United Methodist–Roman Catholic Bilateral Conversations.

JOHN F. HOTCHKIN is Director of the Bishops' Committee for Ecumenical and Interreligious Affairs of the National Conference of Catholic Bishops. Dr. Hotchkin, a priest of the Archdiocese of Chicago, served as associate director of the Bishops' Committee before assuming his present duties. He is an observer-consultant to the COCU Plenary.

FREDERICK D. JORDAN is the Bishop of Urban Ministries and Ecumenical Relations of the African Methodist Episcopal Church, a member of the Executive Committee of the Consultation, and First Vice President of the National Council of the Churches of Christ in the U.S.A.

MARTIN E. MARTY is Professor of Modern Church History at the University of Chicago Divinity School, and an Associate Editor of *The Christian Century*. Dr. Marty, a Lutheran, is author of numerous books including *The Modern Schism; The Search for A Usable Future*, and *Righteous Empire: The Protestant Experience*.

J. ROBERT NELSON is Professor of Systematic Theology at Boston University School of Theology. A United Methodist, Dr. Nelson is chairman of the Working Committee of the Commission on Faith and Order of the World Council, and President of the North American Academy of Ecumenists. He is author of *Church Union in Focus*, and editor and contributor to *No Man Is Alien*.

RONALD E. OSBORN, Professor of Church History at Christian Theological Seminary, is a delegate of the Christian Church (Disciples of Christ) to COCU. He has attended many gatherings of the World Council of Churches, been a lecturer at the Ecumenical Institute at Bossey, Visiting Professor at

Union Theological Seminary in the Philippines, and is author of *A Church for These Times* and *In Christ's Place: Christian Ministry in Today's World.*

JANET HARBISON PENFIELD is a laywoman and Associate Editor of *Presbyterian Life*. She served as a member of the drafting committee of the United Presbyterian Church in the U.S.A. Confession of 1967, and as a delegate of that church to plenaries of the Consultation on Church Union. Mrs. Penfield is a member of the National Board and the World Council of the YWCA.

STEPHEN C. ROSE is Associate Editor of *The Christian Century*, a United Presbyterian delegate to COCU, Coordinator of Network Consultants, Stockbridge, Mass. He is editor of *Who's Killing the Church?* and author of *The Grass Roots Church*.

PRESTON N. WILLIAMS is Houghton Professor of Theology and Contemporary Change, The Divinity School, Harvard University. Formerly Dr. Williams served as M. L. King, Jr., Professor of Social Ethics, Boston University. He is author of many articles including, "The Ethics of Black Power," in *Quest for a Black Theology* (J. J. Gardiner and J. D. Roberts, eds.).

WILLIAM J. WOLF is Howard Chandler Robbins Professor of Theology at Episcopal Theological School, Cambridge. He was an Anglican Observer to the Second Vatican Council, a member of the Plan of Union Commission of COCU, and a member of the Joint Commission on Ecumenical Relations of the Episcopal Church. Professor Wolf is author of *Lincoln's Religion* and *No Cross, No Crown: A Study in the Atonement.*

ROBERT C. WORLEY is Professor of Education and Ministry, and Director of the Center for the Study of Church Organizational Behavior, McCormick Theological Seminary. A United Presbyterian minister, Dr. Worley is author of *Preaching and Teaching in the Earliest Church* and *Change in the Church: A Source of Hope.*

DATE DUE

DEC 7 '83			
DEC 14 '83			
MAY 2 '84			
DEC 21 '84			